GEORGE F. WILL

The Pursuit of Virtue and Other Tory Notions

SIMON AND SCHUSTER

NEW YORK

These articles previously appeared in *Newsweek* magazine and *The Washington Post*.

Copyright © 1982 by The Washington Post Company
All rights reserved
including the right of reproduction
in whole or in part in any form
Published by Simon and Schuster
A Division of Gulf & Western Corporation
Simon & Schuster Building
Rockefeller Center
1230 Avenue of the Americas
New York, New York 10020
SIMON AND SCHUSTER and colophon are trademarks of Simon & Schuster
Designed by Eve Kirch
Manufactured in the United States of America

10 9 8 7 6 5 4 3 2 1

Library of Congress Cataloging in Publication Data

The Pursuit of virtue and other Tory notions.

Includes index.
   1.United States—Politics and government—1945-
—Addresses, essays, lectures.   I.Will, George F.
E839.5.P87   973.92   81-18508
                                AACR2

ISBN 0-671-42393-2

ACKNOWLEDGMENTS

Thanks are owed to William Dickinson, Anna Karavangelos and their associates at the Washington Post Writers Group; to Lester Bernstein, Kenneth Auchincloss and Olga Barbi at *Newsweek;* and to Erwin Glikes of Simon and Schuster. They get what I write to those for whom I write. James A. Miller, my former assistant, is now Senator Howard Baker's assistant. My loss is the Republic's gain.

To err is human, and I am militantly human. To spot as many of my errors as is humanly possible is the difficult task of the divine Lynn Chalmers of Simon and Schuster. If any errors remain, I forgive her.

For Victoria Louise Will

Contents

II. "RIGHTS" AND WRONGS, AND LIFE AND DEATH

III. THE WAR AGAINST THE TOTALITARIAN, 1939–

IV. POLITICS

V. "GOVERNING"

VI. LIVES, PRIVATE AND PUBLIC

VII. PREJUDICES

VIII. ON THE HOME FRONT

INTRODUCTION ❧

"Writing is not hard," wrote Stephen Leacock. "Just get paper and pencil, sit down, and write as it occurs to you. The writing is easy—it's the occurring that's hard." Actually, the "occurring" is not hard for someone blessed with a Tory temperament and sentenced to live in this stimulating era. Today, even more than usual, the world is generously strewn with fascinations and provocations.

What a columnist writes in his capacity as a columnist is necessarily episodic, but there are continuities, and mine are conservative convictions. I call them "Tory" because that is what they are. I trace the pedigree of my philosophy to Burke, Newman, Disraeli and others who were more skeptical, even pessimistic, about the modern world than most people are who today call themselves conservatives.

As the number of such people has grown, so has awareness of the varieties of conservatism. The most familiar and fashionable variety is strangely soothing. It tends complacently to define the public good as whatever results from the unfettered pursuit of private ends. Hence it tends to treat *laissez-faire* economic theory as a substitute for political philosophy, and to discount the importance of government and the dignity of the political vocation.

My conservatism is less sanguine about the supposed ease with which the public good can be produced. All social systems are, in a sense, built on sandy soil. Since the Industrial Revolution, the dynamism of economic and intellectual development has produced a permanent revolution in the physical and philosophical spheres of life. This has made more acute the perennial problem of conservatives: deciding what is to be conserved, and how. That prob-

15

lem is especially vexing for American conservatives. They celebrate the virtues of capitalism, which produces such remarkable, relentless social change. Furthermore, their attachment to *laissez-faire* makes them deeply ambivalent about government, and reluctant to use it as an instrument of conservative values, tempering and directing social dynamism.

But a society that dedicates itself to the pursuit of happiness had better dedicate itself, including its government, to the pursuit of the virtues indispensable to ordered liberty. It has been well said that democracy presupposes that it is better to count heads than to break them. But the success of democracy depends on what is in the heads of the citizens.

There is no more timeless or troubling question in political philosophy than this: What constitutes the proper relationship between law and the beliefs, habits and dispositions that are the real regulators of society? "Manners," said Burke, "are more important than the law. Upon them, in great measure, the laws depend. The law touches us but here and there . . . Manners are what vex or soothe, corrupt or purify, exalt or debase, barbarize or refine us, by a constant, steady, uniform, insensible operation, like that of the air we breathe in." Wise philosophers have come to dramatically divergent conclusions about the extent to which the law should, or can, influence manners, broadly understood. Honorable people of good will will continue to differ about this question. But they will not be able to avoid it. Social and cultural anxieties find their way onto a society's political agenda.

One section of this collection is composed primarily of essays written in response to what I consider the West's reflex of flinching from the awful facts about the totalitarian challenge. Open societies frequently have difficulty comprehending regimes of radically different character. But that state of mind has never been more conspicuous or dangerous. Nothing would please me more than to have a happy posterity read this section with bemusement, wondering how anyone came to be so exercised about a totalitarian peril long since vanished. As Chesterton said, "There is no nobler fate than to be forgotten as the foe of a forgotten heresy." But for the moment, what makes totalitarianism so fascinating is the fear that it has achieved the closest approximation to permanency in politics.

Of course, many of the essays in this volume concern less momentous matters. W. H. Auden playfully produced "academic graffiti," including this:

> *Mallarmé*
> *Had too much to say:*
> *He could never quite*
> *Leave the paper white.*

Mallarmé should have been a columnist. I cheerfully confess to being a compulsive writer. I write constantly. I write (of course) the old-fashioned way, in longhand, with a fountain pen, for the fun of feeling thoughts become sentences. I hope these essays will be persuasive, but I also assume that agreement is not necessary for enjoyment, and I hope that the pleasure I had in writing them will be contagious. The world is tiresome, alarming and too much with us. But perhaps enjoyment—in writing, reading and arguing about the world—is the best revenge.

Part One

CONSERVATISM, RIGHTLY UNDERSTOOD

The Virtues of Boldness

Looking back (Americans do a lot of that these days because it seems pleasanter than contemplating the future), a fascinating aspect of the public's reaction a decade ago was that so many people considered *Apollo 11* the end of something, not the beginning of something.

The moon landing helped to frame the 1960s. At the beginning of the decade, John Kennedy said we would do it by the end of the decade. And we did. It was like Babe Ruth's "called shot" in the World Series. America audaciously pointed to the right-field bleachers and then hit the ball to the spot.

When the words "The Eagle has landed" crackled back to earth ten years ago, a challenge was met. It began on October 4, 1957, when a 184-pound sphere of Soviet technology orbited the earth. One of President Eisenhower's advisers suggested that as a show of national strength, *Sputnik* was less impressive than a U.S. supermarket display in Zagreb. The junior senator from Massachusetts disagreed. John Kennedy's strongest beliefs were about the dynamics and importance of national morale and prestige.

As Eisenhower's term ended, he pruned the space program that was pointing, tentatively, toward the moon. Daniel Boorstin, the historian, believes Eisenhower was moved, in part, by his "Cincinnatus complex." He was "haunted by his military background" and determined to keep America "civilian-oriented." In his farewell address he warned against "the military-industrial complex." It is odd that Ike from Abilene supplied perhaps the most-used phrase of the 1960s radicalism. It is odder still that in another passage he anticipated the growth of anxiety about a "scientific technological elite."

21

Kennedy felt no such anxiety. He was twenty-seven years younger than the man he succeeded; that was the largest age difference in the history of the Presidency. Kennedy was 10 when Lindbergh flew the Atlantic. He was a young naval officer when the first jet flew. He was exhilarated by the rush of things.

Eisenhower thought like a quartermaster. He thought, rightly, that a space program would be useful for developing important hardware, but a moon shot would be unnecessary. Kennedy thought like a general: hardware matters, but intangibles do too. A moon landing became central to Kennedy's space program because, to him, the program was only secondarily about scientific or military benefits. It was primarily about politics, in a grand sense: it was about defining and shaping the nation's spirit and confounding its enemies.

On April 12, 1961, Yuri Gagarin became the first man to orbit the earth. On April 14, Kennedy said to aides, "Is there anyplace we can catch them? . . . If somebody can just tell me how to catch up . . . There's nothing more important than that." On April 17, the phrase "Bay of Pigs" entered the American political language as a synonym for "debacle." On May 8, Kennedy received a memo from James Webb, head of the space agency, and Robert McNamara, Secretary of Defense: "It is man, not merely machines, in space that captures the imagination of the world . . . Our attainments are a major element in the international competition . . . part of a battle along the fluid front of the cold war." On May 25, Kennedy urged Congress to shoot for the moon, and he told some friends that if he died first, "Just remember when it happens I will be sitting up there in heaven in a rocking chair just like this one, and I'll have a better view of it than anybody."

Apollo 11 came at the end of a decade that had been downhill since Kennedy was murdered. It came one year after one of the worst American years, in which his brother was murdered. One of the disharmonies of history is that two days before *Apollo 11* added luster to Kennedy's legacy, his youngest brother had an accident, and millions of Americans now remember the summer of 1969 less for what happened at Tranquillity Base on the moon than what happened on Chappaquiddick Island.

Still, the moon landing was a tonic event. It had a Mount Rushmore quality: it was on a grand scale, was comprehensible and heroic. Unlike, say, recombinant-DNA research, and some other facets of modern science, the space program has been science without a Faustian dimension—without, that is, putting important values at risk. While much of science seems to be quarrying away at mankind's stature, the moon shot was triumphantly human.

The space program has now elevated to a fine art the substitution of mechanical for human functions. We have not brought back a particle of Venus, but the signals sent back are invaluable. The anniversary of *Apollo 11* occurs as *Voyager 2* cruises past Jupiter, outward bound for Saturn and points beyond, sending home breathtaking photographs. It was inevitable that interest in space would wax with manned exploration and wane with mechanical exploration. Still, it is a pity the public is so blasé about what scientists are accomplishing.

Physicists provided, in the Manhattan and Apollo projects, two of the clear-cut successes of modern government. Successes have been so rare that political leaders, in their almost constant bewilderment, continually turn back toward them. The urban disorders of the 1960s produced calls, too many to count, for a "Marshall plan for the cities." In today's energy crisis, with the words "synthetic fuels" buzzing about, leaders warm themselves around the glowing memories of the great collaborations between government and science, the Manhattan and Apollo projects. Perhaps those episodes from wars hot and cold hold the key to winning the moral equivalent of war.

Perhaps, but skepticism surges into millions of minds. F.D.R.'s hot war and J.F.K.'s cold war were real. Not even Carter has behaved as though he believed in his metaphorical "war." Twenty-seven months after Carter declared "war," he was still subsidizing consumption and discouraging production by clinging to price control. Also, no energy project can be analogous to the Manhattan and Apollo projects. They were at the margin of the nation's life. They did not materially affect many Americans; they did not involve broad questions of equity.

Yet because skepticism comes so easily, it should be resisted. True, Carter's Camp David spectacle was a satire of media politics, a broad-brush caricature of leadership. First the skies were dark with helicopters bearing famous people; then there was a dash in the dark to commune with plain folks in Pittsburgh. But perhaps the cunning of history produced the Carter Presidency in order to provoke a more sympathetic appraisal of his predecessors.

The decade since *Apollo 11* has been a decade of second thoughts, about F.D.R.'s idea of government, J.F.K.'s idea of leadership, about the efficacy of government, the benefits of science, even the possibility of progress. But doubt itself has become a dogma. It is time for third thoughts.

July 23, 1979

Freedom, True and False

Of the two calamities that have recently befallen intellectual life in America, one, the American League's "designated hitter" rule, could be repealed easily. Not so the trivialization of higher education.

Belief in "a teaching magic," as Jacques Barzun says, relieves students of the burden of *wanting* to be *taught*, and is an aspect of the "philosophy of permissive rearing—*reciprocity* is not called beneficiary like vaccination." Another and opposite idea is that there is no difference between the teacher and the taught, an idea expressed in bromides about "both being students, learning from each other." A result, Barzun says, is that teachers relax their efforts while students unleash their conceit. Another result is the decline of the humanities as a course of study. The purpose of humanities is to humanize, which presupposes students who acknowledge their incompleteness and teachers who believe that the purpose of education is to put something into students rather than to let something—"self-expression"—out.

In their "Short Education Dictionary," Kingsley Amis and Robert Conquest satirize recent silliness. "**Alphabet**: a set of arbitrary . . . signs which children are still often compelled to learn by rote; usually taught, moreover, in an arbitrary order." "**Examination**: an irrelevant, external test purporting to check a student's knowledge by a set of written questions often repugnant to his personality . . ." "**Standards**: irrelevant academic concept designed to exclude or penalize students distinguished for either concern or creativity or both." The idea that standards are repressive and excellence is a form of aggression is a product of ancient sins, sloth and envy, and modern ideas, such as: assuming that the quantity of pleasure given by each is equal, "pushpin is as good as poetry."

A society that believes happiness is pleasure, and that pleasure is instant gratification, acknowledges no authority higher than the individual, and so believes that any "experience" is valuable if the experiencer says so. Thus students have received academic credits for "experiences." But as Barzun says, "The cliché that education never ends virtually ensures that it doesn't begin." A society that thinks the choice between ways of living is just a choice between equally eligible "life-styles" turns universities into academic cafeterias offering junk food for the mind. Universities devoted to instant utility have produced a professor of "effective living," a course on "The Pleasure Horse: Appreciation and Use" and a dissertation on "Machiavellianism in Hotel Employees." In the Age of Informality, a slovenly curriculum is an institutional analog of undergraduate styles of dress. Small wonder some people consider universities a collection of "mutually repellent particles held together by a common interest in parking."

At some point "pluralism" in the curriculum of the "multiversity" becomes an abdication of responsibility. The attempt to make universities all things to all peoples ignores the fact that not all good things are good for all people. Liberal societies flinch from that fact because much flows from it. *Of course* universities are elitist: a society is judged, in part, by the caliber of elites it produces. A serious university is *inherently* hierarchical and authoritarian: the few who are qualified to be students go there to benefit from supervision by people who know more than students do, especially about what is good for students.

To those who say that this is anti-democratic, the correct response is that the idea of democracy is irrelevant to the idea of a university's purpose. Democracy is a political, not a social concept. It pertains to constitutional arrangements, to the source of sovereignty, not to a "life-style" or a classless society. Indeed, it is the *reverse* of the truth to say that because democracy is a politically egalitarian *regime*, democracy presupposes an egalitarian *society*. It is democratic sentimentality to expect the political process rather than the social system to produce a leadership class. It is a mystification of voting to hope that the casting of ballots will *generate* rather than just elevate excellence. Generating excellence is the task of many institutions, including universities, that best serve an egalitarian political system when they furnish standards, and elites that measure up to them, for all sectors of society.

Fortunately, some universities are having fugitive doubts about "unstructured" education. Harvard has imposed a "core curriculum" of requirements, and some students are unhappy about this unaccustomed whiff of authoritarianism from those in authority. One student says, "It's really in this age presumptuous to think there is any more a common body of knowledge that one generation can define for the next." But it is presumptuous to think that something sets "this age" apart from all others and that this generation can and should start afresh. The point is not that "one generation" defines a body of knowledge for another. A hundred generations have done so. A properly taught freshman knows more physics than Newton did. And the assumption that only scientific knowledge is cumulative is, ultimately, the counsel of despair. Amidst the encircling gloom of such assumptions, the world needs the wisdom of John Henry Newman.

Only one portrait adorns my study. It is of Newman, the great theorist of university life. Newman, philosopher of man's *creatureliness*, insisted that we are smaller than we imagine. Like Darwin and Marx, he was of the generation that first internalized the idea that change is an autonomous process. This led him not to utopian optimism or social pessimism, but to a profound sense of human limitedness in a prodigious world.

Aristotle said the aim of education is to get the student to like and dislike what he ought; Newman said the aim is not to satisfy curiosity but to arouse the *right* curiosity. Education, he believed, is the thread on which received knowledge, jewels of the great tradition, can be strung. A university should be, primarily and for most students, a place that keeps people from getting lost rather than a place where they find things. A university, like any community, presupposes *some* purpose all members share. As Newman said, "greatness and unity go together and . . . excellence implies a center." The center of a university should be a rigorous curriculum of required studies of proven substance.

Requirements do diminish undergraduates' "freedom," as liberals define freedom: "the absence of restraints imposed by others." But true freedom is impossible without comprehension of, and submission to, the natural order. And the most direct path to such comprehension is through the body of knowledge that is civilization's patrimony. What has been lost is the understanding that education consists primarily of arguing from, not with, this patrimony.

May 29, 1978

Misplaced Reverence

When Oscar Wilde said that people do not value sunsets because they cannot pay for them, he was touching, with the stiletto of his cynicism, a difficulty. It is the difficulty a commercial civilization comes to have in assigning values other than economic values—the difficulty it has doing justice to important intangibles. The task of shaping so much of our culture (consider, for example, television) has been so utterly surrendered to the sovereignty of the price mechanism that many people seem no longer convinced of the importance, or even the reality, of things that cannot be assigned a value through economic calculations.

Today's turn toward more hard-edged economic calculation in public policy is called for by common sense, and the electorate. But it is producing a cold climate for environmentalists, and may leave environmentalism intellectually disarmed, to the long-term detriment of American life.

Prudent people will have a presumption against relaxation of environmental standards—not indifference to cost–benefit calculations, but insistence that those advocating relaxation dispatch the burden of proof. Because many environmental rules involve complex economic calculations, and often rest on scientific evidence that is cloudy, and occasionally involve placing a price on human life, there should be constant questioning of whether the rules are rationally related to affordable ends.

But today environmentalists feel special dismay about the conservative tide that swept away the Administration that may have been more hospitable to environmentalism than any since Theodore Roosevelt's. It is, perhaps, odd that it would require a surgical operation to get into the heads of some people who fancy themselves conservative an idea sympathetic to conservation and other environmental values. But there are many such people.

So, environmentalists need a new, or at least enriched, vocabulary of values, a grammar of advocacy that can tap and, in the process, broaden the best impulses of today's conservatism.

They should begin with basics, insisting that what is at stake in defining a basic attitude toward environmental questions is not what you think about redwoods or ducks, but what you think about man. Father Richard McCormick, S.J., of Georgetown University identifies, for example, two sharply contrasting images of man and his relation to nature, either of which, when sunk deep in the hinterland of a person's consciousness, silently shapes, even controls, the way the person lives.

One image is the "power-plastic" model. According to it, "nature is alien, independent of man, possessing no inherent value. It is capable of being used, dominated, and shaped by man. Man sees himself as possessing an unrestricted right to manipulate it in the service of his goals."

In contrast, there is the "social-symbiotic model. In its religious forms, nature is seen as God's creation, to be respected and heeded. Man is not the master; he is the steward, and nature is a trust. In secular forms, man is seen as part of nature. If man is to be respected, so is nature. We should live in harmony and balance with nature. Nature is a teacher, showing us how to live with it."

Father McCormick wrote that in an essay surveying some literature treating questions of bioethics. But the categories fit the contours of the cultural division revealed in many arguments about environmental attitudes.

Indeed, there may be a need for a coalition of reflective environmentalists and persons anxious about the biological revolution, especially the onrushing future of genetic manipulation. Both groups are, whether they know it or not, at the same business: the conservation of certain values against the predations of dangerous thoughts and actions.

Both groups must ground their particular arguments in critiques of the culture which, as Father McCormick says, by the very processes (economic, scientific, technological, ideological) that generate amazing and sometimes fearful possibilities, shapes reflection about those possibilities.

The two groups' common concerns are about misplaced reverence for "impersonal forces" ("market forces," or "the laws of scientific discovery"); mistaken faith in the inherent value and inevitable "progressiveness" of change brought about by technology or scientific endeavor; and especially, thoroughgoing materialism which cannot give the right answer because, preoccupied with tangible things, it cannot frame the question.

The question is: What will be the irrecoverable cost to precious intangibles—our capacity for awe; our moral imagination; our sense of nature, including human nature, as a realm of values—when we regard the world around and within us just as raw material in the service of our (by then necessarily) vagrant passions and imperious appetites?

January 18, 1981

Solzhenitsyn Versus America's Flaccid Consensus

Alexander Solzhenitsyn resembles both the dove in Genesis that found no rest and the prophets who allowed no rest. As a prophet should, he has, with his Harvard commencement address, stirred a reaction that reveals the complacency of society.

The West, he says, has advanced socially "in accordance with its proclaimed intentions," so its thinness of spirit is evidence of a mistake "at the very basis" of thinking in recent centuries. When modern civilization based itself on the "worship [of] man and his material needs," then, "Everything beyond physical well-being and accumulation of material goods, all other human requirements and characteristics of a subtler and higher nature, were left outside the arena of attention of state and social systems, as if human life did not have any superior sense."

During the early ascendance of modern thinking, says Solzhenitsyn, the West was sustained by the spiritual legacy of the preceding millennium. Mankind was understood to have been "endowed" (to use the language of the Declaration of Independence) with certain rights by God, so "freedom was given to the individual conditionally, in the assumption of his constant religious responsibility." Subsequently, "We have placed too much hope in political and social reforms, only to find out that we were deprived of our most precious possession: our spiritual life."

The New York Times, whose spacious skepticism extends to all values except its own, considers Solzhenitsyn "dangerous" and a "zealot" because "he believes himself to be in possession of The Truth." The *Times* wishes he were more like the American Founders—who, the *Times* forgets, committed treason and waged an eight-year war in behalf of The Truth they considered "self-evident."

The Washington Post says Solzhenitsyn's views are "very Russian: They arise from particular religious and political strains remote from modern Western experience."

They are, indeed, unmodern, even anti-modern, but they are not exclusively Russian. His ideas about the nature of man and the essential political problem are broadly congruent with the ideas of Cicero and other ancients, and those of Augustine, Aquinas, Richard Hooker, Pascal, Thomas More, Burke, Hegel and others. Compared with the long and broad intellectual tradition in which Solzhenitsyn's views are rooted, the tradition of modernity, or liberalism, is short and thin.

The *Times*, which accuses Solzhenitsyn of interpreting the world in terms of a crude dichotomy, interprets Solzhenitsyn in terms of an "argument between the religious Enthusiasts, sure of their relationship to the Divine Will, and the men of the Enlightenment, trusting in the rationality of mankind." The *Post* says Solzhenitsyn betrays "a gross misunderstanding of Western society, which has chosen to organize its political and social and cultural affairs on the basis of a respect for the differences among men."

But there is another, less congratulatory, more accurate and quite opposite interpretation of the modern political tradition.

Modern politics emphasizes the sameness, not the diversity, of people. It seeks to found stable societies on the lowest, commonest, strongest passion: self-interest that is tamed by being turned to economic pursuits.

In such societies, law does not point people toward elevated lives. The law's only purpose is to organize and encourage a taming materialism. Modern politics assumes that it is not virtue that makes people free, but freedom that makes people virtuous, at least if virtue is defined as pursuit of pleasure in accordance with minimal legality.

Such a society asks and receives little self-restraint and civic spirit, and produces what Solzhenitsyn calls "an atmosphere of moral mediocrity, paralyzing man's noblest impulses." Solzhenitsyn doubts that a society founded on lightly regulated selfishness can summon the vision and sacrifice necessary for combating determined enemies.

De Tocqueville, Henry Adams, Irving Babbitt, Paul Elmer More, Peter Viereck and others constitute a submerged but continuous tradition that shares Solzhenitsyn's anxiety about American premises and the culture they produce. And Solzhenitsyn's philosophy has a far more distinguished pedigree than does the liberalism which is orthodoxy in societies that owe their success, so far, to the fact that they have lived off the moral capital of older and sounder traditions—capital that is a wasting asset.

America's flaccid consensus about its premises is a study in intellectual parochialism. That consensus lacks the intellectual weight to justify Solzhenitsyn's critics in being as dismissive as they are about his restatement of the most ancient and honorable theme of Western political philosophy.

June 18, 1978

Who Put Morality into Politics?

Pleas for social regeneration, laced with theology, have enlivened America's civic life since the days of Cotton Mather. There was a recent plea in Jimmy Carter's famous "malaise" speech. Carter noted a "crisis of the American spirit" and a "longing for meaning." He suggested, among other antidotes, a synthetic-fuels program. Eugene McCarthy recalls that Ike urged all Americans to spend the first Fourth of July of his Administration in prayer and penance, and on that day Ike went fishing in the morning, golfing in the afternoon, and played bridge in the evening.

But from the fractious Puritans on, religion often has had serious political consequences, and it may today. The conjunction of the civil-rights struggle, Vietnam and Watergate convinced liberals that they had a "moral monopoly." But now evangelical Christian groups, including one calling itself The Moral Majority, are plunging into politics. The public's preoccupation with the evangelicals' finances reflects a preference for diving into the shallow end of every pool. More important than the question of who gets what is the question of why so many people are so aroused. The answer is: they have been provoked.

Many were first provoked by churches that seem to have suffered what Chesterton called "the dislocation of humility," humility not about ambition but about conviction. Many churches have seemed reluctant, as Peter Berger says, "to make statements of faith unprotected by redeeming sociopolitical significance." But what began with the evangelicals' belief that churches should save souls, not society, has become a movement convinced that society is jeopardizing souls and must be changed.

Public policy has become imbued with what is called "the therapeutic ethic," the idea that the morally and practically correct way to cope with aggressive or otherwise difficult people (or nations) is with social services that remove the causes of anti-social behavior. That idea seems fundamentally mistaken to fundamentalist Christians who take seriously man's fallen condition. It has been said that Christianity is too optimistic about this world, but given the record of this world, pessimism is realism. Christian pessimism often has led to political quietism, but many evangelicals are anything but quiet.

As broad considerations of economic class lose their political importance, considerations of ethnicity, sex, culture and religion are becoming more salient. Welfare-state answers to the basic questions about distributive justice have not calmed our politics. Quite different concerns, even more passionately fought over, have broadened the range of political argument. Americans have always been torn between two desires: for absence of restraint and for a sense of community. A culture abandoning restraints has produced among evangelicals a heightened sense of their community, and of antagonism toward the national culture.

As the nation's social pyramid becomes steeper, those closer to the base than to the apex feel increasingly at the mercy of governing and media elites, and are increasingly insistent that those be elites of character as well as achievement. People measure fine character, in part, by shared values. In most societies, most of the time, the most basic values are not much thought about. If questioned, they elicit what sociologists have called "of course" statements, which express the community's "world-taken-for-granted." A dubious achievement of today's elites has been to help diminish the "world-taken-for-granted."

There has been a provocative widening of the unavoidable gaps between values expressed in public policies and values cleaved to by large segments of the public. Questions that touch the quick of our existence, such as the nature of life and the value of sex, recently did, but no longer do, elicit "of course" answers.

Don't blame evangelicals for inflating abortion as a political issue. The Supreme Court did that by striking down laws of the fifty states that expressed community judgments about the issue. Those who opposed those judgments got them overturned by fiat, not democratic persuasion. There were 1.4 million abortions last year, and the forces that made that possible want subsidies for abortions, knowing that when you subsidize something you get more of it. Yet we are told it is the evangelicals who are aggressive about abortion.

Evangelicals did not set out to alter social attitudes about homosexuality. Government has begun teaching, through many measures, that homosexual and heterosexual relations represent only different "preferences" (or, in the language of the Democratic platform, "orientations") among "life-styles." Militant homosexuals are responsible for this, and for making a hot political issue of government attempts to inculcate new attitudes.

The ancient and Christian theories of government held that statecraft should be soulcraft; indeed, that government cannot avoid concerning itself with virtue. Modern theory, however, involves government in unavoidable conflicts between theory and practice. The modern "night watchman" theory of government is that it exists only to protect persons and property. It can be ubiquitous and omniprovident regarding material things, but must be neutral regarding values. It can concern itself with nurturing soybeans, but not virtue.

American public philosophy asserts, untenably, that popular government presupposes especially virtuous citizens, yet cannot concern itself with the inner lives of its citizens. But the government does concern itself—emphatically in public education, but also in what it requires, encourages, proscribes, refuses to proscribe and prevents from being proscribed. As liberalism has become a doctrine of "liberation" it has spawned new "rights," in the name of which government has been empowered to promote certain values by stipulating behavior. Defenders of competing values are castigated for trying to "impose" their values. Evangelicals who are part of the reaction against this sometimes shoot wildly, but as Chesterton said, "Even a bad shot is dignified when he accepts a duel."

September 15, 1980

A Dilemma of Conservatives

In 1960, Governor William Stratton of Illinois told Richard Nixon, "You can say all you want about foreign affairs, but what is really important is the price of hogs in Chicago and Saint Louis." This year it is axiomatic, and perhaps even true, that the bread-and-butter issue is the price of bread and butter.

But this year, Democrats want to emphasize foreign policy, and not just because their domestic policies are failures. Democrats think they can win by mixing candor and hysteria—by saying Carter is dismal but Reagan is dangerous. So Democrats attack Reagan for opposing SALT II agreements that a Democratic-controlled Senate would not ratify. By announcing that they, unlike Reagan, will not engage in an arms race, they remove all incentives for the Soviets to negotiate mutual limits.

The difficulties with the Republican position are less obvious but more interesting. They derive from the fact that foreign policy depends on domestic factors, on values, discipline, confidence, morale—in short, national character. The Republican platform stresses two themes that are not as harmonious as Republicans suppose.

One is cultural conservatism. The other is capitalist dynamism. The latter dissolves the former.

Karl Marx, who had a Reaganesque respect for capitalism's transforming power, got one thing right: capitalism undermines traditional social structures and values; it is a relentless engine of change, a revolutionary inflamer of appetites, enlarger of expectations, diminisher of patience.

A wit has said that the modern American's prayer is "Dear God, I pray for patience—and I want it *right now!*" Republicans see no connection between the cultural phenomena they deplore and the capitalist culture they promise to intensify; no connection between the multiplying evidence of self-indulgence and national decadence (such as pornography, promiscuity, abortion, divorce and other forms of indiscipline) and the unsleeping pursuit of ever more immediate, intense and grand material gratifications.

Republicans sense that manners, meaning conduct in its moral aspect, are as determinative in a nation's life as are materialistic preoccupations. Republicans seem not to sense the effect of such preoccupations on manners.

Today's Republican themes of social decay and national decline are perennial themes of political philosophy, and recurring fascinations for historians. Western philosophy is, indeed, a series of footnotes to Plato, whose *Republic* concerns the myriad ways polities decay. The most famous work of history since the fall of Rome is about the decline and fall of Rome.

Some reflective Republicans believe—rightly, I fear—that a century from now, philosophers and historians will study the trajectory of the United States in the second half of this century as the most striking instance of national decline since that of Spain, centuries ago. This nation may be more than halfway through a decline from the security of 1945 to irremediable vulnerability to, and dictated accommodation with, the Soviet Union.

Republicans are today even more mesmerized than usual by various economic facts. (Or, perhaps, economic theories: Felix Cohen said that the theories we believe we call facts, and the facts we disbelieve we call theories.) They understand that economic vigor is necessary for national survival. They may not understand that the idea that "the economy is king" is just a theory, not a fact.

A characterizing belief of the twentieth century is that we live in an "economic civilization," in the sense that economic supremacy must translate into national security. But economic strength is not sufficient. A more elusive and fragile necessity is confidence, pride, resolve—in a phrase, national élan. What is at issue in this century, and this election, is nothing less than a question of civilization: Has ours the capacity to sustain itself?

Carter's foreign policy reduces to the idea—simple and *a priori*—that we shall prevail because (or if) we are just. Reagan says, with Raymond Aron, that the tribunal of history is not a tribunal of justice. Rather, it tests a nation's capacity for action.

The Republicans' dilemma is the tension between the culture of capitalism and the demands of defending a capitalist nation. The nation's collective discipline—its capacity for strenuous, protracted action in foreign policy—is undermined by the relentless individualism implicit in Republican social policy.

America's individualism has been explicit from the first—from the first paragraphs of the Declaration of Independence. The as yet unanswered, but bound to be answered, question is whether a society so thoroughly given over to the individual's pursuit of happiness is capable of making the unpleasant collective effort necessary to the maintenance of national independence.

August 24, 1980

The Neoconservatives: Melancholy Liberals

Santayana, paraphrasing Plato, said that "unmitigated seriousness is always out of place in human affairs." Santayana and Plato, both of them clever fellows, hit upon that truth even without having had the benefit of seeing the mating dance of Edward Kennedy and the Democratic Party.

The high point of recent merriment came when Rowland Evans and Robert Novak, the columnists, minted a new verb: "to Sherman-out." (It means to declare, as forcefully as General Sherman did, that you won't allow yourself to become President. Evans and Novak do not expect Kennedy to Sherman-out.) But it was also fun to read Kennedy's lecture to James Reston, the columnist, about politics, "the practical approach" thereto:

> I remember . . . when we first put in the first deregulation bill in the Senate. I put it in with Jim Buckley . . . who was the most con-

servative member of the Senate. I think we have to move away from labels, slogans, clichés and try to deal with things by a more practical approach.

Reston probably was too polite to laugh, so I'll do it for him.

"Practical politics," as Henry Adams said, "consists in ignoring facts." But when Kennedy, in full flight from the label "liberal," wraps himself in the golden mantle of Jim Buckley, Kennedy overdoes it.

Until 1977, Buckley was senator from New York, and if God really loves America, Buckley will be senator from Connecticut in 1981. It is more accurate to say that Kennedy is the most liberal senator than it is to say that Buckley was the most conservative. But Buckley is conservative and Kennedy is liberal, and I want to say a word in behalf of those despised things, political labels.

Particular labels, like everything else, come and go. But there always are various labels because they are useful, even necessary: Politics is a varied business. If a politician's behavior is not utterly cynical, or mindless, it will have a pattern that is related, at least a bit, to his beliefs. Political actions tend to cluster; so do political actors. Labels describe how particular people generally cluster.

Most politicians resist things, like labels, that cramp their room for maneuvering. But there is more to Kennedy's dislike of labels.

In 1976, Morris Udall said please, pretty please, if you must call me something, make it "progressive," not "liberal." A sage once wrote, "The dappled deer is said to see the wind; your statesman only sees which way it blows." Kennedy, a dappled deer among drabber statesmen, knows what Udall knew: the label "liberal" is no asset.

Kennedy, who favors expanding the role of the state, increasing the progressive nature of the tax system and nationalizing tonsillectomies, may run as the scourge of government regulation. But seriously, folks, at the center of the cluster of those who are called liberals, Kennedy sits, enthroned and swathed in ermine. Labels identify classes; but people, by acting, classify themselves.

A new label is "neoconservative." I do not know what, precisely, the "neo" is intended to signify, but many spiritual leaders of the "neoconservative movement" were, in bygone days, not at all conservative, and I suspect that splicing "neo" to the sacred word "conservative" is a form of flinching. "Neoconservatives" are solid citizens, but not proper conservatives in the sense of true-blue Tories.

Neoconservatives, unlike we few who comprise the saving remnant of true conservatism, do not have stained-glass minds. Neoconservatives do not really mourn the passing of the thirteenth century: feudal codes, heraldic banners, serried ranks of bishops, the lower orders tugging at their forelocks—that sort of good stuff.

Many neoconservatives are actually melancholy adherents of nineteenth-century liberalism. If we must have liberals, let them be melancholy ones, by all means. But let us note this about neoconservatives:

Most of them adore capitalism. Capitalism means the liberation and incessant inflaming of appetites. But neoconservatives deplore the predictable consequences of capitalism, which include the sorts of social disintegration that should be expected when a culture celebrates instant gratification.

Be that as it may, the label "neoconservative" is useful in this sense: it denotes a cluster of like-minded people.

One of Washington's fashionable haberdashers is advertising a "neo-classic sportswear collection." Everything for the well-turned-out neoconservative? Certainly the prefix "neo" is high fashion in the federal city. Soon we will be told that Kennedy is, and really always has been, not a tacky old liberal, but a neoliberal.

September 20, 1979

Conservative Bridges, Crossed and Burned

It is said that life's crucial judgments concern which bridges to cross and which to burn. Some critics say the Republican platform-makers crossed and burned the wrong bridges.

Platforms are thought to be exercises in the art of insincerity, telling people what they want to hear, and banking on people's forgetfulness. The Republican platform is problematic because of some stands, economic and cultural, that many people do not want to hear.

Much has been made of the Republicans' convening in blue-collar Detroit. But an unremarked irony derives from the fact that Detroit also is an entrepreneur's city, home of the emblematic American industry built by human dynamos named Ford, Chrysler, Dodge, Sloan.

The Republicans promise a purer capitalism, "reindustrialization" by unleashing entrepreneurship from the clammy grip of government. But while Ronald Reagan is saying that the automobile industry needs protection from Washington, not Japan, many industry leaders are calling for closer cooperation with Washington, even a "national industrial policy." As historian Carl Becker wrote, "No class of Americans, so far as I know, has ever objected . . . to any amount of governmental meddling if it appeared to benefit that particular class."

There may not be much of a constituency of capitalists for Reagan's purified capitalism. Everywhere, but with special significance in this entrepreneur's city, the line Reagan wants to draw more sharply, the line between public and private sectors, is becoming blurred, even indistinct.

The cultural conservatism in high tide here is symbolized by the platform pledge that opposition to judicially dictated liberal abortion policies will be among the criteria the Reagan Administration will use in evaluating candidates for judicial nominations. But two points are logically independent of arguments about the ethics of abortion. They are points about the ethics of politics.

First, the 1980 Republican platform did not put abortion on the nation's agenda of questions that shall be debated until a political consensus has stabilized. The Supreme Court did that, in 1973, by forging from a "privacy right" a scythe to mow down state laws that expressed various community judgments about abortion. This was a provocative political act—"political" meaning an authoritative allocation of social values—and not surprisingly, it provoked a political reaction that has not crested.

Second, no one thinks Presidents do or should select judicial nominees randomly. All Presidents have criteria. Jefferson, fighting the Federalists, was but the first to make his criteria explicit in a political program. Liberal critics of the Republican platform profess distress about the mere stipulation of criteria. But would they be distressed by a pledge to seek judicial nominees sympathetic to "race-conscious" (reverse discrimination) programs, or an expansive construction of journalists' First Amendment rights?

Jimmy Carter hints that the winner in 1980 may make four nominations to the Supreme Court, and that his nominees would be better for various interests (labor, blacks, pro-abortion groups, among others). Carter is not long on specifics, but he hints that he will consider sex and race when seeking nominees. Which is more reprehensible, Carter's promise to consider the chromosomes or skin pigmentation of nominees, or the Republicans' straightforward acknowledgment that they will seek certain values in nominees whose values may find their way into the law?

The Republican platform-makers are not political innocents. They know there is not a national majority for their positions on ERA, abortion, voluntary prayer in schools and other matters of cultural conservatism. But serious parties try to shape as well as seduce the nation.

Parts of the platform are studies in seduction. The journalists who think the promise to repeal the federal 55-mph speed limit is peculiar do not, and probably think no one should, drive in Montana. Folks who drive there (rarely under 55 mph anyway) may think that plank is the platform's purest poetry.

But the cultural conservatism in the platform is, to some extent, a noble rarity, commitment to mold rather than merely conform to the mood of the moment. Since the 1960s the nation has been riven by cultural arguments which had to become political arguments because, over time, they influence the kind of lives we lead and the kind of people our children shall be. Republicans believe the nation's moral makeup is, today, soft wax on which national leadership can leave a long-lasting impress.

They may be wrong about that, or about the impress they want to leave. But they are alive to the grandeur, when it is properly understood, of the political vocation.

July 17, 1980

Conservatism's Competing Values

The dullest eye can discern the entertaining irony. Ronald Reagan's transition apparatus (a body politic with a population approaching that of several nations represented in the United Nations) has deprived conservatives of their cherished myth—that enormous bureaucracies are spawned by perverse liberals who, inexplicably, adore bureaucracies. Conservatives are inheriting an enormous government, and the transition apparatus necessarily mirrors that government.

Furthermore, Reagan's people probably will not be able, or perhaps even inclined, to shrink their inheritance. Something—indeed, almost everything—about the modern state causes it to swell. The principal cause is the modern citizenry.

Conservatives correctly indict liberals who, believing in the rationalization of society by central authority, have overloaded government's circuits. But conservatives have not faced the fact that "the public" is a quilt of constituencies for government programs. When—if—Reagan does what some aides say he must, when he asks Congress to prune some of the biggest programs of "big government," he may find that the number of "liberals" in the new "conservative" Congress approaches 535.

Prominent conservatives have encouraged the public to believe that "efficient management" can cure "waste" and thereby make "big government" less big, without pain. Asked what sacrifices people must make, many conservatives respond that government has been living too well and it, not "the people," must sacrifice. This formulation, although rhetorically potent, is analytically confused.

When conservatives promise to get government "off the back" of "the people," who do they think put it there? The people's elected—and reelected—representatives did. The culprits are legislative bodies, the most responsive branches of government, and especially state legislatures, those closest to constituents.

In the seventies, Congress enacted 3,359 laws, which is bad enough. But New York's legislature enacted 9,780. The fifty state legislatures enacted approximately 250,000. (Professor Irving Younger of Cornell suggests, puckishly, an antidote—a court ruling that "no law is validly enacted unless legislators voting for it have read it.")

Every encounter with power pulls American conservatism toward maturity. Eisenhower's conservatism ended the conservatives' pretense that the New Deal's steps toward a welfare state were steps along "the road to serfdom," and reversible. Eisenhower knew those steps reflected realities common to all developed nations—broad acceptance of the ethic of common provision, and the majority's desire to purchase some things, such as certain pension and health services, collectively.

Beginning January 20, Reagan's experiences may continue the maturation of conservatism by ending the sterile practice of defining conservatism simply as opposition to "big government."

The problem is not "bigness," it is unreasonable intrusiveness, which is a function of (bad) policy, not size. Besides, inveighing against big government ignores the fact that government is about as small as it ever will be, and obscures the fact that government, though big, is often too weak.

Many conservatives insist that America's great problem is just that government is so strong it is stifling freedom. These people call themselves "libertarian conservatives"—a label a bit like "promiscuous celibates." Real conservatism requires strong government.

The overriding aim of liberalism, properly understood, is the expansion of liberty. (American "liberals" long since became what Europeans call "social democrats," preoccupied with equality.) Conservatism, properly understood, rejects the idea of a single overriding aim.

Real conservatism is about balancing many competing values. Striking the proper balance often requires limits on liberty, and always requires resistance to libertarianism (the doctrine of maximizing freedom for private appetites) because libertarianism is a recipe for the dissolution of public authority, social and religious traditions, and other restraints needed to prevent license from replacing durable, disciplined liberty.

The truly conservative critique of contemporary American society is that there is too much freedom—for abortionists, pornographers, businessmen trading with the Soviet Union, young men exempt from conscription, to cite just four examples. Regarding the first two, there is little Reagan can do, beyond endorsing a constitutional amendment and appointing judges who will construe the Constitution reasonably. Regarding the third and fourth, about which Reagan could do much, he is inclined to do little. His Jeffersonian (or classic "Manchester" liberal) beliefs render him reluctant to impede free trade or consider peacetime conscription.

Professor James Q. Wilson of Harvard wonders, reasonably, how conservatives can reconcile their idea that government should do less with their desire for the nation to play a more assertive role internationally, a role that may require, in addition to more weapons, more government activism in the management of international trade (of grains, for example) and related facets of the domestic economy.

Liberalism's incoherencies have made American conservatism seem more coherent than it is. After the coming four-year collision with reality, it may more closely resemble traditional conservatism—which is to say, conservatism properly understood.

January 8, 1981

Indiscriminate Skepticism

Beneath the flesh of political rhetoric there usually is a skeleton of principle. Today there is a dangerous principle—dangerous to conservative objectives, among other things—within some conservative rhetoric. This point was brought to mind by a recent episode in the Senate Budget Committee.

The committee, like the Senate itself, only even more so, contains a lot of people whose principal experience with the Federal Government consisted, until recently, of deploring it from afar. Fifty-four of today's 100 senators have served less than five years, and half of the 12 Republicans on the budget committee came to the Senate less than four months ago.

On March 19, the committee was sweeping like a scythe through the budget. Suddenly, Mark Andrews of North Dakota, a Republican rookie zealous about pruning government, reached the limit of his zeal. He did not like a Reagan Administration idea—a "snake" he called it—for diminishing federal support for rural electrification.

Of the 12 budget-committee Republicans, the closest thing to an Easterner is Dan Quayle of Indiana. The rest are from North Dakota, New Mexico, Colorado, Wisconsin, Minnesota, Kansas, Washington, Utah, Texas, Iowa and Idaho. Not surprisingly, urban programs have been criticized with special severity. So when Andrews, joined by others, waxed affectionate about a rural program, Daniel Patrick Moynihan (D.-N.Y.) would have been forgiven if he had delivered a lecture about sauce for the goose being sauce for the gander. Instead, Moynihan lectured (some sort of lecture was inevitable, and called for) on the good that government does.

He said that if the committee was going to have a consensus (and eventually it was unanimous in endorsing cuts larger than Reagan sought), it must refrain from rhetoric about all government being "somehow bad." Then he said, in effect: Huzzah for the Rural Electrification Administration, which helped better the lives of millions, especially in the Great Plains and Deep South. It was proposed, he noted, by a President from New York (Franklin Roosevelt).

Warming to his theme (Moynihan warms to all his themes), he said, in effect: Behold the Imperial Valley of California. Let us now praise government's role in the most striking transformation of the valley since (Moynihan takes the long view) "the receding of the Ice Age." Only God can make an artichoke, but it took government to make the valley into such a splendiferous garden. Specifically, it took the Bureau of Reclamation, proposed by a President from—ahem—New York (Teddy Roosevelt).

"We can agree about the budget," Moynihan said. "But we would ask not to be required, in reducing the budget, to repudiate a tradition of intelligent involvement by American government in the problems of American society."

A reasonable request, that.

Although the vast majority of the proposed budget cuts are sensible, and all are arguable, there has crept into some advocacy of them a tone that is unworthy of, and dangerous for, the Reagan Administration. It is a tone of dogmatic disparagement of government. It suggests that all cuts are morally easy because government cannot do anything right anyway.

If this conservative Administration is to do its most important duty, then eventually—perhaps soon—it must enlist the public's support for strenuous, complex exertions regarding the larger world. This will involve not only procuring complex, expensive military assets, such as the MX missile, but also attempting to change the policies, and perhaps the governments, of nations like Cuba and Libya. At that point, this conservative Administration may learn the cost of supporters who labor at infecting the public with indiscriminate skepticism about the competence, even the motives, of government.

This Administration may reasonably decide to summon the nation for (figuratively speaking) a charge up some San Juan Hill. But its bugle call may be met by the stony skepticism of a nation that has taken to heart what some conservatives say about government being incorrigibly incompetent. Such skepticism cannot be sealed into one compartment of the public mind; it tends to seep. You cannot tell people over and over that government is a klutz that cannot help Cleveland, and then suddenly say, Oh, by the way, give the government $1.3 trillion for military assets, and support its attempt to do something about Cuba.

Earlier in this century, some conservatives achieved a kind of consistency. They advocated a domestic policy of minimal government, and a foreign policy of isolationism. Today that is not an acceptable consistency for conservatism.

March 26, 1981

A Crop of Myths

It was, we now know, an astonishing week, 169 years ago. On February 12, 1809, Charles Darwin and Abraham Lincoln were born. Three days later came Cyrus McCormick. He too transformed the nineteenth century. He was part of the revolution in American agriculture that has led to today's farmers' strike.

A strike is an industrial action, and the farmers' strike, effective or not, should underscore this fact: modern agriculture is a capital-intensive form of manufacturing that refutes some American political and economic myths. Agriculture is, arguably, the most successful American industry, and the one most continuously shaped by government policy. The idea that there is today, or once was, a clear demarcation between public and private sectors is belied by the history of American agriculture.

McCormick's career foreshadowed the evolution of agriculture. He began as a farmer and ended as an industrialist. In six weeks, in his 23rd year, he invented a reaper. And before he died in 1884, he had pioneered many of the mass-production techniques that would be developed by another mechanic, Henry Ford.

McCormick was a model, and almost a parody, of capitalist self-discipline. He did not marry until he was 49, never traveled for fun and relaxed by discussing theology with Presbyterian ministers. He supported the Confederacy, but his reaper helped save the Union: it enabled the North to feed itself, even while conscripting farmers.

A broader paradox of American agriculture is suggested by Thomas Jefferson's life. An exponent of an agrarian republic, Jefferson shared the American suspicion that those who work in cities are apt to be less virtuous citizens than farmers are. But Jefferson, apostle of applied enlightenment, was an early student of new agricultural technologies that eventually would make it possible for a small farm population to feed a thoroughly urbanized nation.

And although Jefferson distrusted energetic government as much as he celebrated agriculture, American agriculture is one of American government's success stories, the product of energetic development policies.

Two hundred years ago, labor was cheap and land was so plentiful that farmers regarded it as something to be "used up," and used it wastefully. Machinery was a plow; energy came from human and animal muscle; fertilizer was animal waste. But federal undertakings, from land distribution through rural electrification and price supports, have made agriculture, in part, a government enterprise.

First, government aimed at broad distribution of cultivable land. But just sixty-four years after Jefferson's death, the census indicated that the frontier was closed. Then government policy aimed at increasing the productivity of land. The land-grant college system, begun by the 1862 Morrill Act, fostered agricultural research and extension services. The National Reclamation Act of 1902 and the Federal Farm Loan Act of 1916 deepened government involvement.

In 1908, the Country Life Commission expressed Theodore Roosevelt's desire to promote the institutionalization of agriculture. "Farmers must learn," he said, "the vital need of cooperation with one another. Next to this comes cooperation with the government. . . ."

Professor Earl O. Heady notes that "By the 1920s the per capita income had risen high enough for the domestic demand for food to have become highly inelastic. That is, incomes had risen to the level where consumers were able to buy all the food they needed and further increases could have little effect on food consumption."

And increased food production was apt to mean decreased prices. Not surprisingly, in 1929 the Hoover Administration committed itself to the task of "preventing and controlling surpluses in any agricultural commodity."

Farmers are thought of as the last vessels of individualism and pristine private enterprise. But, increasingly, they are industrialists whose production processes are science-intensive and capital-intensive, and deeply involved with public policy. Most farmers do not eat what they produce. They eat what they find at the supermarket—that showcase of abundance made possible by two centuries of government promotion of agriculture. The current farmers' strike is interesting principally because of its target: it is a way of lobbying the government.

Those were fortunate pioneers whose wagons sank into the heavy soil of the Midwest, and who did not push beyond that ancient seabed—the world's finest stretch of farmland. McCormick's machine was especially suited to farming that prairie. But perhaps the most important agriculture machinery has been the machinery of government.

February 12, 1978

Democracy and Decadence

Political actions often are less important than the reasons given for them. Consider the case of Congressman Charles C. Diggs, Jr.

Diggs, a Michigan Democrat, has been convicted on twenty-nine counts of mail fraud and receiving salary kickbacks from his staff. He has been sentenced to three years in prison. He is appealing. He also is serving in Congress, having been reelected since his conviction.

The theory that Diggs should not be expelled from Congress reveals much about the condition of democratic government.

Diggs's conviction ended the obligation to presume him innocent, so it is unnecessary to suspend judgment pending appeals. Yet Jim Wright (D.-Tex.), the Majority Leader, probably spoke for the majority when he said Diggs should not be expelled even if his appeal fails:

"Membership in the House is not ours to bestow. . . . The constituents are entitled to have the Representatives of their own choice."

By choosing the word "bestow," Wright blurs the distinction, suggested by a Supreme Court opinion, between expelling and excluding a member. In the case of Adam Clayton Powell, the Court held that, as regards exclusion, Congress is limited to judging members in terms of the qualifications (pertaining to age, citizenship, residency) prescribed in the Constitution. But in a concurring opinion, Justice William Douglas argued that expulsion of a member, once he has been sworn in, is different: ". . . If this were an expulsion case I would think that no justiciable controversy would be presented, the vote of the House being two-thirds or more."

A House committee has held that the power of expulsion is inherent in legislative bodies, and is necessary to the safety of the state. The Constitution says: "Each house may . . . punish its members for disorderly behavior, and, with the concurrence of two-thirds, expel a member."

The power probably is unlimited and unappealable.

The extreme, anti-constitutional and untenable nature of Wright's doctrine is illustrated by this fact: the doctrine implies that the House should not expel a member even for treason or bribery, offenses against the integrity of government, offenses that the Constitution denotes as grounds for impeaching a President. (The House has expelled three members, all in 1861, for the "treason" of supporting the Confederacy.)

Wright's doctrine is grounded not in constitutional reasoning but in a theory of democracy: democratic "entitlement" allows no restriction on the voters' choice of representation. It follows that no offense is so inconsistent with a member's duties that Congress should respond with expulsion in order to protect its corporate integrity. All constituencies evidently have an absolute right to send convicts to make laws and oversee their execution.

The fact that the congressional black caucus has rallied to Diggs's defense is important only as a measure of the decline of black leadership. The issue is philosophical, not racial.

If Diggs's constituents elected him to a legislature that made laws only for them, it would be slightly more arguable that he should be tolerated in office. But Congress legislates for the nation, so voters, ever alert to entitlements, should acknowledge, or be made to acknowledge, countervailing obligations to respect Congress's institutional dignity and national responsibility.

That Wright's doctrine is widely accepted demonstrates how attenuated is Congress's and the public's sense of Congress as a corporate trustee of national purposes. Increasingly, voters regard congressmen, and congressmen regard themselves, as ambassadors dispatched to a foreign province, the federal city, where their only duty is to do the bidding of those who dispatched them.

That duty usually reduces to competing with other ambassadors in the scramble for benefits. Thus the office of representative has lost even the dignity conferred by an elevated theory of its function.

The decay of democratic government, and the permanent economic inflation that is both a cause and a consequence of that, is related to the thoughtless multiplication of "entitlements," and the reduction of democratic theory to a list of entitlements. Most are entitlements to services, but none is as pernicious as the general justifying doctrine that constituents are "entitled" to whatever they can effectively demand.

Wright's rationalization for not expelling a convict from Congress is just a mechanical application of such thinking. But one word describes a democracy that defends an "entitlement" as perverse as that asserted by Diggs's constituents. The word is decadent.

January 25, 1979

Republican Letters

It was time to fulfill the literary function that is central to republican government, so the congressman began a letter to his constituents: "Although no definitive measure of importance hath hitherto taken place in Congress, yet in pursuance of my duty and inclination, I beg leave to furnish you with a short abstract of the state of public affairs. . . ."

The University of North Carolina has published three volumes of "circular letters," newsletters sent by congressmen to constituents between 1789 and 1829. To read them is to sense something we have lost, and to glimpse the elusive relationship between style and substance in politics.

Although the styles of the letters vary, they all seem suited to an age before broadcasting, when the eye was more important than the ear, and people did not expect and require public utterances to be plain and graceless. I will leave aside my firm conviction that the rushing typewriter, with its clackety-clack rhythm, is an enemy of well-crafted sentences.

But I will insist that when those early congressmen dipped quill pens into inkwells they were undertaking a highly regarded art—expository prose—and they aimed for a stately tone appropriate for matters of high moral dignity. The less elevated style of today's political discourse is, perhaps, appropriate for today's servile state that sees itself merely as an undignified broker between clamorous interests.

The subjects taken up in the republished letters include how to cope with Algerian pirates, and Indians, and whether to tax stills or the liquor distilled. There also are perennial themes. A writer boasts about voting against a measure that increased congressmen's compensation to "eight dollars a day and the same for 20 miles travel." In 1818 a congressman expresses fastidious dismay: "All works undertaken by this government are carried on in a manner not remarkable for economy." Another representative, anticipating today's populist dislike of lawyers, criticizes the session just ended because "there was too large a proportion of professional gentlemen, and others not sufficiently conversant with the manner in which the main body of the yeomanry of this country gain their substance."

In the 1790s, when the government was just developing its sea legs, many letters were full of alarm. Americans were "furiously hurling ourselves into the vortex of tyranny." Americans were losing "the Security of their Liberties, for which they have so valiantly fought and so profusely bled." A congressman mentioned "the election of John Adams" and exclaims: "O afflictive words! . . . O the depravity of the times! O the corruption of the manners!"

By the 1820s a congressman's report was more apt to be matter-of-fact: "In giving you a sketch of our session, I have to remark that it commenced in a calm, which approached to indifference."

Communication to and from the central government was difficult in the days before mass and instant communication. When these letters were being written, congressmen were insulated from their constituents by a psychological distance that owed something to physical distance, and something to the philosophic understanding of representation that is the essence of republican government. So it was natural for congressmen to conclude a report as austerely as John Tyler of Virginia did in 1818:

> I have thus briefly, Fellow Citizens, presented you the reasons which have governed me in the course which I have pursued upon those subjects of greatest importance to our future destiny. Should I have been so fortunate as to have coincided with you in opinion, it will be to me a source of gratification . . . [But] should my course not meet with your approbation, I have the consolation to know that I have honestly pursued the dictates of my best judgment, and acted the part of an independent Representative.

When, if ever, have you been addressed by a politician possessing such serenity and dignity? Tyler's course was determined by "reasons," by his "judgment," not his constituents' instructions. He was pleased to present his conduct for approval, after the fact. Given the limited possibility for communication with a constituency during a session of Congress, he could hardly have done more. Given his understanding of his office, he would not have wished to do more.

Tyler expressed the essential, indispensable spirit of republican government, and it seems archaic because we have, in fact, dispensed with it.

October 12, 1978

The Cold War Among Women

At Saint Columba's Nursery School, which has custody of Geoffrey Marion Will, a recent snack time featured corn on the cob, and the sight of the corn being buttered by 4-year-olds was not for the weak. Finding myself seated next to a well-buttered girl, I asked what she intended to be if her parents let her grow up. "A nurse," she replied, briskly. But for her coating of butter, I would have hugged her, so pleased was I that she was unaware that she is supposed to say "neurosurgeon," or something of the sort.

A mother in the school car pool swears she will strangle the next girl who announces an intention to be a lawyer. Suddenly, the world seems infested with Napoleonic little girls who probably read Nietzsche and certainly burn with the desire to right wrongs and unchain the oppressed. Being a full-time mother is hard enough without the implied reproaches of 4-year-olds. And little girls are only half of the little problems. A friend of mine was driving her son to school when he inquired, "Mommy, why did you grow up to be nothing?" No jury would have convicted her if she had tied him to a railroad track. Even as recently as a decade ago, a 4-year-old would have been much less likely to ask such a question. The assumptions that blow like pollen in the social breeze are fertilizing little minds.

A gentleman does not ask a mother, "Do you work?" The somewhat labored, but kinder, question is "Do you work outside the home, for pay?" Mothers who stay at home are understandably sensitive, and one reason is that many men are clods. In social settings these men talk about their jobs, or others' jobs, or the morality of municipal bonds or the originality of Norman Mailer, but confronted with a full-time mother they are dumb, in several senses. They are not much interested in the world's most interesting and important business, which also happens to be men's business: raising children. And they seem to think that mothers who do not work outside the home have no interest in, or nothing interesting to say about, things outside the home.

Furthermore, in this period of "liberation," women are under a subtle despotism of social expectations. A professor at Smith College reports that a generation ago women seeking supportive advice were apt to be those who wanted to enter a profession. Today, the women most apt to feel peculiar and vaguely unjustified are women who want to marry and begin a family without taking the almost obligatory plunge into the job market. Recently, a *Washington Post* report on the social pressure many mothers feel to work outside the home provoked a spirited letter from a woman who says she frequently detects the suspicion that "I am lazy, shallow or just plain crazy for staying home." Speaking, I am sure, for millions, she said:

> Traditionally, the role of a woman was that of wife and mother, homemaker and nurturer. If that stereotype was oppressive to many, its antithesis today is no less tyrannical. The assumption that personal fulfillment for women can be found only in the active pursuit of a career degrades homemaking and motherhood to the status of a desirable but expensive hobby . . . I do not consider all working women (having been one myself) to be child-neglecting, emasculating, selfish vipers. It would be nice if I in turn were not regarded as a mindless, cookie-baking, gingham-clad nitwit.

Many women are longing to get out of the house and into jobs that today are boring men to distraction. For every woman who craves the status of an executive there is an executive who would, if he could, flee to northern Minnesota and open a bait-and-tackle shop. The problem for men is not that employment is more narrowing than ever before, but that the expectations for "fulfilling" work are higher. The problems for women are more complicated. It is said that modern societies alternate between exhilaration about the achieving of progress and disappointment about the fruits of it. Today, in a period of self-conscious "liberation," women are especially apt to live in perpetual anticipation, and hence in unfulfillment.

Before education and employment were open to women, and before affluence diminished the drudgery of domestic chores, the idea that femininity implied domesticity was an attempt to make a virtue of necessity. And after a depression and war, the postwar thirst for stability caused women to embrace domesticity as the chance of a lifetime and a choice for a lifetime. But then two growth industries, academic psychology and sociology, popularized the concepts of "stereotypes" and "roles," and women became increasingly uneasy about lives defined by traditional functions. Women were especially susceptible to the postwar feeling of expansiveness and possibility, and the urgent faith in the flowering of self.

Today's mothers should be forgiven for being restless. They have less authority and more anxiety than ever. They feel that their area of competence is being circumscribed, while their responsibilities are being enlarged. The force of popular culture pulling children away is stronger than ever. But the new "science of parenting," proclaimed in a flood of handbooks (with appalling titles like *Improving Your Child's Behavior Chemistry*), imposes upon mothers the responsibility of measuring up to scientific perfection in raising children. Parenting (in a rational society the use of such ersatz words would be a flogging offense) is another example of the modern assumption that all of nature, including human nature, is raw material for science. And competition among supermoms—they should be wearing white lab smocks—who are determined to concoct the perfect child reaches the grim intensity of an arms race.

Writing in *The American Spectator,* Anne Crutcher says that some contemporary feminism presents "as tragedies the inevitable disappointments of those who want contradictory things at the same time." But she also says, just as truly, that women's handicaps are subtler and more pervasive, and their desires are more mixed, than even most women imagine. There is a special poignancy in the fact that women more often than men face exclusive choices between quite different ways of living, each with intense rewards and deprivations.

Recently, a four-column headline on page 2 of *The Washington Star* proclaimed, with a hint of amazement: HER CHILDREN COME FIRST, SO WHITE HOUSE AIDE RESIGNS. Undoubtedly some feminists shuddered and said "Yucch!" when reading what the mother said about her children: "I told them this morning, and their little smiles were worth everything." And the reassurance that many full-time mothers could receive from the story was diminished by the story's tone of mild astonishment, which suggested that the woman's decision to resign was bizarre. So goes the cold war among women.

June 26, 1978

Gambling with the Public's Virtue

On the outskirts of this city of insurance companies, there is another, less useful, business based on an understanding of probabilities. It is a jai alai fronton, a cavernous court where athletes play a fast game for the entertainment of gamblers and the benefit of, among others, the state treasury.

Half the states have legal betting in casinos, at horse or dog tracks, in off-track betting parlors, at jai alai frontons or in state-run lotteries. Only Connecticut has four (the last four) kinds of gambling, and there is talk of promoting the other two.

Not coincidentally, Connecticut is one of just seven states still fiercely determined not to have an income tax. Gambling taxes yielded $76.4 million last year—which is not a large slice of Connecticut's $2.1 billion budget, but it would be missed, and is growing.

Last year Americans legally wagered $15 billion, up 8 percent over 1976. Lotteries took in 24 percent more than in 1976. Stiffening resistance to taxes is encouraging states to seek revenues from gambling, and thus to encourage gambling. There are three rationalizations for this:

State-run gambling controls illegal gambling.

Gambling is a painless way to raise revenues.

Gambling is a "victimless" recreation, and thus is a matter of moral indifference.

Actually, there is evidence that legal gambling increases the respectability of gambling, and increases public interest in gambling. This creates new gamblers, some of whom move on to illegal gambling, which generally offers better odds. And as a revenue-raising device, gambling is severely regressive.

Gamblers are drawn disproportionately from minority and poor populations that can ill afford to gamble, that are especially susceptible to the lure of gambling and that especially need a government that will not collaborate with gambling entrepreneurs, as in jai alai, and that will not become a gambling entrepreneur through a state lottery.

A depressing number of gamblers have no margin for economic losses and little understanding of the probability of losses. Between 1975 and 1977 there was a 140-percent increase in spending to advertise lotteries—lotteries in which more than 99.9 percent of all players are losers. Such advertising is apt to be especially effective, and cruel, among people whose tribulations make them susceptible to dreams of sudden relief.

Grocery money is risked for such relief. Some grocers in Hartford's poorer neighborhoods report that receipts decline during jai alai season. Aside from the injury gamblers do to their dependents, there is a subtler but more comprehensive injury done by gambling. It is the injury done to society's sense of elemental equities. Gambling blurs the distinction between well-earned and "ill-gotten" gains.

Gambling is debased speculation, a lust for sudden wealth that is not connected with the process of making society more productive of goods and services. Government support of gambling gives a legitimating imprimatur to the pursuit of wealth without work.

"It is," said Jefferson, "the manners and spirit of a people which preserves a republic in vigor." Jefferson believed in the virtue-instilling effects of agricultural labor. Andrew Jackson denounced the Bank of the United States as a "monster" because increased credit creation meant increased speculation. Martin Van Buren warned against "a craving desire . . . for sudden wealth." The early-nineteenth-century belief was that citizens could be distinguished by the moral worth of the way they acquired wealth; and physical labor was considered the most ennobling labor.

It is perhaps a bit late to worry about all this: the United States is a developed capitalist society of a sort Jefferson would have feared if he had been able to imagine it. But those who cherish capitalism should note that the moral weakness of capitalism derives, in part, from the belief that too much wealth is allocated in "speculative" ways, capriciously, to people who earn their bread neither by the sweat of their brows nor by wrinkling their brows for socially useful purposes.

Of course, any economy produces windfalls. As a town grows, some land values soar. And some investors (like many noninvestors) regard stock trading as a form of roulette.

But state-sanctioned gambling institutionalizes windfalls, whets the public appetite for them and encourages the delusion that they are more frequent than they really are. Thus do states simultaneously cheat and corrupt their citizens.

October 15, 1978

De-atomization at West Point

Not long ago, an official inquiry solemnly found that the U.S. Military Academy's shortcomings include an inadequate sense of humor. This finding occasioned some—it must be admitted, rather strained—jocularity at West Point. Now come reports that fun there still is not what it should be.

Female cadets have been pressured to kill chickens by biting the chickens' necks; cadets dressed in Ku Klux Klan garb have held mock trials. It is a pity West Point often makes news with episodes that illuminate neither the virtues of its cadets nor the important questions about its mission.

When I was there this fall it was grand to hear, as the cadets assembled for dinner, soprano voices in the football pep rally: "Napalm North Carolina!"

The appearance of skirts in the long gray line has produced some problems, and some unintended hilarity. (This is the accepted description of a new disciplinary problem: Cadet X is guilty of "gross error of judgment; i.e., having a female cadet in bed in his room after taps and engaging in acts of affection prejudicial to the good order and discipline of the Corps of Cadets.") But as in the past, there are deeper questions about what should be considered the good order of the corps.

Located at one of America's most beautiful spots, on a bluff overlooking the Hudson, West Point is a national shrine that stirs anyone not altogether dead to the promptings of patriotism. And in the nineteenth century, it was a great nation-building institution.

The military made many of the maps, roads and bridges that the wagon trains used. Military forts were part of the infrastructure necessary for the pursuit of our "Manifest Destiny." Many engineers trained by the Army later staffed the private sector. Indeed, the contributions of officers produced in West Point's first one hundred years were as much technical as military.

Today, as always, officers must be capable of handling combat. But officers in a modern army must have many skills unrelated to the discipline of combat, or the technical, engineering curriculum that has been so central at West Point. Such subjects as U.S. and Soviet strategic doctrine, and the policy-planning process, should be at the center of the education of those officers who will engage in close combat in the corridors of the Pentagon and Congress.

Men as different as Thomas Jefferson, one of nature's aristocrats, and Andrew Jackson, one of nature's rabble-rousers, shared a hostility toward military academies, which they feared would be nurseries of a dangerously militaristic elite. My limited exposure to first-year cadets convinced me that Jefferson and Jackson can rest easy.

When asked why they had chosen West Point, the cadets' responses tended to emphasize the matter-of-fact: a free education for a useful career. The spirit of the age has done its dirty work, so they are bashful about saying what is obviously, splendidly true of most of them: they are moved by patriotic as well as personal considerations.

They seem terribly young, these late-teens who have plumped for a life so rigorous and so thoroughly against the grain of America's current culture. But it is at least arguable that officers should be made young: induce the reflexes as soon as possible, because the more a person must unlearn, the harder it is. The rule of life for an aspiring officer must be: You can do more than you think you can, and had better.

Military academies aim not just at endowing their students with particular skills, but also at changing in fundamental ways those who enroll. And never before in this nation's experience have the values and expectations prevalent in society been more at variance with the values and expectations that are indispensable to a military establishment.

In modern society, comfort is high, freedom is virtually boundless and pain is, if not abolished, at least on the agenda for abolition. Military academies must fish young people from this milieu and reverse society's process of atomizing individuals. De-atomization must involve instilling in them the traits made necessary by the timeless fact of life that Oliver Wendell Holmes, Jr., expressed with characteristic concision: "Every society rests on the death of men."

Today this nation flinches from that fact, as from most unpleasant truths, but that does not make it less true. This is a good moment to remember the Marine recruiting slogan: No one wants to fight, but someone had better know how.

November 15, 1979

The Incest Lobby

I cannot catalog all the disagreeable potentialities of the modern mind, but an article attempting to make incest less abhorrent deserves attention because it illuminates, like a flare of sulfurous gas, the darker recesses of that mind.

The article, published by the Sex Information and Education Council of the United States, is by James Ramey, whose biography says he is a researcher whose interests include "incest; the impact of energy, economic and ecological changes in lifestyles in the future; and the positive sexual socialization of children."

In an editorial accompanying Ramey's article, the publishers insist, piously and perhaps even sincerely, that all Ramey is doing is "reportage" and "analysis," not advocacy. They say he is just "clearing the decks, as it were," of misguided "preconceptions and concerns" that impede research.

But Ramey's title—"Dealing with the Last Taboo"—gives the game away. The word "taboo" calls to mind primitive people haunted by irrational superstitions that can't survive deck-clearing research.

"We are," Ramey lectures, "in roughly the same position today regarding incest as we were a hundred years ago with respect to our fear of masturbation." He notes instances of nineteenth-century ignorance about masturbation (such as the theory that it causes insanity or criminality), and he wonders, archly, "Is there a parallel regarding incest?"

He says incest is a matter of "personal morality," and that laws concerning it are "overly harsh," especially considering that "as early as 1936" a researcher "showed" that "incest seldom has anything to do with sexually 'perverse' behavior." He cites a study that purports to show "healthy situations" in which incest "was an obviously appropriate behavior." He cites someone who "found" several families in which "consent openly allowed active, sophisticated lifestyles which included sexual sharing." Ah, "sophisticated" sharing—surely the best sort. No advocacy here, of course.

Ramey says that "several authors concur" in the view of the person who said that

> many girls are, in the truest sense of the word, their fathers' lovers. Many have the same type of relationship that adults have, and some resent community intervention, and are difficult to work with, particularly when professionals carry over a cultural bias that incest is wrong and that by definition the girls should resent it.

Note the phrase "in the truest sense."

Ramey says the "drum-beating" against incest is damaging even those not involved in incest: "American families have been so imbued with prohibitions against incest that they bend over backwards to avoid any possibility of incestuous involvement or the possible accusation that they might become involved. This results either in complete and total abandonment of all parent–child physical contact at puberty . . . or in seductive behavior that never culminates in manifest sexual activity, which James Leslie McCary believed affects the child more negatively than does actual incest." Ramey says this "peculiarly American problem" results from "well meant yet inhuman attitudes" related to incest.

Time magazine recently cited numerous other examples of what it calls the incest "lobby." A Johns Hopkins sex researcher says "a childhood sexual experience, such as being the partner of a relative," need not "affect the child adversely." A professor at Tufts says, "Children have a right to express themselves sexually, even with members of their own family."

A sex researcher distributes questionnaires asking about incestuous experiences, "good or bad." Ramey says we should "abolish" incest laws and rely on rape and child-abuse laws for "those cases" that "warrant" prosecution. In some of the lobby's literature, "positive incest," meaning "consensual incest," is distinguished from "abusive incest." The coauthor of the original Kinsey report says: "It is time to admit," among other things, that incest between children and adults "can sometimes be beneficial."

"It is time . . ." This incantation moves the modern mind: Change is natural, therefore change is progressive, therefore the

natural progression of mankind is through expanding "emancipation" from "taboos" and other "hang-ups" that inhibit "self-fulfillment." The non sequiturs clang together like empty freight cars
on a railroad to barbarism.

There is no labyrinth as unconquerable as the simple mind: an
idea, once in, stays. The simplemindedness of the modern age
manifests itself in the worship of "change."

In the nineteenth century, when there was, perhaps, more excuse for investing extravagant hope in "change," Tennyson wrote:
"Let the great world spin forever down the ringing grooves of
change." We should now know that the key word is "down."

May 22, 1980

Sex Education: Plumbing for Hedonists

These days, everything somehow reminds everyone of sex, and
President Carter's desire to subsidize wood-burning stoves reminds me of sex education. I don't understand subsidies for the
world's oldest use of fuel, and I don't understand intense instruction in the world's oldest obsession. At least, I didn't understand
the latter until I read "Turning Children into Sex Experts," Jac-
queline Kasun's essay in the latest issue of *The Public Interest*.

Kasun, a California academic, argues that sex education has
become a "movement," whose focus is less biological than political.
Its prime movers are mainly psychologists, sociologists and "health
educators" concerned less with the physiology of procreation than
with "value clarification." It seems that being a sex educator is like
being ambassador to the United Nations: a person eager for the job
is apt to be exactly the kind of person who should be kept far away
from it.

Schools are flooding society with young people who cannot read, write or think adequately. But seventh- and eighth-graders in Kasun's community are learning "the four philosophies of mastur-bation—traditional, religious, natural, radical." Those who speak of such "philosophies" are, at best, semiliterate, but they are in careers open to their talents: "Sex is too important to glop up with sentiment . . . Masturbation cannot hurt you and it will make you feel more relaxed."

Kasun reports that the curriculum in Ferndale, California, sug-gests that students discuss in class whether they are satisfied with their "size of sex organs." And she says, "The seventh-grader in my city is advised to set for himself a purely 'personal standard of sexual behavior.' No religious views, no community moral stan-dards are to deflect him from his overriding purposes of self-dis-covery, self-assertion, and self-gratification."

Once upon a time, it was said that sex education would amelio-rate the problem of teen-age pregnancy. But reasonable people warned, and some other people hoped, that sex education often would involve teaching that sex is just another occasion for self-absorption, another arena for "self-fulfillment." This would result in more promiscuity (and more abortions, and other signs of "clar-ified" values).

Recently, a rationale for "sexuality" training has been that it awakens children from the dark American slumber of Puritanism, repression, inhibition, and so on. But surely for every child who needs to be "awakened" to sexuality there are fifty thousand who need reinforcement against the enveloping sexual vulgarity of pop-ular culture.

In C. S. Lewis' *The Screwtape Letters,* the devil Screwtape, tutoring a young friend in the art of corrupting, explains that "nonsense in the intellect may reinforce corruption in the will." The trick, he says, is first to convince people that Fashion should rule them because Fashion is the Tide of History, and hence "pro-gressive."

Then: "We direct the fashionable outcry of each generation against those vices of which it is least in danger. . . . Cruel ages are put on their guard against Sentimentality, feckless and idle ones against Respectability, lecherous ones against Puritanism. . . ."

And so, today, society invests hundreds of millions of dollars, and even more student hours, in sex-education classes. Many of them use the sort of materials Kasun cites, such as the article proclaiming that, "We must finish the contemporary sex 'revolution.' . . . Our society must strive to sanction and support various forms of intimacy between members of the same sex."

The coarseness of the materials she cites (which I flinch from quoting) is intrinsic to the doctrine the material serves. Political arguments, pushed far enough, are about what kind of creatures we are and what we can become, and the doctrine of the sex-education "movement" is this: Man is a sensing more than a reasoning creature; life is a stream of sensations; the good life is the glandular life.

As Kasun says, "In undertaking to finance and promote a multi-million-dollar program of sex education, the government has entered very heavily into the promotion of a particular world view and the establishment of a chosen ideology, a kind of secular religion."

The sex educators she cites treat sex partly as plumbing and partly as recreation. Theirs is an American triumph: plumbing for hedonists. But they should at least remember C. S. Lewis' warning: You can spoil your enjoyment of the finest mountain view by thinking of it in terms of the mechanics of the retina and the optic nerve.

April 12, 1979

Junk Food for the Mind

It has been said that you must swallow a toad before breakfast in order to be sure of experiencing nothing more distasteful before bedtime. But that might not work when CBS broadcasts (October 14) half of a four-hour drama involving incest.

CBS says the program "tastefully" portrays a mother seducing her son at Christmas. Jean Cocteau said tact is knowing how far to go in going too far, and "tasteful" television often involves carefully calibrated excess. CBS excised scenes of the mother passionately kissing and beginning to undress her son. Harry F. Waters of *Newsweek* says the revised scene shows the son "frozen at the bedroom door as Ma glides seductively inside. . . . Mother and son embark on a steamy odyssey to Las Vegas, replete with cheek-to-cheek dance embraces and bed-top nuzzlings."

As Emerson said, we boil at different degrees. Unfortunately, many Americans do not boil at all. But one group is at a rolling boil about this and much else on television. The group is wide open to the ridicule of semisophisticates, first because of its name: National Federation for Decency. "Decency"? Really, how droll. And it is led by a minister—a Mississippi minister, for pete's sake. It all adds up to "redneck"—right?

Wrong. The Reverend Donald Wildmon of Tupelo, Mississippi, is a tranquil, soft-spoken organizer of 10,000 members whose newsletter goes to more than 60,000 individuals, PTAs and church groups. NFD monitors not just television's sexual sleaziness but also gratuitous violence. NFD believes that corporations sponsoring such material should feel the sting of consumer boycotts. It may be, but probably is not, a coincidence that Sears withdrew as a sponsor of the execrable *Three's Company* almost immediately after an NFD protest.

What NFD does is consumerism—consumerism without dragging in government; consumerism applied to one of the most important and toxic things we consume, popular culture. Yet some perpetrators of popular culture accuse NFD of "censorship" and threatening "First Amendment rights."

Americans worry too much about the vigorously exercised right of free speech and too little about the underexercised right of free thought. People who shout "Censorship!" to discredit voluntary economic boycotts directed against commercial entertainment are using libertarian cant as a substitute for thought.

All the "bold, new" departures in popular culture, such as prime-time incest, are praised and defended with old, familiar phrases, because there is nothing bold or new about them. They are not departures from (they are routine facets of) television's business, which is business. Specifically, it is drawing an audience to which someone can sell something.

Just as advertising has depleted the power of most adjectives, movies have exhausted the power of "normal" sex and violence to entertain by shocking. The public, poor thing, is jaded. Poor television: it hardly knows how to keep its audience titillated between commercials. Movies became "bold" to entice people to leave their living rooms and plunk down $4. Such movies are now available in many places on cable television. So network television must scramble to keep up. Hence, "tastefully" done incest.

Newsweek says the incest drama touches "a heretofore taboo subject." The word "taboo" suggests a pre-rational people haunted by shadows and governed by quaint strictures. But taboos are strong proscriptions against certain kinds of conduct (incest and murder, for example), and no society is without them.

It is irrational to accept all of society's proscriptions thoughtlessly, but it is childish to regard all of them as impediments to freedom. And it is folly to think that no subject is too gross and coarsening to be suitable for exploitation as entertainment on an intrusive selling medium like television, for the purpose of peddling fried chicken.

Kentucky Fried Chicken is one sponsor that has resisted requests that it quit sponsoring shows like *Three's Company* and *Anatomy of a Seduction* (middle-aged woman seduces young son of her best friend). That is, perhaps, as it ought to be: a steady diet of television does to the mind what a steady diet of fast food would do to the body. But why do more people worry more about the pollution of the air than about the pollution of the airwaves? More about junk food for the body than junk food for the mind?

The twentieth century did not invent vulgarity, but it did invent sophisticated technologies, such as television, that are often used for the commercial exploitation of vulgarity. A wise man has wondered, "Is it progress if a cannibal uses knife and fork?"

October 14, 1979

Et Tu, Topeka?

Ah, serendipity. Beneath *The Washington Post*'s report of the press conference at which the Coalition for Better Television (CBTV) announced plans to organize boycotts of products produced by sponsors of the sleaziest television shows, there appeared a report by the *Post*'s Tom Shales about a new show:

> A better title for "That's My Line" might be, maybe, "Sick Society." The CBS entry in the amazingly incredible, real-people, variety freak-show genre . . . lurches impishly from a feature about a man who teaches other men "how to pick up girls" for quick sex to a fey hunk of sleazery about a Topeka, Kansas, clothing store where men strip down to their underpants while women ogle and shriek at them. . . . Basically it's another monomaniacal titillation derby.

Et tu, Topeka?

Shales suggests that perhaps the pollution of the prairie by such vulgarity might be television's fault: any entrepreneur knows that if he is sufficiently vulgar, network camera crews will beat a path to his door. I have a less cheerful view of mankind: Topeka or Timbuktu can produce ninnies without the television incentive. Wordsworth, who lived a long way from Kansas and a long time before television, noted mankind's "degrading thirst for outrageous stimulation."

But the pure commercial logic of oligopolistic competition impels three profit-maximizing (which means, basically: audience-maximizing) networks to pander to society's lowest common denominator. And in doing so, they drive it steadily lower. CBTV's aim is to temper that logic by adding a new variable to the economic calculations that control television.

Networks live lives of cheerful, not to say brazen, contradiction. They trumpet their prowess at causing people to buy material goods: Hey, we can modify behavior in thirty seconds. Yet they deny, or disclaim responsibility for, the coarsening consequences of hour after hour of base programs. You can almost—almost, I stress—admire the brass of the tiny coterie of network programmers who complain that CBTV's "narrow" portion of the public—perhaps only a few million citizens—may influence programming.

But more unlovely than the aggressive vulgarity of many programs is the ravening hypocrisy of the programmers as they criticize their critics. It is hard (and hardly obligatory) to credit the sincerity of people who shout "Censorship!"—with that word's connotations of coercive state action—when people are simply planning to practice selective buying of beer and panty hose. A network spokesman decreed that boycotts are "censorship" and are "a totally unacceptable method of trying to influence programming." I called to ask what he considered acceptable. He said—are you ready for this?—"Oh, writing a letter."

Plumbing the shallows of such minds will not dredge up serious arguments against boycotts. Another network theorist called to deploy for me all the stock phrases of First Amendment law. He accused CBTV of planning to "conspire" to create a "clear and present danger" of a "chilling effect" on the "expression of ideas."

Leave aside the inherent disingenuousness of a defense of programs like *Soap* or *Dynasty* or *Three's Company* as vehicles of "ideas." People who argue that way are beyond, or beneath, embarrassment, so they do not blush when quoting Milton, Mill, Jefferson and Holmes to defend their rapacity. It is bad enough that the networks are turning the airwaves into Love Canals of the mind. But a chemical company that recklessly dumps toxic wastes at least spares us the effrontery of claiming to serve civilization's spiritual well-being.

By invoking the noble language of the literature of liberty—"the free expression of ideas," and all that—the networks try to beguile the public into forgetting what networks never forget: commercial television's purpose is to sell rivers of beer and mountains of panty house ("Hey, America—show us your Underalls!"). What CBTV proposes, far from being a "conspiracy," is as public as a calliope and as American as Martin Luther King's boycott of Montgomery, Alabama, buses.

The hysterical network response is heartening. The networks' criterion of an "acceptable" protest is clear: acceptable means impotent. It is acceptable for an individual to write a letter, but unacceptable for individuals to "conspire"—meaning organize—because organizing might work. An advertiser says, "It takes only a percentage-point-or-two shift in the retail sales of washing machines or K-cars to make a tremendous difference in profits." Profits? Quit talking about those, dummy, and start quoting Milton.

Let's all get started. Dial soap helps sponsor the execrable *Flamingo Road*. Aren't you glad you don't use Dial? Don't you wish nobody did?

February 8, 1981

A World of Crushingly Particular Experiences

Odd, isn't it, how the mind works? Or doesn't work, which is much the same thing. One morning recently my thoughts bounced from a tube of toothpaste to Mother Teresa to Paul Volcker.

Volcker is chairman of the Federal Reserve Board. Mother Teresa has received a Nobel Peace Prize for her service to the poor and dying of Calcutta. My tube of toothpaste was empty.

To deal with first things first, consider a dawn that breaks on a day without toothpaste. The horror, the horror. As I stood there, enveloped by Chevy Chase and self-pity, a thought struck me with awful force. In Calcutta, people must frequently run out of toothpaste.

When the Will mind is in high gear, it hippity-hops from one such sunburst to another. In ten weeks I shall have been in Washington ten years, and on a recent morning I came to a conclusion I could have come to anywhere but could hardly have avoided coming to in Washington. It is as follows:

The world's most serious shortage is, we are told, energy. Or protein. Or democracy. Or something. Most nominees for the title of Most Serious Shortage are arguable, but my nominee is better. It is imagination. I mean imagination of a particular kind: the kind that produces social sympathy—the ability to comprehend, however dimly, how other people live. I don't mean just people in other cultures or neighborhoods, but also neighbors who have sick children and other private worries.

The other day Paul Volcker said that Americans may have to lower their standard of living. Imagine how that sounded to those Americans (especially the poor, and especially the elderly who are being impoverished by inflation) who have been lowering their standard of living for a while now, and who will do so again if they fill (or if they do not fill) their heating-oil tanks.

I don't want to make too much of this. Volcker is a very good citizen; and we all say things which, were they put under a moral microscope, would cause us to faint from embarrassment. When Volcker used the category "Americans," we knew whom he meant: the comfortable middle class.

When John Locke wrote that government should rest on the consent of "the people," he meant the consent of a small slice of propertied English males. America's Founding Fathers said that "all men are created equal" and the Father of His Country went on selling slaves until 1798. This wasn't hypocrisy; it was just that "the people" and "all men" were abstractions, categories that took their meanings from peculiar contexts. All categories do; all contexts are peculiar.

The city named after the Father of His Country is, of course, an especially peculiar place, full of people marked by one characteristic of government: abstractness. Washington is a city that thinks in large categories, big blocs getting big bloc grants: the farmers, the consumers, the poor, the elderly, the middle class, the people.

Washington, where big battalions clash over big abstractions, is even farther mentally than geographically from the world of Mother Teresa. Hers is a world of crushingly particular experiences with crushed people, one at a time. How, then, do you explain her, whose life with the tangible suffering—the sufferers—of Calcutta is a triumph over the natural human tendency toward abstractness?

You cannot really explain her life of action by citing her faith. "Faith," wrote Cardinal Newman, "is illuminative, not operative; it does not force obedience, though it increases responsibility; it heightens guilt, it does not prevent sin."

Besides, you can't (or so I am increasingly convinced) "explain" anybody by citing anything. You can't really explain anyone, period.

I know perhaps six adults really well; I am endlessly surprised at their depths, mysteries and courage. And surely there comes a moment when every parent rocks back on his or her heels, figuratively speaking, and exclaims, "What a complicated creature a four-year-old is!" It is extraordinary how extraordinary the ordinary person is.

What distinguishes those, like Mother Teresa, whose extraordinariness is the sort we call saintliness is this: they understand, really understand, and so act as though they understand, what Franz Kafka (fine writer, no saint) meant when he said that "judgment day" is not a "day," it is a court in perpetual session.

October 25, 1979

The Seventies: Illusion of Progress

Experience, some people say, is like a light on a caboose, illuminating only where we aren't going. But we scrutinize the past for its elements of prologue, and consolation. As this decade winds down beneath the dark cloud of the next, consider some calamities that did not happen. Chile and Portugal did not get Communist governments. Eurocommunism crested short of power in Italy and France. No nuclear weapons were used. Baseball's National League did not adopt the designated-hitter rule.

Some people are punished for their sins, others by their sins. In the 1970s, Americans were punished by their penances. As penance for Vietnam, or 1968, or something, they "reformed" the Presidential selection process, and widened the already yawning gap between the skills required for winning and those required for governing. The first "people's convention" picked McGovern, who then lost forty-nine states. Carter's election was a Watergate penance: let's try love. Later, people remembered: a kind heart is no help in poker.

In 1973, the Supreme Court, citing the "privacy right" of women, swung a scythe through abortion laws. By 1979, pornography had done what a million abortions a year had not done: it had given the "women's movement" doubts about the dogma that sexual mores are none of the law's business. Homosexuals demanded laws making their affliction a civil right, and Sweden considered a law allowing children to divorce parents. Coming: 1984.

In Britain and elsewhere, there were moves to the right. The conservative 1970s were called the "Me Decade," especially by people clinging to the myth that the 1960s were years of selflessness. Odd, isn't it, that the slogan of the "selfless" sixties was "Do your own thing"? The 1970s were an odd Me Decade: so many me's were eager to be defined by others, such as *Cosmopolitan* magazine, or Bloomingdale's. "Be a Calvin Klein man." (Mr.

Klein also makes jeans for trendy 6-year-olds.) The sound of the seventies was of joggers panting. Jogging was a facet of the revolt against experts: people were taking their health out of their doctors' hands.

If life is getting better, why are people spending more and more on distractions? Popular entertainment may be the West's last great growth industry. Television in the 1970s vindicated the wit who said that life would be tolerable were it not for its amusements. But some British programs were sublime. The decline of almost everything since 1914 may explain why, in the 1970s, many Americans eagerly fled to Edwardian England in *The Forsyte Saga* and *Upstairs, Downstairs.*

In the 1970s, the largest remaining non-Communist empire, Portugal's disappeared. The Soviet empire spread. Another decade has passed and still, since 1945, Russia's Red Army has been used only against Russia's East European allies. But in the next decade it may be used to creat an ally. Two of the last three leaders of the Second World War, De Gaulle and Mao, died in the 1970s, and when Tito dies in the 1980s, the Red Army may impose socialist solidarity on Yugoslavia.

The great tension of the 1970s involved three men from the Europe between the Iron Curtain and the Urals. The preeminent man of power in the 1970s was Brezhnev. He consolidated his own power and expanded and exported his country's power. He also exported Solzhenitsyn. In Harvard Square as in Red Square, and in the greatest literary work of the decade, Solzhenitsyn fought the West's comforting illusions, about itself and its enemy. Then, in the last year of the decade, in just nine days in Poland, a Slavic Pope gave the world a glimpse of what may be momentous facts of the 1980s, the incurable illegitimacy of the regimes and the quickening religious life in Eastern Europe.

Man is the only melancholy animal because only man can compare what is with what might have been. And only man is perverse enough to feel most alive when the news is most lurid. As Valéry said: "If some great catastrophe is not announced every morning, we feel a certain void. 'Nothing in the paper today,' we sigh." People rarely sighed that way in the seventies.

The United States left Indochina; then the killing accelerated. Hanoi's victory refuted Hanoi's apologists. Cambodia and Laos fell like dominoes. There was a bloodbath that pulled the plug on the smugness of America's critics, and helped give rise to this satire of the Left's catechism:

Question: With Communist Cambodia and Communist Vietnam fighting each other as proxies for China and the Soviet Union, and the Cubans and East Germans deployed as Soviet proxies elsewhere, what country is the threat to peace?

Answer: Chile.

If the record of the human race is anything to go by, and I fear it is, it is likely that in the 1980s, more will be known but worse will be done. By 1979 smallpox was believed to be extinct; medical marvels (such as deciphering the disease mechanisms of cancers) may be just over the horizon. But in this century individual fears (such as infectious diseases, and damnation) have been supplanted by social fears (such as nuclear war and a 15-percent prime interest rate). In the 1980s nuclear weapons will spread, democracy will not and there will be many opportunities for noting this fact: as a starving child shrivels, his eyes seem to become larger. The decade that began with the suffering mirrored in the doelike eyes of the children of Biafra ends with the "Asian Auschwitz" of Indochina. In 1989, who will remember the Cambodians? "Who remembers the Armenians?" Hitler mused, in 1942.

After another decade of technological virtuosity and political brutality, of a test-tube baby and an Ayatollah Khomeini, few people cling to the idea that progress comes, automatically, with the passage of time. Simone Weil wrote that the great mistake of the nineteenth century "was to think that by walking straight on one mounted upward into the air." It is progress, of sorts, that at the end of the 1970s mankind's eyes were so cast down that they noticed the wisp of a woman who has taught the wretched of Calcutta the truth of this saying: Nothing is more beautiful than cheerfulness in an old face. Mother Teresa is proof that a small star's twinkling becomes more noticeable as the night becomes blacker.

November 19, 1979

Part Two 🙖

"RIGHTS" AND WRONGS, AND
LIFE AND DEATH

Crying "Wolf!"

Last week's controversy boiled like surf around the Supreme Court, which did something contrary to the wishes of the nation's most articulate interest group. The Court affirmed a limitation on the privileges of the most privileged profession. Ruling 6 to 3, it held that a plaintiff in a libel suit can compel journalists to answer questions about what their "state of mind" was when they were preparing the story at issue. Some of the press's tartest critics will say that to explore a journalist's mind is to trespass on a wilderness area; and there are, indeed, logical brambles and tangles in the minds of some journalists who are denouncing the Court. They cannot abide a four-word phrase that appears in Justice Lewis Powell's concurring opinion:

". . . The solicitude for First Amendment rights evidenced in our opinions reflects concern for the important public interest in a free flow of news and commentary. On the other hand . . ."

On the other hand, Powell says, there is a "significant public interest" in the right of litigants, such as plaintiffs in libel actions, to seek important evidence, even from journalists. Journalists enjoy reading about the "important public interest" in their rights; they do not enjoy then reading, "On the other hand . . ."

In 1969, Anthony Herbert, a Vietnam veteran, accused the Army of suppressing evidence of war crimes. He has sued CBS, claiming that in 1973, *60 Minutes* falsely and maliciously portrayed him as a liar. He concedes he was then a "public figure." He knows that in 1964 the Court ruled that comment about public figures is protected, except falsehood disseminated with "malice," meaning "with knowledge that it was false or with reckless disregard of whether it was false or not."

81

Journalists rightly regarded that ruling as a sweeping victory. It erected a wall of protection around a vast field of privilege. But a wall protecting a pasture, however vast the pasture, defines the limits of that pasture. And any definition of a right, however sweeping, sets limits to that right. The ruling in the Herbert case only makes explicit a limit inherent in the Warren Court ruling of fifteen years ago: the right to penalize malicious journalism implies the right directly to seek from journalists evidence of a malicious "state of mind." To grant journalists a privilege not to answer questions about motives, intentions and similar relevant aspects of the editorial process would place important evidence beyond the reach of a plaintiff; it would undermine the narrow but vital right of public figures to act against malicious defamation. Hearing journalists complain about even this denial of a privilege recalls Lincoln's story of the farmer who said, "I'm not greedy about land—I only want what joins mine."

Critics of the decision will quote, approvingly, Elizabeth I: "I will not make windows into men's souls." (She did, of course, have men pulled apart on racks to encourage them to volunteer what was in their minds.) But there is nothing inherently wrong with the law requiring testimony about a "state of mind." Justice could not be done without testimony about premeditation in homicide cases; or motives in some fraud cases; or intentions in civil-rights suits about allegedly discriminatory actions.

It is said that the right of libel plaintiffs to require testimony about "states of mind" will have a "chilling effect" on certain kinds of editorial processes. Quite right: it is *supposed* to induce self-censorship of malicious and injurious falsehood, which (in the words of Justice Byron White's opinion for the Court's majority) "carries no First Amendment credentials."

Some journalists are accusing the Court of "judicial Agnewism" and of chopping "ruinous swaths through the First Amendment." But the burden of proof on Herbert in his suit against CBS is still heavy; the construction of the First Amendment has not been changed, and no injury has been done to any constitutional value by not pushing beyond the horizon the boundaries of editorial privilege. Why, then, the alarm? One explanation is the remarkable resilience of a wrong idea, the theory of "absolute" First Amendment rights.

Physiology requires mankind to sleep about a third of the time, and psychology inclines mankind to dogmatic slumbers the rest of the time. The "absolute" construction of the First Amendment is an excuse not to think. It "answers" all questions about journalists' rights, and about much more: the sweep of First Amendment rights cannot be limited by any of the many conflicting values enshrined in the Constitution. But the Constitution is not a mere appendage to the First Amendment. As Powell writes, that amendment's values do not always enjoy "constitutional privilege," and must be "weighed" for proper "balance" with other values. As Edmund Burke wrote, "Political reason is a computing principle: adding, subtracting, multiplying, and dividing . . . true moral denominations." As Alexander Bickel of Yale taught:

> There are no absolutes that a complex society can live with in its law. There is only the computing principle that Burke spoke of . . .
>
> A very broad freedom to print, and a very considerable freedom to ferret out information by all manner of means ought to be, and substantially has been, one of the chief denominations computed in our calculus as constitutional policy. But there are other denominations as well. It is the most enduring instinct of our legal order . . . to resist the assertion of absolute claims and, therefore, a waste of breath to make them . . . Better to recognize from the first that the computing principle is all there is, ought to be, or can be.

Journalists are well remunerated, especially in the coin of prestige. They derive psychic income from the fact that the Republic's fundamental law accords their profession special privileges and immunities. But the public is becoming less deferential toward the elites on which it is, resentfully, dependent. Elites include lawyers, doctors, scientists, politicians. And journalists. Journalists are doubly resented because people feel they must depend on them to watch all the other distrusted elites. It is not prudent for journalists to provoke the public by waxing indignant whenever, out near the horizon, one of the sweeping extensions of their privileges is limited to accommodate another of the public's interests.

The public's confidence in journalists is jeopardized by their overwrought reactions to every small limit on their expansive privileges. The danger is not that the press by crying "Wolf!" when there are no wolves in sight will be ignored should wolves appear. Rather, the danger is that by crying "Wolf!" whenever the law nibbles like a hamster at the edge of privileges the press claims, the press seems immoderate, irrational, self-regarding and antisocial. And the public may come to think that perhaps the press should be gnawed into shape by a wolf or two.

April 30, 1979

Nazis in Skokie: The Right to Speak, the Right to Prevail

During the Second World War, Sol Goldstein lived in Lithuania, where Nazis threw his mother down a well with fifty other women and buried them alive in gravel. Today he lives in Skokie, Illinois, where on April 20, Nazis wearing brown shirts and swastikas will demonstrate to celebrate Hitler's birthday.

Sixty percent of Skokie residents are Jewish, including thousands of survivors of the Holocaust. Aided by the American Civil Liberties Union, the Nazis have successfully challenged the constitutionality of a Skokie ordinance forbidding demonstrations with swastikas, and almost certainly will succeed in challenging ordinances banning demonstrations involving military-style uniforms and incitements of hatred. After sixty years of liberal construction of the First Amendment, almost anything counts as "speech"; almost nothing justifies restriction.

The Nazis say they want to demonstrate in Skokie because

"Where one finds the most Jews, one finds the most Jew-haters."
Beyond inciting hatred, the Nazis' aim is to lacerate the feelings of
Jews. Liberals say that Skokie's ordinances place unconstitutional
restrictions on the Nazis' "speech." But Skokie's ordinances do not
prohibit "persuasion," in any meaningful sense. The ordinances
prohibit defamatory verbal and symbolic assault. What constitutional values do such ordinances violate?

The Washington Post says the rationale for striking down restrictions on advocacy of genocide is that "public policy will develop best through open clash of ideas, evil ideas as well as benign
ones." A typical Nazi idea is expressed on the poster depicti
three rabbis—the Nazis call them "loose-lipped Hebes"—
ducting the ritual sacrifice of a child. The *Post* does not sv
exactly how it expects the development of policy to be impr
"clashes" over ideas like that, or like the idea that Jews
"nigger-ization" of America.

Liberals quote Oliver Wendell Holmes's maxim tha
test of truth is the power of the thought to get itself a
competition of the market." Liberalism is a philoso
the essential task of philosophy—distinguishing
ror—to the "marketplace," which measures preferen
ity), not truth. Liberals say all ideas have an equal "rig
compete in the marketplace. But the right to compete implies the
right to win. So the logic of liberalism is that it is better to be ruled
by Nazis than to restrict them.

Liberals seem to believe that all speech—any clash between any
ideas—*necessarily* contributes to the political end the First
Amendment is supposed to serve. But they must believe that the
amendment was not intended to promote particular political
ends—that there is no connection between the rationale for free
speech and the particular purposes of republican government.

A wiser theory is in *The First Amendment and the Future of
American Democracy*, in which Professor Walter Berns argues
that the First Amendment is part of a political document. There
are political purposes for protecting free speech, and some speech
is incompatible with those purposes.

The purpose of the Constitution, he argues, is to establish a government faithful to the "self-evident" truths of the Declaration of Independence. Holmes said the Constitution was written for people of "fundamentally differing views." That would be an absurd idea about any constitutional community, and is especially absurd about this one. The Founders thought rational persons could hardly avoid agreeing about "self-evident" fundamentals. The Founders believed in freedom for all speech that does not injure the health of the self-evidently proper kind of policy, a republic.

So the distinction between liberty and license, between permissible and proscribable speech, is implicit in the Constitution's purposes. Hence restraint can be based on the substance as well as the time, place and manner of speech.

Berns argues it is bizarre to say the Constitution—a document designed to promote particular political ends—asserts the equality of ideas. There is no such thing as an amoral Constitution, neutral regarding all possible political outcomes.

American Nazis are weak, so liberals favor protecting Nazi swastikas and other "speech." Liberals say the pain to Jews is outweighed by the usefulness of the "clash of ideas" about "loose-lipped Hebes." Were the Nazis becoming stronger, liberals would favor protecting Nazi speech because the "marketplace"—the best test of truth—would be affirming Nazi truth. Besides, restricting speech can be dangerous.

But it is not more dangerous than national confusion about fundamental values. Evidence of such confusion is the idea that restrictions on Nazi taunts and defamations are impermissible because the Constitution's fundamental value is political competition open equally to those who, if they win, will destroy the Constitution and then throw people down wells.

February 2, 1978

Government and "the Cheerleader Problem"

Speaking with the sort of gravity that has become its trademark, the Department of Health, Education and Welfare has showered civil-rights directives upon schools in Oak Ridge, Tennessee. For example, "It also will be necessary that varsity cheerleaders cheer equally for both boys' and girls' varsity teams."

It is unclear whether "equally" means with equal loudness, which can be measured mechanically, or with equal spirit, which cannot be measured. Dear me! And what HEW is pleased to call "a cheerleader problem" is not the only awfulness in Oak Ridge. One civic association "occasionally treats the football team (all male) to steak dinners, but has not provided such services for any female team."

HEW is busy, busy, busy, and not just in Tennessee. That hammer-clang you recently heard was Boston State College being pounded on HEW's anvil. At BSC, HEW discovered, among other things, that "the trophies and pictures in hallways . . . show little attempt to equalize the publicity afforded women's and men's athletics."

HEW's thirst for justice is, we are asked to believe, required by Title IX of the education amendments of 1972. Title IX says that no person "shall, on the basis of sex, be excluded from participation in, be denied the benefits of, or be subjected to discrimination under any educational program or activity receiving federal financial assistance. . . ." That is why the federal brow is knitted with worry about cheerleaders.

What, precisely, did Congress mean when it passed Title IX? One of my heroes, Lord Peter Wimsey, the amateur detective created by the novelist Dorothy Sayers, observes: "It's surprisin' how few people ever mean anything definite from one year's end to the other."

Regarding many matters, Congress is definite only about the

sentiment it wants to be seen embracing. It leaves to various agencies the task of turning a sentiment into a law. This is the task of writing guidelines that stipulate what behavior does, and what does not, conform to the sentiment.

Satan finds mischief for idle hands, and the bowels of HEW are full of guideline-writers, members of society's large and growing class of supervisors. What, I wonder, do these people tell their children when the children ask, "Daddy, what do you do at the office?" "Well, son, I make cheerleaders bow to justice."

The more inefficient government has become in coping with substantial problems, the more peevish it has become with regard to things like "the cheerleader problem." The larger the government's pretensions and vocabulary become, the smaller-minded its behavior becomes, as when it tells Oak Ridge that all-girl "support groups" (cheerleaders) "reinforce stereotypical supportive roles of females" and therefore require—you guessed it—"affirmative action." The school must "take action to recruit equal numbers of male participants in existing support groups" or abolish cheerleaders.

There are ten single-spaced typewritten pages of stuff like "The boys' basketball team travels with the varsity cheerleaders and the 'Stat Cats' (alias 'Towel Girls'). . . . the boys' varsity team is elevated to the main event when they arrive with the varsity cheerleaders and the 'Stat Cats.' " Such childishness is, perhaps, unavoidable in an age when an Ellen Cooperman of Babylon, New York, changes her name to Cooperperson.

But it is strange that Joseph Califano, the Secretary of HEW, does not seem to care about even the political importance of the fact that many communities are fed to the front teeth with petty harassments from his people. Califano is no fool. Neither, Lord knows, is he a conservative wrecker, bent on discrediting government by making it look ludicrous.

Much that HEW does with Title IX and other matters is ludicrous, but not funny. Government cannot make a fool of itself, day after day, wallowing in trivialities, in community after community, without diminishing its ability to deal with matters that are not trivial.

Government has a finite claim on the patience and cooperativeness of its constituents. As unavoidable problems become more serious, complicated and painful, government requires more trust and deference from the public. So no government can afford to act stupidly and make the public irritable. Certainly a government that talks about the moral equivalent of war should not squander solemnity on cheerleaders.

March 5, 1978

Basketball and Human Rights (No Kidding)

On my desk rests an essay that has a title beyond parody: "Six-Player Basketball from a Human Rights Viewpoint." It concerns a matter that is vexing the Department of Health, Education and Welfare: Is it illegal for high-school girls in Iowa and several other states to play six-player basketball?

The "problem" is that the girls' game has only forwards and guards, and the three guards do not shoot. This, it is said, constitutes "sex discrimination" because girls who play guard are marginally disadvantaged in the competition for athletic scholarships from colleges, where the five-player game prevails.

A federal judge can be found to do anything, and a Tennessee girl found one who declared the six-player game unconstitutional, citing the "equal protection" clause. He was overturned. In a similar case in Oklahoma a judge suggested that if the plaintiff did not like playing guard she should try playing forward and should quit trying to drag the judiciary into the gym.

If HEW is to say that six-player basketball is illegal, it must say precisely who is "discriminating" against whom. That won't be easy. Furthermore, it is perverse to suggest that the purpose of high-school athletics is to prepare participants for college athletic scholarships. For the record, among Iowa girls graduating in 1978, 35 guards and 89 forwards won scholarships. One reason for the difference is that the better athletes tend to be forwards. One of the virtues of the six-player game is that it allows more girls to play and provides more roles for those with only moderate athletic skills.

Writing with a directness that is unmistakably Iowan, thirteen girls from North Mahaska have drawn a line in the dust in front of Joseph Califano, Secretary of HEW:

> Dear Mr. Califano:
> Is it true you are pushing five-girl . . . basketball? If so, why? Mr. Califano, have you ever seen an Iowa girls' basketball game? If not, what you basing your convictions on? . . . [Our game] is faster, and has more teamwork than boys' basketball. In Iowa, the Girls' State Tournament is more popular than the Boys' State Tournament.

High-school girls were playing basketball in Dubuque in 1898, just six years after James Naismith invented the game in Massachusetts. Today Iowa is twenty-sixth in the nation in population, but second in the number of girls participating in interscholastic basketball. In no other state does the girls' tournament make more money than the boys' tournament. Because the game is taken so seriously, it produces talent, and Iowa girls are keenly recruited for colleges.

One feminist who wants HEW to intervene by declaring six-player basketball illegal says, "I am sure there will be cries of federal intervention, but the girls of Iowa will be the beneficiaries of such a decision. Ultimately they and their parents will realize this." Study that last sentence. Not only does it concede the obvious (that players and parents like the game they have), it also is a perfect specimen of the bullying arrogance of ideologues.

The Iowa Commission on the Status of Women opposes the six-player game, but the chairperson of the commission has issued an icy dissent: "With the magnitude of some problems facing our country and its women, it is most disquieting to me to see the commission and the federal government spending time and energy in pursuit of amending the rules by which we play games."

Extremists who want government to seem silly and disreputable have reason to hope that HEW's "civil rights" enforcers will declare the six-player game illegal. HEW, and especially its Office of Civil Rights, frequently presents a discrediting contrast between the vastness of its concepts and the pettiness of its practices. HEW does not have so much stature that it can afford to dissipate what little it has. But it has allowed this case to percolate for months, giving moderate Iowans another reason to adjust downward their estimate of the Federal Government's judgment.

The "idealism" of the 1960s has decayed, not surprisingly, into the pedantries of the 1970s. Perhaps HEW's entertaining such pendantries expresses today's frustrations of government. If a "human rights" campaign is impotent against the Gulag Archipelago, try it against Iowa.

October 26, 1978

The Grinch and the American Civil Liberties Union

A Dr. Seuss classic begins:

> Every Who
> Down in Who-ville
> Liked Christmas a lot . . .
> But the Grinch,
> Who lived just north of Who-ville,
> Did NOT!

Dr. Seuss did not say so, but I am sure the Grinch was a member of the American Civil Liberties Union.

Every December, they crawl out of the woodwork, Grinchy people who seem to live for the fun of trying to get Christmas trees, carols and crèches banned from public places. These people advertise themselves as friends of freedom, naturally. Their aim is to get the First Amendment construed to say that carols sung, or trees and crèches displayed, on public property constitute the unconstitutional "establishment" of religion.

The constitutional theory (if it can be so dignified) behind that argument is, to say no more, unpersuasive. But an interesting frame of mind often is behind the attack on carols and crèches.

Tension between religion and the state is perennial because it is inevitable: religion invokes claims to an authority superior to secular authorities. The tension is, in some ways, especially acute in the modern age because the modern state "aspires to an all-comprehending jurisdiction." Those are the words of Peter Berger and the Reverend Richard John Neuhaus, co-directors of the Mediating Structures Project, sponsored by American Enterprise Institute.

The premise of their project is that government tends, inevitably, to expand, and as it does it promotes, and often enforces, social and cultural uniformity. It does so as a rival of structures (families, churches, neighborhoods, voluntary associations) that soften the exposure of the individual to the great megastructure, the state. The growth of the state at the expense of mediating structures—and of the community's right of self-expression—often is, curiously, a consequence of the assertion of certain "rights."

My friend and fellow columnist Joseph Sobran asks, "Why is it that every time somebody asserts a new right, all of us wind up less free than we were before?" He notes that many new "rights" are not protections against power but claims against the freedoms of fellow citizens.

Attempts to silence the singing of "Silent Night" in public schools are attempts to make the state the instrument of truculent people. These people want to use state power to purge the social milieu of certain things offensive, but not at all harmful, to them. There is meanness, even bullying, in this—a disagreeable delight in using the community's law divisively, to abolish traditions enjoyed by neighbors.

There are other examples of rights being asserted in aggressive, almost vicious, ways. The National Organization for Women, which speaks incessantly about freedom and "liberation" and all that, is trying to assert a right to have a judge disqualified from hearing a case pertaining to the ratification of the Equal Rights Amendment: disqualified because he is a Mormon, and his church opposes ERA. What NOW is seeking would violate the constitutional guarantee that "no religious test shall ever be required as a qualification to any office or public trust under the United States."

It is, by now, a familiar process: people asserting rights in order to extend the power of the state into what once were spheres of freedom. And it is, by now, a scandal beyond irony that thanks to the energetic litigation of "civil liberties" fanatics, pornographers enjoy expansive First Amendment protection while first-graders in a Nativity play are said to violate First Amendment values.

Every year at Christmastime we see evidence that there is indeed, as Berger and Neuhaus say, a "growing trend toward legally enforced symbolic sterility in public space." Christmas or Hanukkah lights on the common may be little things, "but of myriad such little things the public ethos is formed." People who seek to use the law to turn out the lights are seeking to impose their aversion to such symbols on communities that cherish them.

This represents an excessive deference toward individual rights and against community prerogatives. Berger and Neuhaus contend that the growing bias of public policy toward the "symbolic nakedness" of public space is deplorable, not only because it abridges the community's right to celebrate the various beliefs that leaven its culture, but also because it gives the state a monopoly on the use of public space for generating and sustaining values.

For some people, strengthening the state in this way is just one manifestation of a disposition to strengthen the state generally, by reducing the social roles of rival sources of authority. For such Grinches, grinchiness is a political program.

December 23, 1979

The "I'm Entitled" Spirit

A glistening gold chain meanders across the expanse of Melvin Belli's vest, and crimson lining lends a dash of flash to his brown suit. From flared trouser legs to silvery hair, the lawyer who has been called "the king of torts" is in fighting trim. He has the girth and aggressiveness of the Oakland Raiders' front four, and today he is especially merry because he has a new case that could devastate an industry, and several states.

Belli is attorney for several people whose mother, a smoker, died of lung cancer. The suit charges major cigarette manufacturers with liability for selling a product that they knew, or should have known, causes cancer.

This is unlike the case involving a woman who broke a tooth on a rock that she could not reasonably have been expected to expect in a can of beans. You buy cigarettes, you get smoke; you buy enough, you should not be startled if you get sick. Or as a judge said to Belli in an earlier attempt to impose absolute liability on cigarette manufacturers:

> Mel, you get what you buy. When you buy a pack of Luckies, you get smoke. I know you say you can get cancer, but I say you get smoke. If that has a side effect, that's tough luck. If I let you get by with this, then pretty soon you're going to be suing Elsie, the Borden cow, for giving too much cholesterol, or Jack Daniel's for giving you cirrhosis of the liver.

Belli's argument is at war with itself. He says it is common knowledge that smoking causes cancer; and he says that the woman "had no knowledge of the . . . lack of fitness for human consumption" of cigarettes. So he simply asserts that advertising "makes" people smoke, and that the addictiveness of tobacco prevents them from quitting.

Of course, millions do quit, and most people never start. But Belli's advertising phobia, although irrational, expresses the theme of individual impotence that is familiar in much modern literature and law.

Writing in *Time* magazine, Frank Trippett reports that a man who survived being struck by lightning is suing the National Park Service for negligently failing to warn him not to stand where lightning might strike. The Park Service won only on appeal against an $84,417 judgment for a man who was bitten by a bear while camping illegally in Yellowstone, where abundant publicity warns about bears.

A woman collected $50,000 from the City of San Francisco, claiming that a fall on a runaway cable car turned her into a nymphomaniac. A woman whose jaw was broken when she was blown against a railing in Chicago's Sears Tower plaza is demanding $250,000 from the architect, whose building, she says, increases wind velocity. Skiers have tried to hold owners of slopes liable for normal injuries.

Trippett wonders, "Must the manufacturer of a knife clearly label it as dangerous or else be vulnerable to damages for a kitchen worker's sliced finger? Could the designer of a dam be blamed if a voluntary swimmer drowned in a lake thus created?" Given the path of the law, it is reasonable to wonder: Might Belli win?

There is much cynicism and avarice behind the "sue-if-possible" attitude, although not on Belli's part. He will give his fee to the American Cancer Society. But the important dimension is that the attitudes exemplified in the cases Trippett cites, and in Belli's case, have political analogs.

The "I'm entitled" spirit expresses what Trippett calls "the utopian dream of a world that is free, if not of risks, then of all individual responsibility for those taken and lost." And if you seek the principal cause for inflation, note the many manifestations of the "I'm entitled" spirit in entitlement programs, and others, in the federal budget.

Even if you believe, as I do, that the tobacco industry is one the world would be well rid of, Belli's suit should be alarming. If the nation believes that society would be served by seriously discouraging smoking, there is much that representative institutions can do.

But Belli's suit is another attempt to make social policy by litigation rather than legislation. And this particular evasion of democratic due process diminishes society's already attenuated belief in individual responsibility.

September 28, 1978

Rape in Marriage: The Law and Intimacy

In the late nineteenth century, a male dean at Oxford addressed, with the delicacy of the day, some women undergraduates: "Inferior to us God made you, and inferior until the end of time you shall remain. But you are none the worse off for that." In the late twentieth century, the emancipation of women from such attitudes continues. But that does not adequately explain, or allay doubts about, the trial in Salem, Oregon, of a man accused of raping his wife.

Intrafamily relationships are not an unexplored frontier of litigation. The family is clearly within the ambit of the state. In 1874, in New York, a group seeking help for a child abused by foster parents had to invoke a law forbidding cruelty to animals. But recently the state has intruded into family relationships to assert a public interest in, for example, necessary medical treatment or education for children whose parents would deny that on religious or other grounds.

The family is society's molecular unit. In modern societies, which lack dominating churches, tribes, aristocracies, monarchies or other traditional structures, the family looms especially large. Furthermore, a liberal society is inherently contractual, and hence litigious; it is given to formalizing and codifying relationships. Family relationships will not be exempt from this.

Increased understanding of early-childhood development gives new urgency to the axiom that "Just as the twig is bent the tree's inclined." As people know, or think they know, more about equipping children to turn the key in the lock of the world, the "rights" of children seem (to some people) more elaborate, and the "rights" of incompetent parents seem more tenuous.

So there is pressure for the state to define and enforce the "rights" of all parties in a family. After all (it is said), incompetent parents do incalculable damage. (Never mind that, as most parents understand, the record of any child's upbringing would be, in no small measure, a catalog of blunders.)

But when you follow the thread of such thoughts about the state's jurisdiction in intrafamily relationships, you sense quicksand all around. When the thread leads from the rights of children to the rights of adults in conjugal relations, the law is drawn into making perilous distinctions, and the resulting litigation requires testimony that pries into the most sensitive intimacies.

When Henry James examined letters pertaining to Byron's incest, he exclaimed (happily): "Nauseating, perhaps, but how quite, quite inexpressibly significant." It is significant that the Salem case is, to say no more, gamy.

The man and woman were living together, tumultuously, when the particular act of sexual intercourse occurred. The question in dispute concerns the kind of force employed. The trial is generating charges, innuendos and rumors (about sexual eccentricity, promiscuity and the sale of movie rights). It is not a tidy seminar on jurisprudence.

Obviously there can be, as a matter of fact, rape—violent compulsion to sexual intercourse—in marriage. The question is whether there should be, as a matter of law, the crime of rape-in-marriage.

The idea that marriage implies or requires perpetual consent, under all circumstances, to sex is grotesque. And a partner in a marriage must have recourse to the law when the other partner resorts to violence. But it is a grave business when the law empowers one partner to charge the other with a felony punishable by twenty years in prison.

The problems of proof relating to the charge of rape in marriage are obvious, as is the potential for abuse of the charge in divorce proceedings. It is less obvious that there are fully compensating social benefits from a law distinguishing from others this particular category of assault.

Less than two hundred years ago in England, it was a form of treason—"petty treason"—for a wife to kill a husband. Such a deed was considered an assault on society's natural and essential structure of authority. Since then, the cake of custom has crumbled generally, and regarding the status of women, the crumbling has been, by and large, for the better.

Inevitably, the state steps in when old customs seem to have become unsatisfactory regulators of relationships. But the Salem case demonstrates how hard it is for the state to bake a cake.

December 28, 1978

Palimony and the Primitives

I am thoroughly married, so I followed the legal fracas between Lee Marvin and Michelle Triola Marvin with the detachment of an anthropologist observing primitives. Never mind the deepest mystery of the matter, the question of what charm either person ever saw in the other. There is sufficient fascination in the public facts.

Ms. Marvin lived with Mr. Marvin for six years. She took his name, cooked, had two abortions and, she insists, acquired a right to $1.8 million of his income.

Neither he nor she is evidence for Edison's axiom that the chief function of the body is to carry the brain around, but she did think up a new wrinkle in the theory of property rights. She says she abandoned a singing career in order to sustain her relationship with Marvin, and she says the relationship implied a "contract" to compensate her with half his earnings. She thought she found this implication in, among other places, his love letters.

Her argument was challenged by testimony that her singing talent was never more than negligible, and that regarding pleasures of the flesh, she neglected to forsake all others.

The judge who endured such testimony may have been addled by the experience. Although he rejected the idea that a "contract" existed, he has ordered Marvin to pay $104,000 to subsidize her "rehabilitation." Marvin may feel $1.7 million worth of relief, but he cannot like the implication that Ms. Marvin's experience living with him was comparable to suffering a disabling accident—an accident that was his fault.

My hero Peter De Vries, the novelist, has written satirically about a church that makes divorce a sacrament in order to serve the spiritual needs of modern man. In religion, these days, it sometimes is hard to distinguish the satirical from the real, and the same is becoming true in law.

Ms. Marvin is to be indemnified, but for what? Leave aside the fact that she entered the relationship with Marvin willingly; and the fact that concubines, like wives, can choose to have careers. But notice Ms. Marvin's aggressive nonsense: she insists upon property rights of the sort that come into existence as corollaries of responsibilities into which she never legally entered through matrimony.

Yet the judge found a way to make the law give her some satisfaction. Although she never incurred legal responsibilities, she somehow acquired a legal right to subsidized "rehabilitation," which is, in essence, alimony of $1,000 a week for two years.

Ms. Marvin did not get most of the money she sought, but she did make her point: she successfully asserted what resembles a wife's right.

The day before the State of California ordered Marvin to finance her "re-education" in "employable" skills, the State of New York held that Peter Frampton, a rock musician, does not owe half his income to his former girlfriend. The girlfriend had neglected to shed her husband before entering into a living arrangement—and an alleged contract—with Frampton. Therefore, she had committed adultery, a crime in New York. Said the judge:

"This contract, as alleged, is clearly opposed to sound morality and is based on the illicit association of parties. Thus it is void and unenforceable."

California is awash with advanced thinking and so cannot be expected to encumber its litigation with illiberal concepts like "sound morality." But California should entertain this thought:

The litigation that involved textual analysis of Mr. Marvin's love letters (*"Hey baby, hey baby, hey baby, hey baby, hey baby, hey baby"*), and speculation about the cash value of singing that Ms. Marvin chose not to do, is the sort of litigation society does not need.

Thoroughly modern people think of freedom as the silence of the law. Ms. Marvin accepted a relationship of maximum freedom with Mr. Marvin. In doing so, she, like him, disregarded society's settled judgment, codified in law, as to behavior that is socially important and morally sound. They had a right to behave as they did. But surely she should have forfeited the right to suddenly demand, when it suited her convenience, that the law speak up loudly for her "rights."

Unfortunately, the spirit of both Marvins—insistence on rights, avoidance of the legal responsibilities that define rights—is, increasingly, the spirit of the age.

April 22, 1979

Richard and Anthony Get Married

When first I heard about Richard Adams and his "spouse" Anthony Sullivan, words failed me, and it is probably good they did. Their story, still unfolding, says something about modern responsibilities.

Sullivan, an Australian, came to America in 1973 on a visa permitting him to stay until January 7, 1974. On January 5, 1974, he married a lady in Las Vegas. He promptly petitioned for permanent residence as an "alien relative." But by September, 1974, he was living alone, his wife's whereabouts unknown. He was told to demonstrate that his was a bona fide marriage. He didn't.

On April 25, 1975, Adams filed a petition on Sullivan's behalf, stating that he, Adams, with the help of a compliant clergyman, had become married to Sullivan in Colorado. The government replied that a same-sex "marriage" is invalid for immigration purposes because it is not real, and certainly Congress never intended a union of that sort to be a basis for a visa petition. So the two fellows went to court to assert their "rights."

They said the validity of a marriage for immigration purposes should be determined by the law of the place where it occurred, and that Colorado law says: "A marriage between a man and a woman licensed, solemnized and registered . . . is valid in this state." They said that because this law "does not specifically prohibit" same-sex marriages, there is an "inference" of permission. The judge replied that the silence of Colorado's law on same-sex marriages permits no such inference and, besides, congressional intent, easily surmised, should prevail.

The government argued that "the basic structure of society and social values rely upon the historical man–woman marital relationship." Therefore, as another court said in a similar case, "there can be no doubt that there exists a rational basis for the state to limit the definition of marriage to exclude same-sex relationships."

That proposition is precisely what Adams and Sullivan deny. They say the government itself has acted in ways that legitimize doubts about the proposition. They argue that "antiquated notions" about male and female roles are falling away fast. And various judicial and executive decisions cumulatively suggest that soon, if not now, homosexuals will be entitled to all the rights, privileges and immunities enjoyed under U.S. law.

A court has held that even if one accepts psychiatric testimony that formal recognition by a university of a homosexual student organization would tend to perpetuate or expand homosexual behavior, such evidence does not justify a university's refusal to grant such formal recognition. This is congruent with the policy of the U.S. Job Corps, which has seen fit to issue a manual on "sexuality," enjoining respect for differing sexual "lifestyles" and stipulating equal respect for heterosexual and homosexual activities. Homosexual parents, of both sexes, have been awarded child-custody rights, and have been found "fit" as adoptive parents.

Sullivan and Adams say the "discrimination" against them is unconstitutional because courts no longer allow "stereotyped and/or antiquated assumptions about homosexuality and gender roles."

In a decision affirming the constitutionality of laws prohibiting same-sex marriages, the Minnesota Supreme Court held that marriage "manifestly is more deeply founded than the asserted contemporary concept of marriage and societal interests for which petitioners contend." Adams and Sullivan argue, in effect, that *nothing* is or should be deeply founded in modern society—except, of course, their rights, as they see them.

They say, "There is no 'important' governmental interest in preserving the moral status quo." Hence there is no justification for the "discrimination" that denies them the legal benefits (such as preferential tax treatment) and other advantages (such as "societal respectability") of state-sanctioned marriages. "Times," they admonished the judge (unsuccessfully; they will now admonish a federal appeals court), "are changing, and they are changing very rapidly."

One thing does indeed lead to another. The fact of change, filtered through the modern mind, becomes charged with value: one thing *should* lead to another. This mischievous proposition is what C. S. Lewis called ". . . the fatal serialism of the modern imagination—the image of infinite unilinear progression which so haunts our minds. Because we have to use numbers so much, we tend to think of every process as if it must be like the numeral series, where every step, to all eternity, is the same kind of step as the one before."

But the life of society is not a numeral series. Infinite unilinear progression is a chimera. It is not infinite. And it can end with what Lewis called "the abolition of man."

May 25, 1980

"Pro-Choice" and the Pretense of Neutrality

America's most triumphant political activists in the 1970s have been those who have produced sweeping changes in abortion laws, changes that have contributed much to the current rate of a million abortions a year. Yet the people who have produced this effect, and who are still working for policy changes that would increase the number of abortions, are interestingly anxious to avoid being called "pro-abortion." They prefer the label "pro-choice."

Political movements always try to justify their programs in terms of the society's fundamental values, and the pretense of a liberal society is that the fundamental value is "freedom of choice." But now a suit challenging one small part of the pro-abortion revolution is also challenging the idea that the revolution is just "pro-choice."

Two Catholic organizations have filed suit challenging the constitutionality of the Pregnancy Discrimination Act. The Act requires employers to pay for time taken off by employees to obtain abortions, including abortions that are strictly nontherapeutic. The Act also requires employers to pay all medical and hospitalization costs of abortions "where the life of the mother [sic] would be endangered if the fetus were carried to term."

The plaintiffs contend that this violates First Amendment rights. It compels employers to treat abortion as a mere fringe benefit, whereas their religious convictions may be that abortion is grave and abhorrent. It compels employers "to participate in the trivialization" of abortion, and to facilitate it by providing economic incentive for it.

Under the First Amendment's protection of the free "exercise" of religion, the freedom to act on religious beliefs is accorded broad protection. The plaintiffs contend that the new law requires employers "to make public acquiescence in a valuation of human life offensive to their religious convictions." And the law does not settle for passive acquiescence but requires "continuing and active participation in an abhorred practice." This is in spite of the fact that the Supreme Court has held:

"Official compulsion to affirm what is contrary to one's religious beliefs is the antithesis of freedom to worship."

The Court has held that First Amendment rights were violated when children of Jehovah's Witnesses were compelled to salute the flag in school. And when employees were compelled to finance political statements they opposed. And even when New Hampshire compelled a dissenting citizen to display the license-plate slogan "Live Free or Die."

Surely the compulsion to facilitate abortions abridges many Americans' First Amendment rights more seriously than did the law requiring display of New Hampshire's slogan.

The plaintiffs argue that the abortion-funding requirement is even worse than a "passive restraint" on free exercise of religion. A law that threatens a person if he speaks his mind can at least be avoided by not speaking. But the Pregnancy Discrimination Act imposes an affirmative duty that compels employers to act. For those wishing to preserve their integrity, and act in conformity with their religious convictions, not even passivity is an option.

Refusal to comply with the funding requirement would trigger sanctions against employers, including denial of federal and state contracts. This in spite of the Court's ruling that "to condition the availability of benefits" upon a person's willingness to violate a cardinal principle of religious faith "effectively penalizes" the free exercise of constitutional liberties.

Those who oppose, for example, public funding of abortions have been accused of trying to "make their morality compulsory."

But this suit demonstrates that where the freedom of many Americans to choose to act in conformity with their religious convictions conflicts with the goal of making it financially easier for women to choose to have abortions, the law is not just "pro-choice," it is "pro-abortion."

The idea that "freedom of choice" is necessarily neutral as regards social outcomes is the characteristic pretense of liberal societies. But liberal societies do not provide "freedom of choice" without having certain expectations as to which choices will be made. And they try to shape choices by shaping attitudes. All societies do this. Only liberal societies pretend to be neutral.

It is a goal, not a collateral effect, of the pro-abortion movement to force people to act upon the assumption that abortion is a triviality. A million abortions a year proves that the movement has achieved its primary goal, which is to transform attitudes. Obviously many people already regard abortion as the birth-control method of first resort, equivalent to taking a pill—in short, as a triviality.

August 19, 1979

Viability and Vagueness

Justice Harry Blackmun may be remembered in connection with abortion the way Chief Justice Roger Taney is remembered in connection with slavery. In the Dred Scott decision, Taney tried to use judicial power to "settle" the slavery issue by removing it from legislative arenas. Instead, he hastened civil war. Blackmun seems to want to "settle" the abortion issue similarly, but his injudicious opinions may provoke an anti-abortion amendment to the Constitution.

Blackmun wrote the 1973 abortion decision, which was a scythe mowing down state restrictions on abortion. Now Blackmun has written the opinion in a 6–3 ruling striking down a 1974 Pennsylvania law requiring doctors to use whatever abortion method is most likely to spare the life of any fetus that "may be viable." Blackmun finds that phrase unenforceably "vague."

Blackmun also faults Pennsylvania law because "it is uncertain whether the statute permits the physician to consider his duty to the patient to be paramount to his duty to the fetus." This suggests, obliquely, the real incompatibility of Pennsylvania's law and the 1973 ruling, an incompatibility that has nothing to do with the concept of "viability."

The Court's labored analysis of "viability" obscures, in 1979 as in 1973, what the Court is doing. It is concocting an expansive right to abortion, a right not significantly limited by considerations of fetal viability.

Justice Byron White, dissenting, says the latest ruling "withdraws from the states a substantial measure of the power to protect fetal life that was reserved to them" in the 1973 decision. But in fact the latest ruling only makes clear that the 1973 ruling virtually stripped the states of such power.

The logic of the 1973 ruling is this: A woman who wants an abortion has a virtually unlimitable constitutional right to purchase a procedure that will result in a dead fetus. The 1973 decision held that at no point in pregnancy are fetuses "persons" in the whole sense. The Court said that states may not forbid an abortion that a doctor determines is "necessary to preserve the life or health of the mother."

The Court established, in effect, a right to abortion on demand when it said that doctors may make that determination "in the light of all attendant circumstances—psychological and emotional as well as physical—that might be relevant to the well-being of the patient." Doctors can be found who will construe "health" broadly enough to include, for example, the absence of "distress."

Pennsylvania's law was odd. To require abortionists to use the method safest for fetuses is to require abortionists to risk failing at their vocation, which is killing fetuses. But given today's moral and legal climate, it is unclear what must be done when fetuses do survive abortion procedures. There are bound to be many such cases in a nation with a million abortions a year.

True, some states require that babies born after abortion procedures must be given life-sustaining treatment appropriate for premature births. And many hospitals have neonatal intensive-care units that can prolong, if not always preserve, the lives of infants that survive abortion procedures. But an abortionist might be sued for malpractice if he failed to kill his patient's fetus.

For centuries many societies considered abortion permissible before "quickening" (when a woman feels fetal movement) because they did not think the fetus was alive until then. Strict abortion laws developed as the science of embryology developed in the nineteenth century.

Today there is no doubt that pregnancy is a continuous process: what begins at conception will, if it escapes natural misfortune or deliberate attack, become a child. And what abortion kills is an organic system distinct from the woman's system. Abortionists do not deny that a fetus is alive and biologically human (meaning that it belongs to that category of life). They argue that an unwanted fetus has no value.

In *The Ambivalence of Abortion*, Linda Bird Franke reports that many women who have had abortions say, "I felt like I'd killed something." Of course. The feeling is reasonable. In every abortion, something living is killed. That is an indisputable biological fact, not a moral judgment. The moral argument today concerns whether Blackmun and his colleagues shall be allowed to define as nothing the status of that "something."

January 18, 1979

The Case of the Unborn Patient

A character in a John Updike novel says, "Life, that's what we seek in one another, even with the DNA molecule cracked and our vitality arrayed before us as a tiny Tinkertoy." But as science explicates the chemistry of life, many people flinch from some facts. They seek not life but reasons to deny that some life exists. They sense, I think, the moral incompatibility between some facts of modern science and some practices of modern society.

Recently a boy underwent brain surgery six times in the nine weeks before he was born. An ultrasound scan in the twenty-fourth week of gestation revealed hydrocephalus, a damaging concentration of fluid in the brain. A hollow needle was inserted through the womb, and into the fetal skull, to the fluid. Nearly a quart of fluid was drained in six operations.

Prenatal medicine can detect and treat various forms of fetal distress and genetic problems, with the help of ultrasound pictures that can show all fingers and heart chambers at eighteen weeks. A fetus's inability to assimilate an essential vitamin has been detected and treated by the administration of large vitamin doses to the mother. Babies likely to be born prematurely can receive drugs that hasten maturation of the lungs, thereby combating hyaline-membrane disease, a killer of premature babies. Drugs such as digitalis can be delivered to a fetus through the mother's bloodstream to correct irregular heart rhythms. Excess fluids have been drained from the chests and abdomens of fetuses, and blood transfusions have been given to fetuses.

Prenatal medicine should raise troubling thoughts in a nation in which abortion is the most frequently performed operation, a nation in which last year 1.5 million abortions ended about one-third of all pregnancies. Science and society are out of sync. The most humane of sciences, medicine, can now treat as patients those who the law says lack an essential human attribute: rights. Mothers may kill any fetus that medicine can treat.

This is not widely understood. Some defenders of the Supreme Court's 1973 abortion decision may have been so busy applauding it that they have not read it. *The New Republic* recently praised the decision as "fair," explaining it this way: "Abortions are freely available in the first trimester, subject to medical determination in the second trimester, and banned in the third, when the fetus is viable." But the Court actually decreed that there can be no serious impediment to even third-trimester abortions. It said that even in the third trimester, states may not prevent any abortion deemed necessary to protect a mother's health from harm, and that harm may include "distress."

There is, effectively, abortion on demand at every point. So just as prenatal medicine was beginning to produce marvelous lifesaving and life-enhancing achievements, Supreme Court Justices made it the law of the land that the patients for such medicine have no right to life.

Not surprisingly, some pro-abortion forces are increasingly anti-scientific, in the name of "humility." They say: Let's all be properly humble and admit that the matter of when human life begins is a mystery beyond our poor power of understanding, so the answer "birth" is no more arbitrary than any other. This argument is too anti-scientific, and too convenient to the pro-abortion position, even to seem ingenuous. It has aroused Walker Percy, an M.D. and a novelist of distinction. He notes that it is a commonplace of modern biology that the life of an organism begins "when the chromosomes of the sperm fuse with the chromosomes of the ovum to form a new DNA complex that thenceforth directs the ontogenesis of the organism," producing the undeniable "continuum that exists in the life of every individual from the moment of fertilization of a single cell." Percy adds:

> The onset of individual life is not a dogma of the church but a fact of science. How much more convenient if we lived in the thirteenth century, when no one knew anything about microbiology and arguments about the onset of life were legitimate . . . Nowadays it is not some misguided ecclesiastics who are trying to suppress an embarrassing scientific fact. It is the secular juridical-journalistic establishment.

Stephen and Amanda, twins recently born in Australia, were conceived *in vitro*. Two eggs were fertilized in a laboratory and implanted in the mother, who wanted twins. Perhaps the *status* of life begun *in vitro* is unclear prior to the implantation that is necessary for the continuum. (Necessary today but perhaps not tomorrow, when there may be artificial wombs.) But surely two-year-old Louise Brown in England is famous because she is the first child whose *life* began *in vitro*.

In 1946, before Planned Parenthood became a pro-abortion lobby, an officer referred to the being produced by fertilization of an ovum as "the new baby which is created at this exact moment." In 1964 a Planned Parenthood pamphlet said, "Abortion kills the life of a baby, once it has begun." What has changed is not biology but Planned Parenthood's agenda.

In 1973 the Supreme Court, feigning humility as it arrogantly legislated, said it could not "resolve the difficult question of when life begins." Actually, the Court knew what every high-school biology student knows. So it quickly inserted the telltale adjective "meaningful." It defined viability as the point at which the baby can have "meaningful" life outside the womb. Speaking of such life, recently at a Phoenix abortion center a woman in her second trimester was injected with a saline solution and sent home. Three nights later she went into labor and was told to go to the hospital to "deliver the fetus"—dead, of course. Instead, she delivered a live girl.

The argument about abortion cannot be about when human life begins. It must be about the status of life at various early stages—a matter about which decent people can disagree. But denial of elementary biology is the way some pro-abortionists duck the difficult issue of gradation. However, whatever one thinks should be the status of the life that exists at conception, surely any civilized sensibility should be troubled by the status of life later in pregnancy. Under the law the Supreme Court has made, a mother need not treat as human a being that prenatal medicine can treat as a patient—a being that can become, if the attempt to kill it fails, a pediatrician's patient.

June 22, 1981

A Death in Pennsylvania

Twice in eighteen months, Philadelphia doctors deliberately killed infants. I say "killed" because this story should not be muddied by euphemisms. The doctors acted responsibly and with moral valor in cases that were both sad and inspiring.

The cases, superbly reported by Donald Drake of *The Philadelphia Inquirer*, both involved Siamese twins, girls, joined at the chest. They shared a liver and a complete four-chambered heart fused with an incomplete two-chambered heart. Consider the October, 1977, case.

Baby Girls A and B appeared to be hugging. No babies joined that way have lived more than nine months. (Siamese twins occur once in 50,000 births; twins with joined hearts occur once in 100,000.) Such one-and-a-half hearts cannot stand the strain. Without separation, both babies would die. Separated, the one given the indivisible heart would have a slight chance.

The parents were spared an awful choice: the heart could function only with Baby B's circulatory system. Surgeons believed they could build for Baby B a chest cavity to hold the heart, perhaps using grafts from Baby A's ribs.

The parents are devout Jews; the chief surgeon, a Presbyterian; six of the seven nurses who assisted in the operation are Catholics. At three weeks, both babies were alertly making eye contact. Nurses saw personality differences emerging. Everyone agonized about the idea of "sacrificing" either baby.

A rabbi wondered: Are there two babies? Could Baby A be considered an appendage? The chief surgeon said there were two brains and nervous systems, thus two babies.

Lawyers sought grounds for holding the surgeons safe from homicide charges. They argued that Pennsylvania law says death occurs when the heart stops; thus, because there was only one heart, there was only one life involved. The court rejected this route to classifying Baby A as an appendage. Then the lawyers argued that no crime occurs if an act is done under a court order issued because the good anticipated from the act outweighs the bad. They cited an argument similar to one the rabbis had been pondering:

A mountain climber falls and is saved from instant death only by hanging from a rope attached to his partner. But the partner's hold is not secure enough to keep both himself and his friend from falling to their deaths. Either one climber must die or both will; so the climber with the more secure hold is justified in cutting his partner's rope.

The different groups considering God's and Pennsylvania's laws agreed: the operation should occur. It did. Baby A was sacrificed; Baby B lived, but only three months. The survivor of a similar operation last month is alive, and is the first such survivor to leave a hospital.

Now, what I am about to cite, from Dennis Bloodworth's *The Chinese Looking Glass*, is ghastly, but germane:

> Somerset Maugham tells us . . . how he came upon a little tower on a Chinese hillside with a single small hole in its wall, from which came a nauseating odor. This was the baby tower, and it covered a deep charnel pit into which parents threw their unwanted children through the aperture, or, if they were more gentle, lowered them in a basket on a piece of stout string. . . . Perhaps nothing [better] measures the enormous abyss between Chinese living and Western understanding than a passage from a Chinese book of travel . . . in the last century: "England is so short of inhabitants that the English rear every child that is born. Even prostitutes who bear children do not destroy them."

This passage refers to China during a period of hideous privation. The point is not that it is in "the nature" of any people to treat life casually. On the contrary, the point is that the value placed on life is to some extent contingent, socially rooted, changeable.

The Philadelphia cases attest reverence for life. But that reverence may be moral capital inherited from another age and dissipated in this age. Our society has suddenly decided that abortion can be a mere convenience, a morally insignificant form of birth control for the careless. There are a million abortions a year in America, a society that does not understand how fast and far it is moving from the sensibility that dignified the deliberations in Philadelphia.

April 8, 1979

Trading Jimmy for a Corvette

Even allowing for the fabled American love of automobiles, and for columnists' tendency to discover large portents in small episodes, you will, I hope, entertain the thought that some peculiar significance attaches to the story of the New Jersey couple charged with child abuse for allegedly trying to trade their 14-month-old son for a three-year-old sports car.

I know that the foremost modern value is open-mindedness about all values except open-mindedness. I acknowledge not merely that everyone is innocent until proved guilty, but even that, to a really modern thinker, anyone is innocent even after being proved guilty. Maybe you need to know the infant, or the sports car, to evaluate the episode *The New York Times* reported.

Allegedly the couple (he is 29, she is 21) approached the dealer about trading James, Jr., for a black-and-silver Corvette valued at $8,800. The dealer, who contacted the police and played along at their request, says of the parents: "They had the keys and the papers for the car and we were putting the license plates on. They left the baby in the showroom on the floor."

I leave to others the task of exploring a possible connection between this matter (and the one I come to in the next paragraph) and two phenomena: the casual contracting and dissolving of marriages in a society in which divorce is epidemic, and the casual conceiving and disposing of life in a society in which there are 1.4 million abortions a year.

The story about the baby and the Corvette appeared two days before a story about "throwaway" children in the Washington area. A suburban welfare agency reports that troublesome children expelled by parents from their homes comprise a significant and growing portion of its case load. A director of a shelter for runaway and "throwaway" youths says: "The whole '60s idea of 'do your own thing' has moved into the '70s and '80s with disposable relationships—if it doesn't work, if it's not perfect, I want something else.' " So, reports a social worker, at least once a week a parent drives up and drops off a child "with a suitcase and a quick goodbye."

I leave to others the task of arguing the possible connection between this phenomenon and the prevailing theory that the highest purpose of the modern state is to facilitate the individual's pursuit of his or her preferred "life-style." However that may be, there clearly is a dilemma for government: A child rejected by parents may need assistance more immediate and certain than a public agency's attempt to reform or compel the parents into acting more like parents. But the state's readiness to act *in loco parentis* can diminish parents' sense of urgent responsibility for acting as parents.

There are many mentally handicapped children who should be with their families, but who are in institutions, or foster homes, because a too-solicitous society sometimes wrongly offers parents the option of being less than parents to their handicapped child. Of course, some children must be institutionalized. And many extraordinary men and women provide splendid homes as foster parents of even seriously retarded children with serious physical handicaps. But regarding the retarded, society sometimes acts in ways that can work to weaken the natural threads of affection between parents and an infant.

I know of a couple who, immediately after the birth of their child with Down's syndrome (a chromosomal defect that involves widely varying degrees of retardation and physical abnormalities; whether the difficulties will be mild or severe usually cannot be known for years), were advised by a kindly physician that a foster home could be found for the child for a few months while the parents considered whether to take the child into their home.

Surely it is generally wrong to offer parents that choice at that time. Wrong because it can insinuate a sense of distance, an unnatural, unhealthy tentativeness into the magic moment of parent–infant bonding. Wrong because it is apt to derive from, and encourage, pessimistic prejudgments about the child's problems and the parents' ability to cope with them.

Providing parents with a period for detached reflection about the relationship they want to choose to have with their child suggests that the child is owed less than the unconditional attachment that healthy parents feel for their children, handicapped or not. Society weakens its molecular unit, the family, when it suggests, even unintentionally, that the caliber of love owed to a child is somehow a function of parents' calculations of convenience.

September 11, 1980

The Definition of "Health" and the Probable Medical Imperialism

A few years ago, a woman had a healthy breast removed surgically because it interfered with her golf swing. The interesting question is not whether what she did was censurable, but whether what the surgeon did was medicine. The distinction between true and false ends of medicine is germane to the annual debate about public funding (primarily through Medicaid) of abortions.

Opponents of funding for most abortions have a decisive argument that is logically independent of views about the general morality of abortion. The argument is that few abortions are, properly speaking, medical procedures, and so should not be subsidized by funds appropriated for medical programs.

Dr. Leon Kass of the University of Chicago argues for what he calls "the old-fashioned view" that health is the true goal of the physician's art. If his argument is correct (and it is not easily assailed), most abortions are not acts of medicine, properly understood. The vast majority of abortions are nontherapeutic, in that they are not performed to ensure the health of the woman (who surely should not be called a "patient"). Although they are performed by persons licensed to practice medicine, they serve not the pursuit of health, but rather the woman's desire for convenience, absence of distress—in a word, happiness.

Kass gives other examples (less bizarre than that of the woman golfer) of physicians' skills put to nonmedical purposes. Amniocentesis, a diagnostic technique which reveals many fetal disorders, also reveals the sex of the fetus, and abortions have been performed because the fetus was not of the desired sex. Some doctors specialize in pharmacologically induced "peace of mind," and dispense amphetamines to physically healthy but discontented people seeking mood "elevation."

Such doctors are not practicing medicine—the pursuit of health—any more than are narcotics peddlers. Doctors who perform artificial insemination may or may not be doing good; they certainly are not doing medicine, any more than are practitioners of the "cosmetic surgery" that corrects other than inborn or acquired abnormalities. Such practices, says Kass, "the worthy and the unworthy alike, aim *not* at the patient's health but rather at satisfying his, albeit in some cases reasonable, wishes." They are acts not of medicine but of gratification: for consumers, not patients.

Another false goal of medicine is "behavior modification," using physicians' skills to produce "social adjustment." Kass warns that biological manipulation (such as psychosurgery or sophisticated drugging for violent people) is apt to increase as more is learned about the biological contribution to behavior. But even if such manipulation by "biobehavioral conditioners" has "socially useful" outcomes, it is not medicine.

Kass notes that when medicine's powers were fewer, its goal—health—was clearer. And the World Health Organization has muddied things by defining "health" as "a state of complete [*sic*] physical, mental and social [*sic*] well-being." This means that happiness is a medical commodity; happiness is the doctor's business. That, in turn, means that almost everything is the doctor's business, so "medicine" becomes a classification that excludes nothing, and hence does not classify.

What Kass calls "creeping medical imperialism" is encouraged by a definition of medicine that is not properly related to health—or more precisely, is related to an overbroad definition of health that includes "happiness" and "contentment" and "good citizenship."

From the fact that physicians have a monopoly on the right to perform surgery, it does not follow that surgery is always medicine. Nontherapeutic abortion is the second-most-common surgical procedure, after circumcision. Most abortions are "birth control of last resort"—or more accurately, of first resort.

Most women seeking abortions are unmarried, and neither they nor the men attempted contraception. According to one study, 1.7 million of the "sexually active" teen-age women do not use any contraceptives. Most abortions are measures of relief from the consequences of pleasure pursued irresponsibly.

Supporters of subsidized abortions argue that such relief not only is a social good, but also is an individual right that must, as a matter of equity, be subsidized for those who cannot afford it. But no such argument can establish the propriety of using funds appropriated for medical services to promote such a goal, which, whether defensible or indefensible, is not a true goal of medicine. Most abortions have no more to do with medicine than did the golfer's mastectomy.

June 25, 1978

"Coercive Incentives" and Related Confusions

Aside from the outcome itself, perhaps the best thing about the Supreme Court's action affirming the constitutionality of the Hyde Amendment (which strictly limits funding of Medicaid abortions) is that not even a single dissenter in the 5-4 decision had a kind word to say for the most audacious argument against the amendment.

That argument was that the amendment constitutes "establishment" of religion because values embodied in it are congruent with the beliefs of certain religious groups, and—the most ominous attack—because members of those groups had been important participants in the debate that preceded passage of the amendment. Justice Stewart, for the majority, curtly noted that a statute is not unconstitutional because it happens to harmonize with some or all religions: the fact that the Judeo-Christian religions condemn stealing does not mean government violates the "establishment" clause by legislating against larceny.

The attack against Hyde on "establishment" grounds is another example of extremism from people who, having lost a political argument in a legislative arena, attempt to abridge their opponents' right to participate in such arguments. It is gratifying that the Court gave that short shrift. But it is sobering to note that the Court was narrowly and sharply divided on philosophic fundamentals.

Opponents of Hyde argued a double negative: that Congress cannot not subsidize all therapeutic abortions. That proposition is as philosophically untenable as it is syntactically awkward. I say philosophically rather than just constitutionally untenable because the attack on Hyde involved confusion about elemental concepts, those of rights and freedom, and about the sort of affirmations a polity can legitimately make through its political process.

The dissenters seemed to say that an individual's incapacity to exercise a right constitutes governmental denial of that right. Justice Brennan, joined in his dissent by Justices Marshall and Blackmun, asserted that by refusing to subsidize abortions more broadly, government "coerces" indigent pregnant women, that it "burdens" their "freedom to choose." He spoke of "the coercive impact of the congressional decision to fund one outcome of pregnancy—childbirth—while not funding the other—abortion." Justice Stevens, dissenting separately, agreed that subsidizing childbirth but not abortion imposes a "governmental burden" on a woman's choice. Brennan said that the government's unequal subsidizing involves "coercive financial incentives."

That last phrase, especially, betrays deep confusion. Generally, and rightly, the use of incentives is sharply contrasted with the use of coercion. The concepts should be kept distinct, lest we lose an important standard by which we judge free societies: to what extent are they committed to reliance on incentives rather than coercion in achieving social objectives?

Coercion compels; incentives encourage. Free societies are inclined to resort to coercion only where freedom to choose is impractical or intolerable because only one choice is acceptable (for example, as regards paying taxes, or refraining from murder). Incentives (for example, the deductability of mortgage interest payments to encourage home ownership; subsidies to encourage production of particular agricultural commodities) are used when societies want to influence the uses to which freedom is put. When, that is, societies want to encourage certain values by encouraging people freely to choose certain courses of action.

An incentive acknowledges, it does not negate, freedom of choice. Surely we do not want to start equating subsidization, or its absence, with "coercion."

It is one thing to possess a right in the sense of an entitlement not to be actively prevented from doing something. It is something else to claim an entitlement to public resources to facilitate the exercise of that right.

Brennan asserts the unconstitutionality of "any scheme of granting or withholding financial benefits that incidentally or intentionally burdens one manner of exercising a constitutionally protected choice." But the right to choose to read pornography has been granted broad constitutional protection. Under Brennan's formulation, when the state subsidizes—in libraries and schools—only the reading of nonpornographic material, it unconstitutionally "burdens" the protected right to choose to read pornography.

Blackmun says that with the Hyde Amendment the government "punitively impresses upon a needy minority its own concepts of the socially desirable, the publicly acceptable, and the morally sound." His use of the adverb "punitively" violates the logic of our language. The Hyde Amendment "impresses" no course of action on anybody. Rather, it expresses a legislative majority's judgment, arrived at after protracted and repeated debates, about certain values that are desirable, acceptable and sound. That is the essence of politics, and Blackmun should not begrudge the political branches of government a part of the political action.

July 6, 1980

Wombs for Rent: The Rise of "Surrogate Parenting"

Such, evidently, is her passion for anonymity that the surrogate mother used a surrogate name ("Elizabeth Kane") in her press conference, in her article written for *People* magazine and in her appearances on *Good Morning America* and the *Donahue* show. Kane, 38, is the woman who, for an undisclosed fee, had herself artificially impregnated with the semen of a man whose wife was unable to bear children. The biological father and the adoptive mother were with Kane's husband (and the photographer whose pictures appeared in *People*) in the delivery room.

Kane lives in Pekin, Illinois, a town hitherto famous as the home of Everett M. Dirksen, whose comments on "surrogate parenting" must be enlivening his Heavenly press conferences. Folks in Pekin are, apparently, hidebound and reactionary regarding human reproduction. Kane says many of them will not speak to her. And children tease her children, saying that their mother is "selling babies." That is neither nice nor precise. It would be more accurate to say that a surrogate mother rents her womb.

The times are indeed out of joint. There are approximately 1.4 million abortions in America each year. But so strong is the unsatisfied demand for adoptions that there is a black market in babies. And now there is a Surrogate Parenting Association whose leader says he is overseeing "about a hundred" pregnancies like Kane's. So summon the lawyers. There are going to be some interesting tangles.

During the pregnancy, Kane said: "It's the father's child. I'm simply growing it for him." But was it "the father's child" at that time? She says that before leaving Louisville, where she had the baby, "I went to court and signed papers dissolving any legal rights I had to the baby." Oh? That sounds tidy, and as easy as giving away a Buick. But consider some problems that can derive from "surrogate parenting."

Suppose that early in the pregnancy the surrogate mother decides she would rather go skiing, or would rather not have morning sickness, and decides to have an abortion. Can a contract with the biological father be an impediment? Arguably. Thanks to the Supreme Court, the biological father, even when married to the biological mother, has no rights—absent a contract, at least. Absent a contract, what matters is the biological mother's "privacy right" which the Supreme Court in 1973 discovered in the Constitution. That right makes her as sovereign over an unborn child as she is over her appendix. But perhaps the surrogate mother can waive, by contract, her "privacy right."

Kane says that "because of my age, I had amniocentesis." That is a diagnostic procedure for determining whether an unborn child is genetically normal. It is often recommended for women over 35, at which age women become progressively more prone to bearing children with Down's syndrome, a genetic disorder involving retardation and physical abnormalities. Kane's amniocentesis results were good.

But suppose a surrogate mother's amniocentesis reveals, say, spinal bifida, and the contracting couple decides it does not want the child. Can the couple walk away from all responsibility for the baby?

Suppose the contract between the couple and the surrogate mother stipulates that the couple can demand an abortion of an "unsatisfactory" baby—and suppose that when the clause is invoked, the surrogate mother refuses. Would a court enforce such a contract? If not, to whom would the baby belong, once born—the couple for whom the surrogate mother was (in Kane's words) "growing it," or the surrogate mother who prevented the abortion?

Suppose no amniocentesis is performed, and the baby is born defective. Does clear responsibility for the child reside on either side, or can all three people agree to abandon the baby to some public agency?

Suppose a baby is born and the surrogate mother is so seized by maternal feelings that she decides she wants to keep the baby. Is a court going to wrest it from her?

There is no end to attempts to "broaden" or "transcend" the traditional role of the family. And there is no end to the moral conundrums and menacing ambiguities that arise when people improvise changes in the family's functions regarding procreation and child rearing.

At a press conference called to "carry the standard for surrogate parenting," Kane urged women "to share their bodies for nine months." Her language (like the pro-abortion slogan about "women controlling their own bodies") reduces to a purely individual and physical matter something that is irreducibly social and spiritual, something that radiates subtleties which reach the core of our sense of what it is to be human.

December 14, 1980

Bilingual Education: Misplaced Solicitousness

Exasperated by difficulties deriving from the influx of Latin immigrants, voters of Dade County (Miami), Florida, picked up a blunderbuss on election day and shot, perhaps, Saint Patrick. As Yogi Berra said when told that Dublin had elected a Jewish mayor, "Only in America!"

It is unclear whether public support for Miami's Saint Patrick's Day parade is illegal now that the following language has been enacted into law by referendum: "The expenditure of county funds for the purpose of utilizing any language other than English, or promoting any culture other than that of the United States, is prohibited." A bit sweeping, that.

The main purpose of proponents of the ordinance was defensible. It was to reverse a 1973 decision making Dade officially a "bilingual county." But the ordinance not only threatens to rain on the Saint's parade; it might, if taken a tad too literally, curtail such vital services as bilingual assistance on the 911 emergency telephone number.

Excesses happen when the masses make laws by referenda. Excesses also happen, regularly, when bureaucracies make laws. Consider the nation's sleepwalk toward bilingual education. In 1974 the Supreme Court held that . . . well, let Henry Catto, who has watched the policy evolve, pick up the narrative. The Court held:

. . . that Chinese-speaking students in San Francisco were being discriminated against by being taught in English. It ordered relief, but did not specify what form the relief should take. The Office of Civil Rights of the Department of Health, Education and Welfare could have gone two ways to implement the decision: increase special English instruction or impose teaching in Chinese. With an unerring instinct for disaster, it chose the latter.

Now the Department of Education has proposed rules that would impose bilingual education on many school districts—rules which violate existing law, and which probably will be blocked by Congress. Thus does DOE confirm its critics by acting like a "national school board"; thus does it strengthen the determination of those who want to dismantle it.

In no other nation has the history of society been so bound up with the history of schools. In this nation of immigrants, schools have transmitted the essentials of citizenship, often beginning with the language.

The modern push for bilingual education began before the 1974 Court decision. It began in the 1960s, when, in some circles, the very idea of "Americanization" was regarded as arrogantly "ethnocentric," when cultivation of ethnic "consciousness" was regarded as rebellion against "negative stereotypes" imposed by the "racist society" and when public policy began to assert that rights belong not just to individuals but also to certain government-approved ethnic groups.

Abigail Thernstrom, writing in *The Public Interest*, argues that bilingual education grew, in part, from the "revolution against American culture." She says it began, and not coincidentally, at the time of "black power" rhetoric; it was rationalized, in part, as necessary to the "self-esteem" of America's "victimized" groups:

> Black power advocates had reversed the Supreme Court's argument in *Brown* v. *Board* [of Education of Topeka], and white liberals in the 1960s had adopted that reversal. Children who are racially segregated suffer irreparable psychological damage, the Court had contended. . . . Black militants and their liberal sympathizers turned this argument around. To *assimilate* children into an alien culture, they said, creates feelings of inferiority.

Dade County's ordinance, however flawed, reflects a defensible intuition: what is done regarding language shapes the culture, and hence shapes the politics of the society. Bilingualism can lead to biculturalism, and hence to social schisms. In some areas—parts of Florida, Texas and California—bilingual education is part of what may become, inexorably, the institutionalization of two languages. If you doubt the intractable nature of the problems that such a development can produce, consider Quebec; consider Belgium.

"America," says Thernstrom, "the most ethnically heterogeneous nation in the world, is one of the most linguistically homogeneous. Yet today the ideological underpinnings of that homogeneity are largely gone." The basic underpinning is belief in a distinctive and admirable American culture, and insistence that a certain minimal immersion in it is a prerequisite for proper citizenship.

The drift toward bilingual education represents yet another triumph of enthusiasm over lucidity—enthusiasm for the sort of "rights" that we are multiplying with unbridled license, at great cost to the social fabric.

America has been a beckoning haven for brave and determined people because it promises stability, equality and social mobility, all of which are, in part, by-products of cultural unity. Misplaced solicitousness for recent immigrants could undermine the attributes that have made the nation a magnet for millions.

November 27, 1980

Experimenting with Racism

The Supreme Court has closed for the summer, so the Constitution is safe until October. But before the brethren departed, they damaged it considerably by affirming, 6–3, the constitutionality of the first law by which Congress created a legislative classification for entitlement to benefits based solely on race.

Speaking for the majority, Chief Justice Burger said "appropriate deference" to Congress requires acceptance of the law reserving 10 percent of certain public-works funds for contracting firms controlled by members of six government-preferred minorities ("Negroes, Spanish-speaking, Orientals, Indians, Eskimos, Aleuts"). This even if the firms are not the lowest bidders and fail to satisfy other criteria that nonminority competitors must satisfy.

Burger says the constitutional power to provide for the "general welfare" gives Congress "latitude" to allocate special rights to certain racial or ethnic groups. This in spite of the Fourteenth Amendment's guarantee of "equal protection of the laws" for all persons. And in spite of the constituting doctrine of all open societies, on which the Fourteenth Amendment rests—the doctrine that rights belong to persons, not races.

Burger recognizes that discrimination in behalf of the preferred minorities will injure some competitors who are entirely innocent of wrongdoing. Astonishingly, he says, complacently and wrongly, that this is an "incidental consequence of the program, not part of its objective." But injuring some of the competitive firms is not "incidental"; it is the essence of a program designed to give privileges to uncompetitive firms.

Justice Stewart, dissenting, noted that only twice before has the Court found constitutional a government program that imposes injury on the basis of race. That was during the Second World War, in the infamous Japanese-American curfew and exclusion cases. But when Stewart upholds forced busing, which involves assigning children to schools on the basis of race, he helps diminish resistance to official actions based on race.

Justice Powell sided with the majority, in spite of the fact that in his Bakke opinion he said: "It is far too late to argue that the guarantee of equal protection to all persons permits the recognition of special wards entitled to a degree of protection greater than that accorded others." Now Powell seems to say that to be constitutional, a "race-conscious" program must at least be "temporary," so that it "will not last longer than the discriminatory effects it is designed to eliminate." But Congress can renew such programs, thereby renewing its call on the Court's "appropriate deference." There hardly can be criteria for determining when all ethnic groups have received recompense for all injuries inflicted by history on their ancestors.

By creating privileges based on race, the government reinforces—

even teaches—the noxious habit of thinking of people as mere parts of classes. And as Justice Stevens asks in dissent, "What percentage of Oriental blood or what degree of Spanish-speaking skill is required for membership in the preferred class?" Now the government must devise its version of the Nazi laws that defined who is a Jew. Stewart says "our statute books will once again have to contain laws that reflect the odious practice of delineating the qualities that make one person a Negro and make another white."

This "splapdash" law (Stevens' description) is unlike, say, the Voting Rights Act. It is not designed to remove barriers to free competition. It is designed to curtail free competition. As Stevens says, "A comparable approach in the electoral context would support a rule requiring that at least 10 percent of the candidates elected to the legislature be members of specified racial minorities."

Powell says, incongruously: "The time cannot come too soon when no governmental decision will be based upon immutable characteristics of pigmentation or origin." But by joining the majority, he said: Now would be too soon.

Eighty-four years ago, in a noble dissent against a ruling that segregation was constitutional, Justice John Marshall Harlan insisted that "our Constitution is color-blind." It wasn't then; it isn't now; and because of what the Court has done, it may never be. To the civil-rights movement—when there was a civil-rights movement; before it became just another movement maneuvering for economic redistribution—Harlan was a hero.

Burger concluded his opinion with a bromide from Justice Brandeis: "To stay experimentation in things social and economic is a grave responsibility." But the law the Court has condoned just puts a different, "progressive" spin on the familiar evil of conditioning government favors on the basis of race. The Chief Justice bears grave responsibility for rationalizing, as Congress did not bother to do, congressional "experimentation" with racism.

July 10, 1980

Reverse Discrimination and the "Foot-Race" Analogy

"You cannot spill a drop of American blood without spilling the blood of the whole world," Herman Melville wrote in 1849. ". . . Our blood is as the flood of the Amazon, made up of a thousand noble currents all pouring into one. We are not a nation, so much as a world." But government policy has been, increasingly, to divide the majestic national river into little racial and ethnic creeks. If that policy succeeds, the United States will be less a nation than an angry maelstrom of factions scrambling for preference in the government's allocation of entitlements.

That policy was endorsed by the Administration's brief against Allan Bakke, a brief which urged that the nation should cultivate "race consciousness." The brief did not suggest how the government will decide, someday, that persons who have been "victims," personally or through "their forebears," have been "restored"—a strange choice of verb—"to the position they would have occupied" but for discrimination. The *Bakke* decision pleases the Administration.

Bakke won because a medical school, with no record of discrimination to rectify, adopted a numerical quota for certain minorities, and admitted some who were dramatically less qualified than he was. The *Bakke* decision has made little law. Therefore, most existing policies will continue, so the law can be riddled with racial considerations. With regard to higher education, the decision suggests broad tolerance for reverse-discrimination policies that are less raw than that which excluded Bakke. And Justice Powell's opinion for the Court can be read plausibly as somewhat permissive regarding considerations of race and ancestry in the allocation of other government benefits generally.

The opinion says racial and ethnic distinctions are "suspect" and require "exacting judicial examination." But when state distribution of benefits "hinges" on race or ethnicity, the racial and ethnic classifications are acceptable if they are "necessary" to promote a "substantial" state interest, such as diversity in enrollments. Four Justices even assert the constitutionality of programs like the one that excluded Bakke, programs that do not just use "minority status as a positive factor," but "set aside a predetermined number of places" for minorities. These Justices say, not groundlessly: "For purposes of constitutional adjudication, there is no difference between the two approaches."

Powell says that the "equal protection" clause precludes "recognition of special wards entitled to a degree of protection greater than that accorded others"; he rejects a "two-class theory" of equal protection. But then he says there can be compelling state interests served by constitutional forms of discrimination which disadvantage whites for the benefit of preferred minorities. This necessarily means distinguishing two classes of citizens.

Powell says there is a distinction of constitutional dimension between an "explicit racial classification" that "totally" excludes members of some groups from full participation in a program, and "properly devised" racial considerations that are "flexible" in treating race or ancestry as a "plus." But this can be a distinction without a significant difference. For most professional schools, the pool of qualified minority applicants is shallow. Schools that dip too deeply will produce striking disparities between the test scores and academic records of the minorities and the whites they accept. At some point such disparities must be *prima facie* evidence of a quota, whether it is acknowledged or surreptitious.

The *Bakke* decision does not necessarily mean the Court will say that reverse discrimination in employment and awarding of contracts is "necessary" to a "substantial" state interest. But the Court may not seriously impede the bureaucratic drive to transform the core concept of American justice from "equal opportunity for individuals" to "statistical parity for government-approved groups." There is indeed a substantial state interest in broadening membership in the middle class, and especially in professions. But the Fourteenth Amendment guarantees equal protection to "persons," and any reverse discrimination grants special entitlements to preferred groups. Nevertheless, the *Bakke* decision will leave unscathed an array of programs by which the government encourages or compels public and private institutions to consider ethnic quantities more, and individual qualities less, when conferring benefits.

In 1954, the Court seemed on the way to saying what Congress subsequently seemed to say in the 1964 Civil Rights Act: race is an inherently unacceptable basis for state action. But now, in the *Bakke* case, the Court has refused to find that principle in the 1964 act, and the Court rejected that principle in cases before *Bakke*. For example, it held that states may tailor redistricting plans racially to create or preserve legislative districts that enhance the electoral power of preferred minorities (in the particular case, blacks and Puerto Ricans). The plan in question diluted the electoral strength of Hassidic Jews, who do not enjoy government preference.

Reverse discrimination began as a means of ameliorating the condition of blacks, but it was quickly claimed as a "right" by groups defined by race, ancestry or sex. It is demanded in spite of the fact that it devalues the achievements of its beneficiaries and stigmatizes them as wards of the state, unable to compete. This taint is not disguised by tactical euphemisms, such as saying that employers must "differentially validate" employment tests when they are required to set lower passing scores for preferred minorities than for whites. Whether called "affirmative action" or (as in the 1976 Democratic platform) "compensatory opportunity," reverse discrimination and the quest for statistical parity for "underrepresented" groups involve what Professor Ben L. Martin calls the "sensory" theory of representation: "only personal qualities crude enough to be obvious to sense perception, such as skin color, language, or sex, are acceptable bases of representation." Martin explains reverse discrimination in terms of "the foot-race analogy":

> In a fair race, none is disadvantaged at the starting line. But if all begin with equal advantage, then all should finish together, because contemporary liberalism leaves virtually no personal quality—not character, personality, motivation, self-discipline, or any other personal trait—as the responsibility of the individual.

The premise behind reverse discrimination is this: an unfair start can be inferred from an unequal outcome. The traditional American premise is this: the equal status of citizenship is the basis on which a structure of inequality *should* be built by a population in which talents are neither equally distributed nor equally rewarded. Reverse discrimination is a betrayal, not a fulfillment, of American values.

July 10, 1978

My Ancestor Charlemagne and the Census Bureau

Because I may be a descendant of nobility, or even of an emperor, I try to view democratic government with an elevated detachment that any venerable ancestor would have considered seemly. So I am only bemused by reports that the Census Bureau, acting at the behest of proud or acquisitive (or proudly acquisitive) ethnic groups, wants all members of all seventy-three million households to be classified under one of fourteen "races" (including Eskimo, Hawaiian, Samoan, Aleut) listed on the 1980 questionnaire.

This racial inventory involves more than a natural curiosity. It is "necessary," given the government's determination to bestow special entitlements on certain approved minorities: those which government certifies, implicitly, as victims of society. That determination will survive, and will probably be encouraged by, the *Bakke* decision.

Although that decision addresses only reverse discrimination in admissions procedures in higher education, the tone and substance of the decision are broadly permissive regarding consideration of race and ethnic background in the allocation of entitlements. Much the most important aspect of the decision is a forceful assertion that, in many cases, racial considerations (put plainly, forms of discrimination) that disadvantage whites can be constitutional.

As government gets deeper into the business of allocating "just shares" of wealth and opportunity to approved victims, membership in those groups becomes valuable. As the core concept of justice changes from "equal opportunity for individuals" to "statistical parity for government-approved groups," leaders of those groups want to swell the government's count of the members of their groups.

Alas, some souls are condemned to loneliness. There are few ethnic companions for the eminent New York lawyer who says he is a WASP: White Armenian-Swiss Protestant. Perhaps he can form a coalition with the Washington lady who is Scottish-Armenian-Cherokee. A friend of mine from England is planning to give the Census Bureau this recipe for the bubbling broth that he is:

English, French (a dark stain he has hitherto concealed), Spanish and Portuguese (the residue of mercantile ancestors), Dutch, German, Italian, Swedish, Scottish, Cornish (whoever doubts that this is a separate race has not lingered in Cornwall), Arab (from some feisty Crusaders) and Welsh. Because Welsh ladies fraternized shamelessly with Roman legions that were rotated through Britain in the first four centuries after Christ, the recipe for my friend should also probably include a dash of Moroccan and a pinch of Rumanian.

When my friend's questionnaire has reduced the Census Bureau's whirring computers to puddles of melted transistors, the sweet stillness will enable us to contemplate this fact: most people are tossed salads. I intend to tell the Bureau that I place myself in this category: "Possible Descendant of the Nobility of Charlemagne's Day, and Perhaps of Himself." To understand why, you must contemplate some large numbers, a chore that is tedious but perhaps rewarding because it may enable you to claim membership in this exalted class.

Assuming that there are about 3.5 generations to a century, there were about 42 generations between the birth of Charlemagne and the birth of George F. Will. It takes two humans to produce a human, so on the impossible assumption that there was no intermarriage among my ancestors, my ancestors alive twelve centuries ago would have numbered two to the 42nd power, or more than four trillion.

But there were at most eighty million people in Charlemagne's Europe. So there had to be considerable intermarrying among my ancestors, as among the ancestors of most people of European extraction. Europe's population is a tangled ball of twine, and many who lived in Charlemagne's Europe, including Himself, are related—in many ways—to many people who today are of European extraction.

Although it is jolly to think that one may have noble lineage, there is a mild drawback. Remember that America, ever the land of opportunity, today does offer prizes, in the form of entitlements, to those minorities which have won from the government the increasingly coveted status of victims. And obviously, those who may be descended from nobility are ineligible for such status.

July 2, 1978

Alphabetism: A Case of Terminal Earnestness

Connecticut, I regret to report, is now in the vanguard of advanced thinking about what constitutes correct government. Through Barry Zitser, the state's consumer counsel, Connecticut has pioneered a new dimension in fastidiousness about the protection of its citizens.

Zitser has asked the Southern New England Telephone Company to consider "the compelling logic" of the idea that listing companies alphabetically in the Yellow Pages "provides an unfair advantage to those with names at the beginning of the alphabet."

"When most people pick up the telephone book to look up a business, attorney, etc., they start with the A's. . . . Why should we force such individuals either to change their names or suffer economic detriment?" Zitser urges the telephone company to consider combating "this blatant discrimination" by printing the Yellow Pages "so that one half of the subject listings are in alphabetical order, and one half are in backwards-alphabetical order." And "to avoid the temptation to change one's name *after* the listings are so changed, a provision could be made to rotate such alphabetizing every other year."

The injustice of "alphabetism" is, of course, a thorn in the Zitser side, and he playfully promises to assign the problem to "alphabetically neutral" aides (named Koss, Little and Matthews). But he is, at bottom, serious, and some of his assistants are marvelously so.

Some companies have, indeed, changed their names to the Ace or Acme or Aardvark Widget Company to gain "alphabetical preference." But what really troubles Zitser and his helpers is what one helper calls a "potential problem." We want, he says, "to make people aware that they should not be selecting companies or products on an alphabetical basis."

This aide (who would, I guess, be classified a "dove" in the war against alphabetism) is not hoping for a "bullet-proof solution to this problem-situation." He indicates that he might feel that Connecticuters were adequately protected if the telephone company were to scatter through the Yellow Pages warnings that the order of listing does not constitute ranking by merit.

I asked, incredulously, if he thought anyone was in doubt about that, and he replied, ingenuously, that, "We have some concern that there are some people—we don't know where they are"—who might think that "the A's are better than the Z's."

There, I submit, you have a crystalline expression of the spirit of today's regulating, paternal government. Such government is benevolent in intention, diligent in application, scrupulous with regard to detail—and frequently ludicrous, because lacking a sense of proportion.

The issue of alphabetism is, of course, trivial, but what government does is often less important than why government does it. What is dismaying about the war on alphabetism is not any conceivable outcome, rather its premise. The premise is that government should try to make society risk-free for even irrational people.

Discussing "what sort of despotism democratic nations have to fear," De Tocqueville foresaw the "immense and tutelary power" of a benevolent state that would cover "the surface of society with a network of small complicated rules, minute and uniform."

"That power is absolute, minute, regular, provident, and mild. It would be like the authority of a parent if, like that authority, its object was to prepare men for manhood; but it seeks, on the contrary, to keep them in perpetual childhood. . . ."

One of the wonders of the modern world, and of the modern state, is this: adults will soldier through law school, making a considerable investment of their own time and other people's money, and when they have been initiated into the majesty of the law, they are content—nay, they are eager—to apply their skills to the strangest, smallest matters. Still, in a letter to me, one of Zitser's helpers seems a tad defensive:

"It should be noted that this is not a priority issue . . . but we do feel it is a realistic problem. Therefore, even though it may be difficult to find an equitable solution to the problem, it is deserving of some earnest consideration."

This is how the world will end: not with a bang, or even with a whimper, but in the awful silence of billions of lips pursed and brows furrowed by terminal earnestness.

November 5, 1978

Part Three ❧

THE WAR AGAINST THE TOTALITARIAN, 1939–

Remembering an "International Kiss"

Fifty years and many wars ago, the United States took the lead in an effort to make war a thing of the past. On August 27, 1928, representatives of fifteen nations met in Paris to sign the Kellogg–Briand pact, thereby renouncing the use of war as an instrument of national policy.

Today the name Kellogg–Briand is like the memory of wind whistling in a chimney, in an old house, long ago. But it is wrong to regard the pact banning war as just another example of the featherheadedness typical of a nation that was simultaneously trying to enforce a ban on alcohol. It was more than a pale flame of idealism in the closing dusk of American innocence. It expressed aspects of the American temper that still exist.

Warren Harding, the first postwar President, declared, "I don't know anything about this European stuff" and left all such stuff to his Secretary of State, Charles Evans Hughes, whose successor was Frank Kellogg. In the mid-1920s, the State Department's staff of just six hundred professionals disposed of a budget of just $2 million. In Europe, the most ominous figure was Mussolini, who preached the virtues of war to an inattentive nation.

Most Americans did not care about foreign policy in the decade after the "war to end war," but there was a significant "peace movement," two ornaments of which were Columbia University President Nicholas Murray Butler and Professor James Shotwell, also of Columbia. Shotwell suggested to Aristide Briand, the French Foreign Minister, that the United States and France should sign a treaty to "outlaw" war.

Briand fastened upon the idea as a way of beginning to bind the

139

United States in a bilateral relationship with France. But Briand did not anticipate Kellogg's deftness.

Kellogg disdained the "peace movement," but Briand's offer compelled him to act, and he knew a political opportunity when it was handed to him. Kellogg turned it into a multination extravaganza. And by 1934, sixty-four nations had endorsed its provisions. A decade later, most were at war.

Prior to 1928, the last event that had stirred public interest in foreign policy had been "the first SALT talks"—the Washington Naval Conference of 1921. The opening of the conference coincided with interment of the "Unknown Soldier," a ceremony broadcast nationwide by the magic of radio.

The assumption sustaining the Naval Conference was that naval limitation was the key to peace. A few years later, when the Senate ratified the Kellogg–Briand pact 85–1, that body promptly voted to authorize fifteen new cruisers.

The pact banned only "aggressive" war; it lacked enforcement mechanisms; and the Senate Foreign Relations Committee tacked on an "interpretation" which affirmed the U.S. right to "enforce" the Monroe Doctrine.

Nevertheless, the pact satisfied those—and there are always many of them—who believed that diplomatic parchment could do the work of blood and iron in guaranteeing national security. Kellogg received the Nobel Peace Prize in 1929.

As today's President understands too well, there is always an American audience for the theory that a particular problem is the intended result of scheming by this or that "special interest." In the 1920s, a significant audience was eager to believe that the "Great War" had been caused by "munitions makers" and other "merchants of death." People who believed that were prone to believe that conspiracies of ill will would be blocked by open expressions of goodwill.

The Kellogg–Briand pact accorded with three beliefs that recur in America: the world is in the "mood" for peace; moods are decisive; moods last. Anyone who thinks that those beliefs died long ago has not been paying attention to more recent history.

One critic, who had a way with wounding words, dismissed the

Kellogg-Briand pact as "an international kiss." But it is not obvious that the pact was more vacuous, more of an exercise in deception (including self-deception) or more of a dead letter than is the U.S.-Soviet document explaining the principles of détente (1972) or than are the human-rights provisions of the Helsinki accords (1975). In the year 2028, the assessment of these may be similar to today's assessment of the Kellogg-Briand pact: worthless, but not harmless.

August 24, 1978

War: *Swift Solvent of Inhibition*

If (to end this year with conjecture about the next) the nation faces a protracted debate about nuclear weapons, then 1979 may be an educational experience. It may be the year when, at long last, people think hard about the technology and morality on which their security, such as it is, rests.

The proximate cause of this will be the proposed strategic-arms-limitation agreement. But the time is ripe for reflection about matters which are so familiar that they no longer seem, as they should, astonishing and disquieting.

It is said that since the summer of 1945 the world has lived "in the shadow of the bomb." But the shadow is, of course, metaphorical, and the assumption that mankind has been weighed down by thoughts of nuclear weapons is false. Such weapons are part of the wallpaper of the age, unnoticed and, to almost everybody, uninteresting.

The flood of fiction about nuclear holocaust (*On the Beach, The Fallen Sky, Alas, Babylon, A Canticle for Leibowitz* and more) has virtually dried up. Thirty-three years is a long time in the experience of nations, and John Lukacs, the historian, notes that the nuclear age is the only age many people have known:

In 1945 the Prime Minister of Great Britain was a man born and brought up under the reign of Queen Victoria. In 1945 . . . there were still millions of Germans who had been born and brought up during the age of Bismarck; there were at least one million Frenchmen who had been born under the reign of Napoleon III, and at least three million Americans, including President Truman's mother, who had been born when Lincoln was alive. At the time of this writing [1978] less than half the people in the world were born before the Second World War.

Actually, we may already be entering the third "nuclear age."

In 1945, when nuclear weapons were used, they were just big tactical weapons, enhancing the effectiveness of a familiar weapon, the bomber. Two atomic bombs did the work of two air raids over Japan. (The railroad station at Hiroshima was operating again within forty-eight hours after the attack.) In 1945, the only nation with nuclear weapons had neither the number of weapons, nor the will, nor, it turned out, the need to use them strategically (to dominate an entire theater of war).

The second nuclear age began, symbolically, in 1957, with *Sputnik*, which underscored the primacy of missiles. The lesson was this: More important (because harder to come by) than "the bomb" is the delivery system.

But today it no longer seems clear that the most likely users of nuclear weapons are the few superpowers capable of developing sophisticated delivery systems. The third nuclear age may see the broad democratization of nuclear force. A small nation with limited conventional resources but sufficient physicists (actually, engineers will do) can be a political entity without precedent: a small nation that no other nation, large or small, dares to back into a corner.

It is impossible to anticipate how any nation's leaders would behave in nuclear war. In 1914 the world lived "in the shadow" of the First World War, yet the New York Stock Exchange closed for three months after the war began, so bewildered were the world's financial leaders.

Europe's military classes had thought long and hard about war, but about half of France's corps and divisional commanders had to be replaced in the first two months. The French experience was especially severe, but other nations' commanders also proved unprepared for the shock of reality. And in June, 1941, Stalin—who was as hard as his name: "Steel"—came unglued for more than a week after Germany attacked.

War is a swift solvent of inhibitions. In September, 1939, Britain's Secretary of State for Air learned that Britain's military men were contemplating using incendiary bombs on the Black Forest, which the beautiful summer of 1939 had turned to tinder. He exclaimed, "Are you aware that this [the forest] is private property? You will be asking me to bomb the Ruhr next." And, indeed, they did.

But leaders, officers, and men and women get used to things. We all have got used to basing national security on a form of nuclear "deterrence" that is in fact a practice universally condemned for centuries—holding civilian populations hostage.

December 31, 1978

"The Last European War"

It is regrettable, if understandable, that September 1 will pass with much less notice in the United States than in Europe. At dawn September 1, forty years ago, German troops crashed into Poland. Twenty million people were to die in the next six years. But John Lukacs writes: "The outbreak of no other great war in the modern history of Europe caused so little surprise." And in contrast to 1914, Europeans went to war with resignation rather than enthusiasm.

It is arguable (and A. J. P. Taylor does argue) that the Second World War actually began in April, 1932, when Mao Tse-tung declared war on Japan in the name of the Kiangsi soviet. Americans think the war began December 7, 1941.

What did begin forty years ago was (in the words of the title of Lukacs' superb history) "The Last European War: September 1939/December 1941." This war, as Lukacs says, was the decisive phase of the larger war. If Hitler had beaten Britain or Russia then, he would have won the war.

He came close in Russia. On October 15, 1941, there was the first traffic jam in the history of the Soviet Union as government officials and others privileged enough to have cars fled east. Others scrambled to buy Russian–German dictionaries. Lukacs believes, "A single German parachute regiment could have taken Moscow." After 1941, with the United States in the war, Hitler could not win, and since 1941 the destiny of Europe has depended on two extra-European powers, the United States and the U.S.S.R.

In 1917, Germany sent Lenin into Russia. In 1939, Germany, with the Nazi–Soviet pact, brought Stalin into Europe. These two deeds help explain why, as Lukacs says, the rising importance of the eastern, relative to the western, half of the continent is a major theme of European history in this century.

The war in the West began slowly. Six years before Hiroshima, the British pulled three-hundred-year-old howitzers from museums, the French sent to Finland some guns used in the Crimean War, and the Norwegian navy included a warship commissioned in 1858. King George VI practiced pistol shooting in the garden at Buckingham Palace.

British and German troops did not meet until April 20, 1940, in Norway. In the first fifteen months of the war, there was only one small Allied victory on land, at Narvik, Norway. But Hitler's victory in Norway brought Churchill to power, and his invasion of Norway and Denmark helped dissipate isolationist feelings in the American Middle West, home of many people of Scandinavian extraction.

Hitler understood better than his enemies the revolution in warfare wrought by the internal-combustion engine. Some of his troops even used Michelin guides in their invasion of France. But Germany's use of mechanized forces does not fully explain its devastating successes early in the war.

In 1938, Britain was, for the last time, the principal factor in world politics. In 1938, France had five allies, at least in theory, and Germany had none. But it is widely and wrongly assumed that the German army swept to early victories in the West because it had overwhelming material advantages.

It had some. But in 1939, German aircraft production was about the same as British production. German tank production was less than British production. The British and French navies were larger than the German navy, and Germany did not launch a ship larger than a destroyer during the war.

The crucial point is that in the last European War, as Lukacs says, equipment told: but never apart from the martial qualities. As Lukacs says, Hitler "was one of the most terrifying creators of national confidence."

The Second World War began because of the moral more than the material weaknesses of the democracies. The two kinds of weakness often go together. Forty years later, there is rising anxiety about the provocative weakness of the West. Consider, for example, the swift transformation of the SALT II debate. During three weeks of hearings in July, it became a debate about how to rectify the U.S. military weaknesses that SALT II reflects and ratifies.

It is another sign of the uneasy times that on the fortieth anniversary of the beginning of war in Europe, the nonfiction bestseller list includes a novel written as a warning by some British NATO officers and advisers. Its title is *The Third World War: August 1985.*

August 30, 1979

Kissinger and the End of Innocence

Henry Kissinger's memoirs are an elegant literary achievement and a political act of, I hope, profound consequence. His aim is to purge foreign policy of sentimentality.

The book, which covers just 1969–1972, is fat (1,521 pages) yet lean; it will disappoint today's ravenous appetite for gossip. The author is frequently eloquent, gripping, droll, ironic, sarcastic, tetchy and aphoristic. But throughout, he makes readers wade waist-deep in detail. Like Monet, he covers a large canvas with small strokes that have a remarkable cumulative effect.

Some works of literature can be read in snippets. Others, like Kissinger's, should be experienced as a steady march. Read relentlessly, his book conveys an overwhelming impression of the grinding, exhausting weight and density of things at the juncture of international and intragovernmental politics. No book better reveals the texture of experience at the highest levels of the modern bureaucratic state.

See Kissinger flail against a monster slug. (The Kremlin? No, the State Department.) See him at daggers drawn with a wily foe. (Le Duc Tho? No, silly: Secretary of Defense Melvin Laird, for whose deviousness Kissinger felt something like the admiration Michelangelo must have felt for Raphael.) Kissinger does not tell even half of his side of the many-sided conspiracies, jealousies and maneuvers in what is called, antiseptically, "the policymaking process." As Mark Twain said, confession is good for the soul but bad for the reputation.

The greatest political memoirs of this century begin: "All my life I have thought of France in a certain way." De Gaulle knew where to begin: with national character. It has been said that anyone who has seen the same opera performed before Italian and English audiences knows how different national characters can be. Kissinger's memoirs are, in part, a meditation on the character of his adopted nation. He believes that because America became great by assimilating disparate groups, it believes too much in the possibility of tolerance and compromise, too little in protracted conflicts over unbridgeable differences. He hopes America is losing its "innocence" and coming to terms with the practice of "balance of power" diplomacy.

People have been announcing the end of American innocence since Yorktown. Innocence? John Adams? James K. Polk? Lincoln? The Founders built a "balance of power" into the constitutional system of checks and balances, and did well in diplomacy. Last century, Americans fought often to consolidate the nation and suffered proportionately more casualties than any European nation. This century, Americans learned childishness (which, any parent knows, is not innocence).

Kissinger notes that in 1919, Americans withdrew from the world because they thought the world too evil for America, and fifty years later the intelligentsia wanted to withdraw because they thought America too evil for the world. The Marshall Plan and Point Four expressed the faith that our moral and material resources could overwhelm all problems. It was the New Deal internationalized: economic progress would dissolve political conflict. Peace, people thought, is "normal" and is the final result of diplomatic goodwill. Kissinger says that finality is a chimera. "History knows no resting places, no plateaus," because "the management of a balance of power is a permanent undertaking, not an exertion that has a foreseeable end."

Kissinger admires De Gaulle, who also faced, simultaneously, problems of a withdrawal (from Algeria; he too took four years) and restoration of national confidence. De Gaulle, "the son of a continent covered with ruins," knew that a statesman must sense the "trend of history." History, Kissinger senses, has trends, but is neither a prison nor an alibi. There is "a margin between necessity and accident" in which one can act to "resist the decay that besets all human institutions."

Kissinger believes that the hinge of the history he helped make was autumn, 1970. Jordan was disintegrating; the Soviets had troops in Egypt and were building a submarine base in Cuba; and Allende came to power promising to turn Chile into a Cuba. But two great events of 1970 involved no human volition. One was Nasser's fatal heart attack, which led to the ascendancy of Sadat. The other was the cyclone that devastated East Pakistan and set in train civil war, then the India–Pakistan war, during which the United States "tilted" toward Pakistan to show, to China and the Soviet Union, a commitment to balance-of-power diplomacy. But historical accidents only make possible what other events have prepared. In nurturing events, the statesman must "rescue an element of choice from the pressure of circumstance."

If you culled from Kissinger's tome all his maxims, you could assemble an essay as slender and pithy as Machiavelli's *Prince*. Machiavelli stressed *fortuna,* meaning the capriciousness of history, and *virtù,* the ability to show mastery amidst the flux of things. But on page after page, Kissinger demonstrates that a leader of the American democracy is apt to be bound down with many cords, like Gulliver among the Lilliputians. The chief impediment to creative diplomacy is not, as has been said, the turbulence of the people, but the sluggish, clogging bureaucracy, which "confuses wise policy with smooth administration and has an incentive to exaggerate technical complexity and minimize the scope and importance of political judgment." How can a leader show *virtù* when *fortuna* dishes up something like the State Department?

It was an epochal event when, responding to the Soviet threat to China, the United States decided that it had a strategic interest in the survival of a major Communist country. The "triangular diplomacy" made possible by the opening to China reflects Kissinger doctrine: the multiplication of diplomatic variables creates opportunities for a subtle and supple Prince. The more intricate the game of nations becomes, the more opportunity there is for creative leaders to compensate with cleverness for what their democratic societies lack in discipline.

Yet leadership exercised—even a decision taken—at the center of the U.S. Government often trickles away and disappears like rain on sand. No theory of the "imperial" Presidency will survive

Kissinger's descriptions of the Executive Branch busily inventing "backchannels" around itself. And Kissinger's book is an antidote to frivolous talk about its not mattering who is elected President. It matters very much that a President have the tenacity to radiate his energy through the government.

James Joyce expected his readers to devote their lives to understanding his writings. Kissinger has a bit less brass, but he thinks people should devote many evenings to understanding how he thinks history happens. If enough people do, this will be a more mature nation when it enters a decade that threatens to demand more maturity than the nation has recently shown.

October 29, 1979

The Need for Nationalism

A young but eminent member of the Carter Administration, a diplomat with a taste for lost causes, recently lured me from my hearth to a breakfast rendezvous. He hoped to correct some of my worst underestimations of the Administration's foreign-policy achievements. Several eggs and muffins later we parted, he with a new sense of just how lost a lost cause can be, I with an even deeper admiration for Charles de Gaulle.

A week or so earlier I had pushed the diplomat past forbearance by writing that Carter had given much and got little in negotiations with Peking over normalization of relations. With the patience of a priest catechizing a slow seven-year-old, the diplomat explained to me that Peking had not gotten all it wanted. For example, we continued selling arms to Taiwan, and were allowed to end our defense treaty with that ally a year later, rather than immediately.

I replied that if full diplomatic relations between Peking and Washington are not as important to Peking as we think they are (with all that would imply about China as a geopolitical asset), then we should find that out, fast. And we would have found out if Peking had refused normalization because of U.S. insistence on preserving more of our relations with Taiwan than, in the event, we were allowed to preserve. The diplomat responded that I had to understand how strongly Peking feels about Taiwan.

I replied with a statement that I prefaced by saying that I meant it "ninety percent facetiously," but which the horrified diplomat said was not facetious enough. I said: We should not have agreed in 1972 to reversion of Okinawa to Japan. This because when a nation is in retreat, as the United States was beginning to be then, and has been since then, perhaps the best way, even the only way, to stop retreating is just to stop, all at once, everywhere. The diplomat responded that I had to understand how strongly Japan felt about Okinawa.

His references to the strength of other nations' feelings, although correct regarding the feelings in both cases, is symptomatic of a national deficiency. The problem is less that we are too understanding of other nations' sticking points than that we seem to have none of our own. Occasional obduracy is good for a nation's soul, and standing. This would be a safer, better world if more nations had more occasions for muttering to themselves, "We just have to understand how strongly the United States feels about this."

Professional diplomats from liberal societies are inclined to equate good relations with smooth relations; they generally aim at reducing noise and friction in the international system. So liberal societies need political leaders who can supply nationalistic impulses that diplomatic corps usually lack. In that regard, De Gaulle was a model.

In 1958 he returned to power in a nation not yet recovered, spiritually, from the calamity of 1940, and lacerated nearly to civil war by the issue of Algeria. Michel Jobert, a Gaullist, writes:

> The General taught us—or revealed to us—that the *attitude* with which one approaches a difficulty is more important than the actual result. That a people's will is more significant than its present circumstances. That the collective consciousness needs to distinguish, to see in

the half-light of history, a few clear points, a few simple notions, and that this clarity and simplicity must have a galvanic power which leads to the power of self-transcendence.

Jobert argues that De Gaulle's insistence on his, and France's, right to the aura and gestures of grandeur was intensely practical. Foreign policy, "an area which highlighted common and exclusive social membership," became, under De Gaulle, an irritant to many nations, including the United States. But it was

in the first place a way of uniting the French on clear objectives, and it was no bad thing that the attempt was provocative. It was also a way of showing the face of France more clearly to other nations, and consequently of making the French more aware of their own existence, by seeing it through other people's eyes.

Jobert uses the words "simple" and "simplicity" to describe—to praise—aspects of the policies adopted by one of the most complex men and effective leaders of this century. Consider that the next time Jimmy Carter—the sophisticate who says that a President's principal task is to make government as good, decent, loving, and so on, as the American people are—exclaims that a Ronald Reagan idea involves "simplicity."

September 18, 1980

Shame

For several decades, since the Soviet Union lost its allure, many "progressives" have admired Asian Communism—from a safe distance, of course. For such people, 1979 is becoming tiresome.

In January, Vietnam attacked Cambodia: War really is hell for a "progressive" when neither side can be called fascist. Cambodia's slaughtering Communists were an embarrassment; but so too was Vietnam's attack. It refuted the myth of "peace-loving" Hanoi, a myth concocted to serve the supreme myth: that Hanoi's war of aggression against South Vietnam was merely a welling-up of nationalist ardor.

Then China, which "progressives" have said "has so much to teach us," attacked Vietnam, destroying villages to "teach them a lesson." And in Paris, Jean Lacouture, a prolific journalist revered by Hanoi's Western friends, denounced himself and others for having been "vehicles and intermediaries for a lying and criminal propaganda . . . spokesmen for tyranny in the name of liberty."

Lacouture confessed "shame for having contributed . . . to the installation of one of the most oppressive regimes [Cambodia's] history has known." And "with regard to Vietnam, my behavior was sometimes more that of a militant than of a journalist. I dissimulated certain defects of [North] Vietnam at war against the Americans. . . . I believed it was not opportune to expose the Stalinist nature of the [North] Vietnamese regime."

Michael Ledeen, writing in *Commentary,* says Lacouture's recantation is part of "the debate among French intellectuals over the nature of communism—a debate which has now reached historic proportions." In France, philosophy, like wine, matures slowly, and some French philosophers, having read Solzhenitsyn, have concluded (better late than never) that the Gulag is the essence, not an accident, of Communism.

It is quite French, this lighting upon the obvious with a proud sense of original discovery, but it is nonetheless welcome, especially because the debate is spilling into Italy. The debate there is helped along by an irony: as an Italian commentator has noted, Rome has a Communist mayor who knows nothing about real Communism, and a Pope who knows everything about it.

And now comes another affront to "progressive" sensibilities—the movie *The Deer Hunter,* winner of the Academy Award as best picture of the year. It is, primarily, a sympathetic treatment of the working-class, young Americans who fought the Vietnam war. Although it deals admiringly with some martial virtues (such as bravery, loyalty and disciplined ferocity), it is in no way a celebration of war or of America's Vietnam involvement.

Nevertheless, it has been denounced by those among Hanoi's friends who cling to the old cause as if clinging to life. They detest the movie's stirring love of country, and even more its portrayal of Vietnamese Communists as brutal, especially in the treatment of prisoners. That their many brutalities did not include one shown in the movie—forcing prisoners to play Russian roulette—is not the principal point of controversy. Those who denounce the movie as "reactionary" reveal how much their opposition to American policy was rooted in anti-Americanism and a romantic assessment of Asian Communism.

Captain John McCain of the U.S. Navy has not seen the movie. He saw too much of the reality. He was a POW for nearly six years, and experienced some of the "defects" of the North Vietnamese that the likes of Lacouture thought it would be "inopportune" to expose.

One day his captors told him he would be taken to meet someone identified only as "an American actress who is for peace." He refused to see the actress—in part, he says, because he did not expect her to be the sort of person who would go home and tell the truth.

He also refused because of the experience of a POW who had agreed to meet with some other Americans in the "peace" movement. The "peace" people commanded the POW to confess war crimes. When he refused, repeatedly and adamantly, he heard a "peace" person suggest to his captors that "this young man needs to be straightened out in his thinking." He was hung by his wrists until an arm pulled from its shoulder socket.

For refusing to see the actress, McCain was confined for four summer months in an unventilated cubicle five feet long and two feet wide, and he was beaten and starved. Other prisoners suffering similar abuse also were made to suffer Jane Fonda's voice: the North Vietnamese piped into the cells recordings in which she urged prisoners to actively oppose U.S. policy, and told the world how well the prisoners were being treated.

McCain recounts this without passion. He is a professional who understands that he must know the enemy, but not take things personally.

April 15, 1979

Enemies

Republican lions and lambs have lain down together, a spectacle as rare as it is Biblical. All thirty-eight Republican senators have joined in a stinging criticism of President Carter's foreign policy. Their declaration reflects the public's growing suspicion that the Cold War did not end when the United States pronounced it over in the name of détente. The Republicans avoid noting which party was in power when that pronouncement was made. But their declaration supports the belief that this is the fourth decade of the Cold War rather than the ninth year of détente.

The Republicans say Carter has failed to comprehend the nature of the Soviet threat. The Soviets want military superiority, not equality, and believe a nuclear war is winnable, not unthinkable. The Republicans criticize Carter's failure to respond to the Soviet buildup, with special reference to naval forces. Even before the Vietnam war ended, wise people warned that the "lessons" Americans would choose to draw from the war would be as dangerous as the war itself. The Administration's attack on the Navy reflects values and perceptions shaped by Vietnam "lessons": the Navy projects U.S. power and gets into "harm's way," so it poses the danger that the United States will sail into "another Vietnam." And the Republicans cite the definitive *Jane's All the World's Aircraft:* " . . . 1977 might be recorded as the year in which the seeds of defeat for the Western powers were sown . . . The fragile coexistence maintained for a generation by balanced East-West military power is being allowed to slip inch by inch from our grasp."

The Republicans decry Carter's "lack of resolve" in the face of "a powerful adversary whose goals are incompatible with our own and which, judged by its actions, appears bent on imposing its social and economic system on the world." This rediscovery of the Cold War comes nine years after a Republican President seemed to redefine "resolve" to conform to détente. In his new book, *The Soviet Syndrome,* Alain Besançon writes: "Since Germany's surrender, Western policy has set up for itself objectives that coincide miraculously with those of Soviet policy." The policy of "containment" established a defensive cordon while the Soviets digested their conquests. Détente, the West's unilateral commitment to "relaxation of tensions," came at the moment when the Soviets had recovered from war, consolidated their hold on their conquests and acquired military strength sufficient to make it awkward for the West to resist more aggressive Soviet behavior.

"Starting in 1970," the Republicans say, "the time when most experts agree the Soviets began to approach strategic parity with the United States, Moscow became much more strident in its political and military adventurism." What also started around 1970 was the myth that a new era had begun, in which Soviet behavior would be measurably improved. This myth, propagated by a President who detested liberals and was detested by them, was congruent with a change in liberalism.

For many years, the nation's anti-Communist consensus meant that the distinction between liberalism and conservatism was drawn almost exclusively in terms of domestic policy. But that consensus was a Vietnam casualty. The decline of liberal anti-Communism was manifest in the nomination of George McGovern, who blamed Vietnam on "Cold War paranoia." Ridicule heaped upon "paranoia" about the "domino theory" of Communist conquest in Indochina, and upon warnings about bloodbaths, has been silenced by the sounds of suffering from within the fallen dominoes, and the ridiculers' silence about the suffering is deafening. But many still believe that a "lesson" of Vietnam is that U.S. policy toward Communist aggression should be benign neglect.

Republican anti-Communism was diluted by Richard Nixon, whose most treasured moment, his visit to China, complete with applause for propaganda ballet and toasts comparing the Chinese and American revolutions, moved William Buckley to note that Nixon might be "the most deracinated American who ever lived and exercised great power." But the decline of Democratic anti-Communism is more important. The Democratic Party has been the central player in the central drama of this century, the irrepressible conflict between the totalitarians and free peoples. Woodrow Wilson was Lenin's *enemy*. Franklin Roosevelt was Hitler's *enemy*. Harry Truman was Stalin's *enemy*. John Kennedy was Khrushchev's and Castro's *enemy*. Lyndon Johnson, to his credit, was Ho Chi Minh's *enemy*. But today, the Secretary of State describes President Carter and Brezhnev as men who "have similar dreams and aspirations about the most fundamental issues."

The real significance of Secretary Vance's "Foundationspeak" is precisely that it is reflexive. Vance has lived in an environment of earnest, modulated, well-meaning liberalism. He calls to mind Randall Jarrell's fictional college president: "President Robbins was so well adjusted to his environment that sometimes you could not tell which was the environment and which was President Robbins." Vance is the gentleman of the Western world, reluctant to see that people do not all agree on "most fundamental issues." No wonder the Administration is often surprised and bewildered. The nineteenth-century ascendancy of liberalism meant faith in moral and material progress, and the conviction that war and other forms of conflict are aberrations in the "natural" harmony among peoples. Most Americans, regardless of party, are products of modern liberal culture that finds the international frightfulness in the world *unbelievable*.

Besançon explains détente as practiced by Western powers: "They are treating the U.S.S.R. as if it were just like any other state, in the hope that it will finally behave that way, will actually be what they want it to be. In short, their action is pedagogical." The use of détente diplomacy as pedagogy is a compound of complacency and condescension. It assumes that the Soviets are slow learners but are ready to learn from Western tutors. Obviously

Solzhenitsyn is widely read and his conclusions are widely resisted in nations slumbering in the faith that the U.S.S.R. is "just like any other state." It is not. It is not even a classic despotism. It has the implacable dynamism of a state permanently waging war on human nature, pulverizing and impoverishing civil society to satisfy militarist ravenousness. It is founded on a pseudoscience, enveloped in a pseudoreality of ideology and sustained by terror and lies. It has been said that the four words for which the initials U.S.S.R. stand contain four lies, and that the Soviet constitution contains more lies than articles. The Republicans' declaration is an inoculation against the contagion of comforting lies the West tells itself about the Soviet Union.

May 15, 1978

The "Ordinary" Soviet Leaders

For generations, the world has been awash with potent ideas about the impotence of ideas, and theories of history that discount individuals as makers of history. The most contagious of these doctrines is vulgar Marxism, a materialist theory of cause and effect which asserts that history is governed by an iron law of inevitability, and that ideas and ideals are, in Marx's words, "phantoms of the human brain," mere by-products of material forces. But John Lukacs, in his new book *1945: Year Zero,* notes an exhilarating demonstration that history, which is the history of the human mind, is unpredictable:

. . . Something happened in 1945, in a most unlikely place: in the pine forests of East Prussia . . . under the cap of a Soviet captain, into the gray fur on which the metallic red star was deeply impressed. Something had crystallized in his head. A cold, crystalline thought which . . . eventually led this man far, far enough to reject the entire mental system of the world in which he was born and in which he lived, to the point where the very rulers of that enormous empire began to worry about him and to fear him, while to many millions of other people he became that new thing, a Light from the East. Truly a single event in a single mind may change the world. It may even bring about—and not merely hasten—the collapse of the Communist system which is inevitable, though only in the long run. If so, the most important event in 1945 may not have been the division of Europe, and not the dawn of the atomic age, but the sudden dawning of something in the mind of a ragged Soviet officer, Alexander Solzhenitsyn . . .

When Stalin said that a single death is a tragedy but a million deaths are a statistic, he, a proper materialist, did not reckon on the power of literature. Solzhenitsyn finished writing *The Gulag Archipelago* in 1967, the fiftieth anniversary of the Communist Revolution and the one hundredth anniversary of the invention of barbed wire. It is a tragic epic, woven from millions of deaths. He has now published the third and final volume, which is especially powerful because it recounts the resistance, rebellions and deaths of people who refused to be *only* victims.

Concentration camps are this century's distinctive contribution to the art of government, and they are inappropriately named. The word "camp" suggests impermanence. But Nazi Germany's camps embodied the primary purpose of the man who embodied the state. Soviet camps are as permanent as the Soviet postal service and as important as the police to the functioning of the state. As Solzhenitsyn says, "Rulers change, the Archipelago remains." It is fitting that we have a detailed, reliable picture of life in the concentration camps (and prisons and "mental hospitals"), but not in the factories of the "workers' paradise."

In 1910, Charles Péguy wrote: "It will never be known what acts of cowardice have been motivated by the fear of not looking sufficiently progressive." Since 1917, such fear has produced cowardly apologies for Soviet barbarism. But today, as Robert Conquest says, the world "Gulag" has entered every language, thanks to Solzhenitsyn, and for the first time since 1917, it is impossible to find in the West serious defenders of the Soviet system.

Conquest has just published *Kolyma,* a shattering report on Siberian camps near the Arctic Circle. A poet who died there called the camps "cold Auschwitzes." At first, their primary purpose was gold mining. But between 1937 and 1954, an equally important purpose was the killing, by general abuse, of millions of people. Then every kilogram of gold cost a human life. As Conquest says, the camps of the Kolyma region exemplify the background against which Stalin's successors made their careers, and that of their system as a whole. But the Gulag is not history. It lives on in today's system of camps, and in the soul of the society. In addition to approximately 1.5 million prisoners still in camps, there are many millions whom the Gulag has processed and returned to society as broken reminders that the state has no mercy. An uncountable number of Soviet officials over the age of 50 stepped into dead men's shoes and are implicated in the making of the corpses that were their stepping-stones.

Recently in *Encounter,* an indispensable magazine, George F. Kennan ignited a controversy by deploring people who portray the current Soviet leaders as "a terrible and forbidding group of men." Kennan thinks those leaders are "quite ordinary men," and that Brezhnev is "a moderate . . . a man confidently regarded by all who know him as a man of peace." In response, Richard Pipes of Harvard noted that Brezhnev lapsed from perfect peaceableness when he "invaded Czechoslovakia, threatened to invade China and Romania, conspired twice with Egypt and Syria to attack Israel, assisted North Vietnam to conquer South Vietnam and a pro-Soviet government to seize Angola" and launched his ongoing imperialism in Africa. And Bernard Levin of *The Times* of London, responding to Kennan, icily recalled what befell the leaders of the "Czech spring" after Brezhnev's invasion. Those moderate Czechs who had urged their countrymen not to resist the invasion were hauled off to Moscow:

> There, while the moderate, peaceful Brezhnev and his quite ordinary colleagues finished their dinner, the Czech leaders were kept in chains—not metaphorical chains but real ones—forbidden to wash or eat or drink or use a lavatory and when the ordinary moderates of the

Kremlin were ready, they came out and walked around the fettered group, abusing and jeering at them.

This vignette of moral squalor is not just fascinating for its repellence. It is important because, as Kennan rightly says, at the heart of the dispute about how to cope with the Soviet Union lie "these two conflicting views of Soviet leadership," the view that Soviet leaders are "quite ordinary," and the view that they are "a terrible and forbidding group of men." Rivers of blood, and mountains of other evidence, constantly expanding, confirm the latter view. The system presupposes and produces coarse, cruel leaders.

The alarming and sorrowful fact is not that evidence for the correct view is scanty, but that such evidence must be produced so constantly, in such abundance, with such genius and at such terrible cost in order to convince the West, which is eager to disbelieve. The unimaginable bravery and suffering of Soviet dissidents is indispensable to the West because it forces the Soviet regime to advertise its essential nature. And Solzhenitsyn's relentless Light from the East illuminates the indissoluble connection between the internal savagery of that regime and the external aims of the terrible and forbidding men who constitute it.

June 12, 1978

Believing the Unbelievable

Television viewers of what the Kremlin calls "news" recently saw an edited "confession" by a dissident, a writer from Soviet Georgia. He confessed to the crime of slandering the state. Andrei Sakharov, a leader of the dissidents, remarked, "It is a heavy thing to see a man broken." Heavy indeed.

Robert Conquest's history of Stalin's purge, *The Great Terror*, recounts a conversation between Stalin and one of his aides, Mironov, who was failing to get a confession from a prisoner named Kamenev:

> "Do you know how much our state weighs, with all the factories, machines, the army, with all the armaments and the navy?"
>
> Mironev and all those present looked at Stalin with surprise.
>
> "Think it over and tell me," demanded Stalin. Mironev smiled, believing that Stalin was getting ready to crack a joke. But Stalin did not intend to jest. . . . "I am asking you, how much does all that weigh," insisted he.
>
> Mironov was confused. He waited, still hoping that Stalin would turn everything into a joke. . . . Mironov . . . said in an irresolute voice, "Nobody can know that. . . . It is in the realm of astronomical figures."
>
> "Well, can one man withstand the pressure of that astronomical weight?" asked Stalin sternly.
>
> "No," answered Mironov.
>
> "Now then, don't tell me any more that Kamenev, or this or that prisoner, is able to withstand that pressure. Don't come to report to me," said Stalin to Mironov, "until you have in this briefcase the confession of Kamenev!"

Now as then, the Kremlin is sunk in cynicism about the "scientific socialism" that was supposed to legitimize the regime as the midwife of History. There is so little faith within the regime that the regime needs, for its peace of mind, the contrast of victims compelled to confess having no faith.

The Bolsheviks who stood Czarist officials against walls were not interested in "confessions" any more than were the confident fanatics who administered the Terror of the French Revolution. But sixty years after the imposition of Communism on the "Soviet people," the regime is preoccupied with its lack of legitimacy. One reason for that lack is that the "Soviet people" is a fiction. The Russians have always been detested by many of the other nations that make up most of the U.S.S.R. Were the Kremlin to become weak, the U.S.S.R. would disintegrate through a series of secessions.

In 1921, during negotiations between Irish rebels and the British Government, Michael Collins, speaking for the rebels, used the phrase "the Irish nation," and Lord Birkenhead responded, "That is not conceded." The Soviet regime, by speaking of "the nationalities question," has always implicitly conceded that the U.S.S.R. is composed of what are—ethnically, linguistically, religiously and culturally—undigested nations, like Soviet Georgia.

Decade after decade, the West blames a "thug element" in the Kremlin for episodes like the televised "confession" by the Georgia dissident and the "trial" of Yuri Orlov. Actually, such episodes express the essence of a Stalinist state.

"An up-to-date comprehension of the U.S.S.R. requires continual effort," writes Alain Besançon.

> Not because fundamental changes are occurring within the regime: quite the contrary, its extraordinary stasis is one of the reasons why we find it hard to keep our comprehension up to date, since we expect a regime, a country, sooner or later to follow the historical rhythm of other countries. The chief problem confronting the expert in Soviet affairs is not to keep his information up to date, as it is in other fields. His main difficulty lies in accepting as true what people deem improbable, in believing the unbelievable.

Solzhenitsyn's *Gulag Archipelago* is an attempt to force the West to face evidence. Reviewing the final volume of *Gulag,* Robert Conquest writes:

> The last section has an epigraph from the Book of Revelation, "Neither repented they of their murders. . . ." This was strikingly confirmed at a ceremonial meeting for Soviet Army Day on Feb. 22 this year, when 6,000 of the elite were assembled to hear a speech by Defense Minister Dimitry Ustinov, and interrupted twice with prolonged applause when he mentioned Stalin. Though so many of his murders and falsifications had long since been exposed publicly in the Soviet Union itself, this clearly does not matter to the ruling class.

That fact should matter to the West.

May 25, 1978

The Soft Cushion of Détente

In a story, Tolstoy described Nicholas I stipulating punishment for a student who had attacked a professor:

> He took the report and in his large handwriting wrote on its margin, with three orthographical mistakes: "Diserves deth, but thank God, we have no cpitle punishment, and it is not for me to introduce it. Make him run the gauntlet of a thousand men twelve times.—Nicholas."
>
> Nicholas knew that twelve thousand strokes with the regulation rods not only were certain death with torture, but were a superfluous cruelty. . . . But it pleased him to be ruthlessly cruel, and it also pleased him to think that we have abolished capital punishment in Russia.

It must please Leonid Brezhnev that torturing Yuri Orlov is consistent with Soviet "law" and not inhibited by the Helsinki accords. "Terror," wrote Engels to Marx, "consists mostly of useless cruelties perpetrated by frightened people in order to reassure themselves." The maximum sentence imposed on Orlov expressed fear of those within the Soviet Union who advocate freedom, and contempt for the forces of freedom outside the Soviet Union.

At Helsinki, the West ratified Soviet domination of Eastern Europe, in exchange for Soviet ink on papers affirming human rights. Orlov organized a committee to monitor Soviet compliance. To suggest that the Soviet Union should fulfill international undertakings is to commit the crime of "anti-Soviet agitation and propaganda." Dissidents and Western journalists excluded from the courtroom were showered with expressions of the regime's anti-Semitism: "You have a kike's snout!" "Jews, we'll shoot you!"

The arrest of Andrei Sakharov outside the courtroom dramatized the impotence of the West's "human rights" campaign. Although President Carter's campaign has become primarily a matter of hectoring weak allies, its glistening moment occurred early on, when Sakharov and Carter exchanged letters. Carter has subsequently made clear that the Soviets need fear no "linkage." Neither adventurism abroad nor repression at home diminishes U.S. readiness to negotiate arms agreements or to subsidize the Soviet war economy by subsidizing trade.

The Soviets feel no need to disguise the contempt they feel for the United States. The sentencing of Orlov expresses contempt for "human rights" rhetoric, and is an analog of Brezhnev's contemptuous "response" to Carter's decision against producing the neutron weapons needed to counter the Soviet advantage in conventional forces in Europe. Brezhnev's declaration that the Soviet Union too will forgo such weapons has prompted this comparison: A man plagued by rats considers purchasing a cat. The rats respond that if he will not purchase a cat, they will not purchase a cat.

For a while there seemed to be as many theories of détente as there were advocates of détente, and as many advocates as there were reasons for wishing that détente would be a blessing. But all theories of détente, whether rooted in the desire to think well of the Soviet Union or the desire to think ill of the United States for "provoking" the Cold War, held that détente would result in improved Soviet behavior.

"There are still from one million to one and a half million people in concentration camps," writes Raymond Aron, "and from five thousand to ten thousand dissidents confined to insane asylums. Compared with the other phases—the phase of the Great Purge and that of the last years of Stalin—the current period is one of détente. . . . This does not mean that the Bolsheviks have made peace with society and human nature."

Domestically, Brezhnev's Russia is somewhat less ghastly than Stalin's Russia. Internationally, it is more reckless. "For the past few years," writes Alain Besançon, "we have been resting our heads on the soft cushion of 'détente,' and no urgent issues involving us have forced us to refine our concepts." That testifies not to the absence of urgent issues, but to the extraordinary amount of forcing required to get the West to reexamine comforting concepts.

Since November 8, 1917, every assumption adopted, every premise clung to by people eager to rationalize a policy of accommodation toward the Soviet Union has been shredded by events. Today, the Soviet regime is so grotesquely ignorant and arrogant, so boorish and bullying, that its cruelty and recklessness may awaken Americans from their dogmatic slumber.

May 21, 1978

Struggling

In a speech announcing his new enthusiasm for defense spending, a speech that an aide said marked "the end of the Vietnam complex," Jimmy Carter said: "We have learned the mistake of military intervention in the internal affairs of another country when our own vital security interests were not directly involved." In spite of all the evidence as to what has happened in and around South Vietnam since Hanoi completed its conquest of that nation, Carter still believes that that war of conquest was an "internal affair" of the late South Vietnam. The "Vietnam complex" is alive.

Explaining why he now proposes defense increases that he adamantly opposed three months ago, Carter said that Iran is a "reminder" that America must be strong and must take "the world as it is." I do not know which is more disturbing, the evidence that a national leader needs to be reminded of such things, or the suggestion that suddenly, somehow, times have changed.

Asked to explain the changes in defense policy, Harold Brown, the Secretary of Defense, said the changes "relate to an appreciation that we are in for a long pull of adversary relationships" with the Soviets. From what springs this new "appreciation"?

When shown a draft of John Kennedy's inaugural address, Walter Lippmann suggested that references to the Soviet Union as "the enemy" be replaced by "adversary." They were. Still, Kennedy did summon the nation to "a long twilight struggle" with the "adversary." Nearly nineteen years later, Brown has reannounced a "long pull of adversary relationships."

But Brown was part of an Administration (Lyndon Johnson's) that radically misunderstood the nature of Hanoi's motivations. That Administration conducted a war of subtle "signals"—diplomatic feints, finely calibrated escalations and "pauses"—that were unintelligible, or perhaps just ludicrous, to the other side.

There are no reasons for thinking that Brown and his colleagues understood the constancy and dangerousness of Moscow's motivations. People who have to be "reminded" by Iran of an obvious truth, or who come, in their fifties, "to an appreciation" of an elementary fact of twentieth-century life, are not people who should be trusted to conduct "the long pull of adversary relationships" with the Soviets.

Intellectual parochialism causes the leaders of liberal Western societies to think of the Soviet Union as just a political adversary rather than as an enemy culture. Robert Conquest, in his book *Present Danger,* notes that in the fifteen years since Khrushchev fell, all the slight tendencies toward a moderated tyranny have been reversed by a regime committed to something like "restalinization." That is not surprising, given that the regime is run by men "whose moral and intellectual qualities enabled them to pass through the bloodbath of 1937–1938 [the purges] unharmed; and the process of selection, stretching over fifty years, has produced a very definite human type."

They are "men whose attachment to the Leninist attitude is part of their whole personality, rather than a matter of the 'opinions' they hold." As Conquest says, it is not that Brezhnev reads Marx before bedtime (any more than Richard Coeur de Lion went around constantly reciting the Athanasian Creed), but that Brezhnev has Leninism in his bones. Such civilized Russian spirits as Mandelstam, Sakharov and Medvedev believe that the rising generation of Soviet rulers, now in their forties, is, if anything, even more socialized to myopia and intolerance.

Are Carter and Brown the sort of people to lead "a long twilight struggle"? Or Cyrus Vance, who says Carter and Brezhnev "have similar dreams and aspirations about the most fundamental issues"? In 1946, when less prescient people thought the darkness was lifting, T. S. Eliot wrote, in "The Dark Side of the Moon," about the future of liberal societies:

"The frantic attempt, either through assembling representatives of more and more nations in public, or through discussions between leaders of fewer and fewer nations in private, to find a political solution to what is not merely a political problem, can . . . only lead to temporary and illusory benefits, unless the deeper problem is faced and pondered."

Face the deeper problems? As this is written, the U.S. Government is bursting with pride and pleasure over its latest achievement, the deporting of the Shah of Iran, a man once useful but now used up and discardable, to exile on a Panamanian island. This nation is untroubled by the spectacle of its government's using the denial of political asylum as a tactic for dickering with a distant mob. The twilight deepens, and American behavior cannot be dignified as a "struggle."

December 20, 1979

The End of the Hostage Fiasco: Celebrating and "Feeling"

The movable feast of celebration about the hostages has abated a bit, so perhaps it will not seem intolerably churlish to ask what, precisely, people have been celebrating. Clearly, more is involved than just gratification about the hostages' deliverance. At the risk of seeming stone-hearted, I suggest this:

The crisis that began because of weakness, and was prolonged by confusion, and ended in extortion, has been followed by a national hysteria of self-deception symbolized by a sign carried by a celebrator: "AMERICA 52, IRAN 0." When calamity is translated into the idiom of sport and christened a victory, when victims are called heroes and turned into props for telegenic celebrations of triumph, then it is time to recall George Orwell's axiom that the great enemy of clear language is insincerity.

Much of the emotionalism, although not consciously insincere, has been synthetic in the sense that it has been a psychological mechanism to keep unpleasant thoughts at bay. Beneath the intense, almost fierce focus on the ceremonies of victorious homecoming, there was, I suspect, grim determination to have fun rather than face facts.

The hostages were used by Iran, for the humiliation of America and the consolidation of Iran's revolution, and now the former hostages have been used by America in a pageant, whose effect is to prevent the country from thinking about how it allowed Iran to succeed.

The Carter Aministration's penchant for striking poses and calling them policies matched the public's penchant for yellow ribbons, candlelight vigils and other gestures that were explained by the gesturers on the grounds that "we just felt we had to do something." The public supported Carter's policies of "doing something" with the likes of Ramsey Clark and Kurt Waldheim, and the public tied yellow ribbons and called that "doing something." Such activities were cathartic for the nation, but a nation that confuses catharsis with the defense of its interests is a nation that cannot distinguish between attitudinizing and acting.

Some Americans even say the crisis was "a good thing" because it "brought the country together." But so did Pearl Harbor, which was not a good thing and would have been worse if America's response had been vigils and ribbons. Perhaps Americans are so starved for a sense of "togetherness," and so covet the warm feeling of shared emotions, that they care not whether the emotions are ersatz, or disproportionate, or whether they are suitably occasioned.

I cannot erase from my mental retina what I saw at 1 A.M. at the

Dakota apartment building on the second day after John Lennon was shot there.

A crowd, bathed in television lights and tears, was keeping a vigil in front of a large gate covered with flowers and photographs. The unintended but striking effect was of an altar. A pent-up yearning for public witness found release in worship of a rock star. For days, twenty-four hours a day, news shows, talk shows and radio disc-jockey shows were clogged with people having fun explaining how they "loved" John Lennon, and their grief at their "deeply personal loss." Love confessed to disc jockeys, like grief expressed to Merv Griffin, is, however real the psychic need it nourishes, still synthetic.

Even worse than the inflation that is debasing the currency is the inflation debasing the language. It is cheapening the words that are the currency of thought. A nation that was built by muscle and preserved by blood is increasingly fueled by hyperbole and sustained by euphemism. (Remember the "incomplete success" at Desert One?) It has an economy increasingly geared to the manufacture of frivolous appetites (How many Calvin Kleins in your closet, America?), an entertainment industry geared to the manufacture of the lowest moods (using bathos and titillation). And now the nation may be becoming addicted to manufactured "feelings."

In the 1960s, professors noticed the growing tendency of students to answer questions with statements like "Well, my feeling about Hamlet is . . ." and "My reaction to the Renaissance is . . ." The language of "reaction" and "feeling" was evidence of a culture losing interest in reason, celebrating sentiment, obsessed with "authenticity" and defining it in terms of strong emotions, warm feelings. Descartes's *"Cogito, ergo sum"*—I think, therefore I am—became "I feel, therefore I am."

In an acute dissection of the nation's recent mood, Thomas Bray of *The Wall Street Journal* notes that "How does it feel?" was the emblematic question of the hostage crisis, asked of everybody, about everything. The celebrating will end when the thinking begins.

February 1, 1981

The Workers Who Dare to Unite

In Poland a public servant's lot is not a happy one. The public is such a nuisance, and it is so hard to get good work done. Recently a Communist official who was being pestered by people who wanted to reopen a nineteenth-century church had a most tiresome time organizing a demolition team willing to dynamite the church.

What a spectacle! A regime committed to indoctrinating everyone with the intellectual junk of dialectical materialism reduces an old building to rubble in order to fight what materialists disbelieve in—the autonomous life and the power of ideas. And now another specter is haunting the regimes that are trying to keep a sinewy grip on Eastern Europe: the workers of their world might unite.

To those of us who believe that Western democracies are, whether they know it or not, in the fifth decade of a war with the totalitarians, there is satisfying historical symmetry in the fact that the specter rises from Poland, and especially from Gdansk. Forty-one Augusts ago Gdansk was Danzig, and appeasers were down to their last slogan: "Why die for Danzig?" Forty-one years ago last Sunday the Soviet Union became Hitler's ally, preparatory to raping Poland. In 1939, Danzig was the last inch of Europe's fuse. In 1980, Gdansk is a sputtering fuse of unknown length.

Poland has sputtered intermittently for three decades, but what now gives the world reason to hold its breath is that some of the strikers' demands threaten the regime's roots—or, rather, its buttresses; it has no roots. Today's troubles are no more about food prices than the American Civil War was about Fort Sumter. On other occasions of labor unrest, the regime has bought peace with economic concessions. This time not even a regime that believes everyman is "economic man" and believes history is a story of economic forces can believe that it faces an economic challenge.

True, some demands (such as abolition of special shops open only to police and Party officials) pertain to relatively mundane idiocies and mendacities of Communist life. But shopping is not a minor matter in a country where the typical woman spends two hours and ten minutes a day waiting in lines. Anyway, the workers' critical demands attack the ligaments of totalitarianism: access for all religious groups to the mass media; guaranteed free expression for all; free trade unions.

The name of a dissidents' organization may seem stilted, but it defines the issue: Committee of Social Self-Defense. Polish society is at war with Poland's government. Totalitarianism means total domination of society by the state; suppression or politicization of all mediating structures—such as churches and labor unions—that act as buffers between the individual and the state. Totalitarianism is a twentieth-century disease, dependent on modern bureaucracy and other potential instruments of social control, such as broadcasting.

Today's drama in Poland is riveting because it says—it shouts: "Totalitarianism doesn't work. Indoctrination is less potent, human beings are less malleable, mediating structures rooted in the social soil are more resilient than totalitarians think." But thinking is not something totalitarians do elegantly. Totalitarianism is tyranny with delusions of grandeur, delusions rooted in intellectual rubbish about *Herrenvolk* or New Socialist Man. Intellectually, totalitarians are the most loutish tyrants. To signal confidence in its marionette in Warsaw, Moscow has just announced plans for a spanking-new edition of the writings of Edward Gierek. Imagine, if you can bear to, curling up with one of those books.

Poland is the Soviet Union's largest "ally" (if that description can be used of a manacled nation). So it is delicious that strikers decorated the gates of Lenin Shipyard with Polish flags, portraits of Pope John Paul II and blue-and-white banners of the Virgin Mary. Lenin: founder of a "dictatorship of the proletariat" in which the proletariat is denied trade unions. Polish flags: dear me, didn't Lenin say workers have no fatherland, no country but the "socialist movement"?

The Pope: the most consequential statesman of our time is a Pole living abroad and governing a city-state 1/1,000 the size of

Andorra, from which he governs Poland more, in a sense, than does the government planted by bayonets in Warsaw. The banner of the Virgin Mary: religion is the *opiate* of the masses? Building Bolshevism is not all beer and skittles in a nation in which thirty million of the thirty-five million citizens are Catholics whose Catholicism is an undiluted fighting faith.

The Polish Government is arresting people. The Kremlin too is acting in character, jamming broadcasts from the West. Both are violating the Helsinki agreements on human rights and freedom of information. But then, the point of the Helsinki meeting was less those pieces of paper than the West's formal acquiescence in Soviet domination of Eastern Europe—in the outcome of the 1939–1945 phase of the war against totalitarianism.

Poland is surrounded by Soviet satellites and Soviet divisions, so the current drama, which is yet to be played out, can hardly come to a happy conclusion. Perhaps the fact that justice and power are so entirely on opposite sides encourages romantic and sentimental judgments. Viewed from afar, the Polish workers may seem nobler than any lot of people can be. But on the other hand, the democracies, increasingly cynical about their leaders and themselves, are incapable of crediting anyone with virtues that they, like cattle at twilight, plod along without.

One would have to be made of marble not to be moved by the glimpses we get of Polish workingmen and -women organizing themselves against a leviathan. A grainy, black-and-white photograph of those people seated at a table, quietly taking their lives into their own hands by talking about organizing, is a reminder that the simple decencies of life seem banal only to people who owe their enjoyment of those decencies to the bravery of previous generations. To paraphrase what Dean Acheson said of Louis Brandeis, the Polish workers may receive some undiscriminating praise, but they are worthy of the urge that gives rise to it.

September 1, 1980

Sorry, Mom, but That's Dialectics

The Soviet *Literary Gazette* has honored me with an attack that is, so experts tell me, remarkably coarse, even considering the source. To its calumny I reply: Sticks and stones may break my bones, but words will never hurt me—although when a Communist says I once was a "run-of-the-mill" professor, he goes beyond what is permissible even in the death struggle with capitalism.

The attack is worth noting, not just because it contributes to the public stock of harmless pleasure, or because it reminds us of what we cannot be reminded of too often—the vulgarity of the Soviet mind. It also dramatizes the shocking decline in the caliber of Communist invective.

The article, which nominates me for a place in the Soviet "Gallery of Slanderers," says that the "military-industrial complex" is not only the hand that feeds me: it is "the hand that gives him food and drink, strokes him, scratches him behind the ears and takes care of him in every way. It is necessary to lick that hand. . . ." It goes on like that, but you get the picture.

"What comes from his pen depends on who gives him the orders, and it is evident from the output who the prompters are. It is a kind of dialectics."

Bingo! When a Communist deep thinker is really ready to get down and boogie, out comes the key concept: dialectics. Don't ask me, or him, what it means; but bear with me, and him.

He says I gave the game away when, last December, just before the full-scale Soviet invasion of Afghanistan, I said, correctly, that some Soviet troops already were engaged in Afghanistan. This, my critic says, was a lie, and a blunder because it betrayed my fear that Soviet troops would enter Afghanistan to forestall the CIA's overthrow of the Afghan Government, which, my critic says, I knew was "planned for December 29." To frustrate that overthrow, my critic says, the Soviet Union extended fraternal socialist assistance to the Afghan Government. (And murdered the head of it. Perhaps that is applied dialectics.)

My slip, which revealed my guilty knowledge, proves that I am close to, indeed a pawn of, "the Washington faction that is making every effort to foment tension." My critic thinks that faction includes almost everyone, and meets weekly in Katharine Graham's living room.

The "huge editorial-commercial enterprise known as the 'Washington Post Company' " belongs to "Mrs. Boss," who commands "Will's reckless and evil thoughts about the unthinkable." Furthermore, I am, dialectically speaking, her man in the CIA and the CIA's man in *Newsweek*.

Actually, I suspect that *Newsweek* and my newspapers regard me the way Ronald Reagan's staff are coming to regard him— with the trepidation aroused by randomness. Still, I am chagrined, if not surprised, that my Soviet critic reduces me to the status of an "epiphenomenon." My critic does not use the term—he seems innocent of any understanding, even of Marxism—but it is a favorite of Marxists, denoting something that is a mere reflection of vast, impersonal forces. That's the way my critic regards me—pretty much the way Marx regarded Louis Napoleon; an appraisal almost as wounding as "run-of-the-mill professor."

To the charge that I am a mere reflection of social forces, I respond, "So's your old man!" In fact, so is everybody, according to Marx. A whole academic industry exists trying to read Marx otherwise, but he said that everyone is a mere cork on the currents of History.

Frankly, I am saddened to note the decline of Marxist invective. Marx himself, who probably considered civility a bourgeois affectation, was always unloading on someone as a "sentimental petty-bourgeois social fantast," and stuff like that.

That's a denunciation with a doctoral degree, full of sociological gravity and the tang of high learning. The *Literary Gazette* can't rise above saying that I'm a fellow with "a completely soiled soul" (do Marxists now believe in souls?) and "a pathologically evil mind," and one who "knows no limit to his inhuman calculations."

My critic, who probably needs the job, is no doubt unwilling to face the fact that personal abuse makes no sense in the Marxist scheme of things, in which nothing is personal. He knows perfectly well that I, although repulsive, am not to blame.

I am a plaything of, and destined for the ashcan of, History. I am a mere necessity, a by-product of this passing stage of the development of the means of production. Sorry, Mom, but that's dialectics.

September 7, 1980

Part Four ॐ

POLITICS

Politics and "Cheat the Prophet"

Clock radios, like most things thought of since the death of Queen Victoria, are menaces to serene living, especially during election campaigns, when you are apt to be awakened by political commercials.

A few days before the elections, I was jolted into astonished wakefulness by a commercial for a candidate who advocated schools that would produce "Beethovens and Einsteins." The candidate did not realize that most voters would consider it progress if their children learned to spell "Beethoven."

But Wisconsin voters, at least, found a candidate attuned to their lowered expectations. Governor-elect Lee S. Dreyfus campaigned on the slogan that Washington has only three duties: "Deliver the mail, defend the shores and get the hell out of my life." Washington eagerly awaits Dreyfus' visit, during which he will, presumably, beg that Wisconsin be released from the bondage of dairy subsidies, and that Washington get the hell out of the lives of Wisconsin communities by withdrawing aid to education and revenue-sharing.

I do not have a smidgen of evidence, but I believe (for the same reason that many people believe many things: I hope it is true) that some playful souls cast their ballots for the pleasure of confounding the polls. They believe that if they are part of a process in which the outcome is predictable, then they are somehow less than fully autonomous. This is, of course, irrational, but the spirit is right.

It is a spirit G. K. Chesterton understood. In his enchanting novel *The Napoleon of Notting Hill*, published in 1904, Chesterton explained the game of "Cheat the Prophet":

The players listen very carefully and respectfully to all that the clever men have to say about what is to happen in the next generation. The players wait until all the clever men are dead, and bury them nicely. Then they go and do something else. That is all. For a race of simple tastes, however, it is great fun.

But the twentieth century has been hard on this, as on most other forms of innocent merriment:

. . . in the beginning of the twentieth century the game of Cheat the Prophet was made far more difficult than it had ever been before. The reason was, that there were so many prophets and so many prophecies, that it was difficult to elude all their ingenuities. When a man did something free and frantic and entirely on this own, a horrible thought struck him afterwards; it might have been predicted. Whenever a duke climbed a lamp-post, when a dean got drunk, he could not really be happy, he could not be certain that he was not fulfilling some prophecy.

One prophecy that was fulfilled in 1978 was that "single-issue voting" would be important. And before the 1978 elections become just another beautiful but faded memory, consider the element of special pleading in some of the condemnations of such voting. The principal cause of the condemnations is the defeat of Senator Dick Clark, an Iowa liberal who was vigorously opposed by the right-to-life movement. But in the 1960s, when the streets were alive with "single-issue voters" whose passions were civil rights or Vietnam, many of the people who now complain about "single-issue voters" considered them admirably single-minded.

Anyway, it is probable that for many "single-issue voters" the alternative is "no-issue" voting, or not voting. It might be "no-issue" voting because, without a single salient issue to simplify the welter of political arguments, they might allow their votes to be determined by the flickering images of thirty-second television commercials. Or they might not feel strongly enough about anything to take the trouble to vote.

This year, the electorate felt strongly about "change." It

pounded its chest with clenched fists, demanding "change." And two days after the reelection of New York's somewhat dour governor, Hugh Carey, the New York *Daily News* filled half its front page with this headline, spelled in heavy black letters 1.5 inches high:

Gov. Carey Vows:
I'LL CHANGE
MY PERSONALITY

Even in an age of extravagantly personalized politics, New Yorkers may feel that although Carey's change is, of course, part of his duty, it is by no means all of it.

November 16, 1978

The Denim Presidency

While the mists of sleep were enveloping Washington, Hamilton Jordan, Jimmy Carter's helper, was in a bar where, according to a news report, he rubbed a woman's back, wrote her a racy limerick, spat a drink at her and got slapped. Because Jordan *is* a known live wire, and occasionally *has* been too buoyant for polite society, the White House considered it prudent to attack the report. It did so with one of the most remarkable documents in an age of remarkable White House documents. It included an apparently unedited twenty-four-page interview with a bartender. Ten years ago, George Wallace complained: "Hell, we got too much dignity in government." But just when things seemed to be looking up for people who subscribe to Wallace's complaint, the White House muddied the water with its ringing assertion of Jordan's gentlemanliness.

The Washington Star, tongue in cheek, paraphrased the report: "As he sought to enjoy a quiet beer, a steak and a liquor *crème*, he was accosted by a monstrous regiment of tiddly women and fled in self-defense."

When the Israeli and Egyptian ambassadors dined together for the first time, Jordan's deportment produced, on following days, an enchanting spectacle: several people who had attended the dinner, all of them *very* Establishment, lied valiantly to exonerate the man who symbolizes unbuttoned disdain for Establishment proprieties.

Another irony is that Jordan, who seems to fancy himself an anti-cosmopolitan, would not be so scrutinized if Washington were not still a village *becoming* a mature capital. As recently as the 1950s, there was farmland within the District of Columbia, and Washington picnickers rode trolleys to the woods at the Maryland line, eight miles from the White House. Today, that spot is planted thick with department stores, and is much closer to the center than to the fringe of the metropolis. As is normal with adolescents, emotional maturity has not come as quickly to Washington as has physical growth. In a mature capital, like Paris or London, there are many old, established, confident elites, in industry, finance, the arts and universities. In Washington, nothing is old, and no countervailing elites offset the prominence of the political.

Washington is celebrity-struck, thirsts for gossip, dissolves the distinction between journalism and voyeurism, and cares that Joseph Califano hired a chef. But there is nothing new about attention paid to trivia of public life. TV coverage of the 1960 campaign included:

JOURNALIST: Oh, isn't she darling?
MRS. KENNEDY: Now, look at the three bears.
CAROLINE: What is the dolly's name?
MRS. KENNEDY: All right, what is the dolly's name?
CAROLINE: I didn't name her yet.

The Nixon camp fired its own volley:

JOURNALIST: I am so fascinated with that little kitten. Does the kitten have a name?
JULIE: Yes, its name is Bitsy Blue Eyes.

Perhaps (as Murray Kempton wrote) Kennedy won because Caroline did not name the doll. In any case, in May, 1961, she was the subject of a *Newsweek* cover story.

On August 20, 1962, Caroline's daddy went for a swim at Santa Monica, and a crowd, including a fully dressed woman, followed him into the Pacific. Perhaps the dawn of such political delirium was January 30, 1958, the opening of *Sunrise at Campobello*, Dore Schary's play about Franklin Roosevelt's recuperation from polio. It imagined this saccharine exchange between F.D.R., who in real life had a full measure of vitriol in his veins, and his sandpapery adviser, Louis Howe:

HOWE: Franklin, you have too many interests. You've got to cut down.
F.D.R.: I will not discontinue my work in the Boy Scouts. Their aims are damned important.

The audience did not guffaw; the nation was ready for fairy tales, and soon got Camelot.

In the second month of Camelot, *The New Republic* happily reported that "Washington is crackling, rocking, jumping" and "is a kite zigging in the breeze." It was a novel idea that good government resembles a kite. So when rushing to work on Sunday mornings, aides to Robert McNamara, the Secretary of Defense, anxiously touched the hood of his car to see if it was warm (indicating he had just arrived). Usually it was cold.

Those were the days of studied strenuousness, of a carefully cultivated aura of heroism in the trenches of government. Since then, Washington's sense of competence has shrunk as its sense of importance has swollen. The celebrity syndrome has grown apace, especially regarding the Presidency, whose dazzling social preeminence is unaffected by the abundant evidence that politically, it is not as preeminent as it is cracked up to be. Celebrity, not mastery, is the fruit of victory. Those who, like Jordan, blaze with the reflected glory of the Presidency are not offstage just because they consider themselves off duty.

Jordan is intelligent and, much more often than not, nice. But there are more kinds of arrogance than were hatched beneath H. R. Haldeman's crew cut; and it is arrogant for a powerful person to be scruffy and boorish in order to advertise his exemption from little conventions and courtesies. Besides, Jordan's comportment reinforces the growing belief that many of the most important people in the Administration, including the most important person, are out of their depth as well as their element.

All Presidents must eat some of their words, but this President is consuming an enormous tossed salad of his promises about balancing budgets, cutting defense spending, aiding parochial schools, reforming taxes, not raising taxes and many other matters. He is having enough trouble with his measures; he does not need trouble from his men. Anything that makes the Presidency seem shabby is serious trouble.

A President is disarmed unless he can seize the nation's moral imagination. Carter cannot seize it with his rhetoric: remarkably, fifty-three years with the King James Bible has not given him a flair for stirring cadences. So he needs all the help he can get from what remains of the nation's reverence for the Presidency. After an Administration of Prussian arrogance and Sicilian corruption, it was fine for Gerald Ford to invite the networks to watch him toast muffins. But in other times, the Presidency should be clothed in majesty, not denim.

Although it goes against the American grain to say so, Nixon had a serious idea when he put White House guards into those unfortunate uniforms. His idea, shared by De Gaulle, was that *especially* in a democracy, the authority of government, and particularly of the Executive, depends on an element of grandeur. His idea deserved a better tailor.

March 6, 1978

Carter and the Silverware Criterion

The battle hymn of President Carter's energy "war" should be the country song with the enchanting refrain "I don't know whether to kill myself or go bowling." The "war" still resembles the European war in the winter of 1940. There is anticipation of fearful battles, but little bloodshed yet.

When F.D.R. wanted to galvanize the nation, he went on a hundred-day dash, doing things like closing the banks. Bang! Three days after he took office his impact was visible on Main Street.

Carter flinches from the one obvious action that would have an immediate bite of seriousness: he will not decontrol gasoline prices. Having advertised his readiness for "tough" decisions, and having said he would "make absolutely certain that nothing stands in the way" of energy goals, he left in place policies that subsidize consumption and discourage production.

The ceiling on oil imports is calibrated to be unnoticeable in the near term. But Carter's long-term plans are noticeable indeed. They call for expanded collaboration between the public and the private sectors in producing energy. Call it "state capitalism," or "socialism," or a "mixed economy," or what you please, three things are reasonably clear:

Such collaboration would be a significant step away from free enterprise. Much of the business community would like it. And whether or not it would be wise, it would not be un-American.

Anyone who thinks an anti–free-enterprise, pro-business policy is a contradiction in terms has not been paying attention to modern politics, or to the modern businessman. Collaboration between the state and private capital is routine in all industrial societies. The U.S. economy is heavily subsidized, and the subsidies were not enacted over the bodies of businessmen who preferred to perish rather than benefit at the hand of the state.

In the nineteenth century too, when the national interest was involved, so was government. Building the railroads that united the United States was not just the moral equivalent of war; it occasionally was war. First the cavalry tamed those Indians who did not see the romance of railroading. Then government gave rights-of-way to railroads, and set rates that were not onerous to railroad operators. The profits were private; the enterprise was collaborative.

The fact that Carter's energy program envisions a hugely expanded role for government makes it especially unfortunate that he has remounted his anti-Washington hobbyhorse. He is inciting distrust of the government that he proposes to entrust with "wartime" powers. The gap between his rhetoric and the implications of his policies is becoming eerie. It would not be so scary if he were cynical, but he really seems to believe that he is an enemy of Washington's power.

However, Carter may understand one thing perfectly: Thinking coherently is not the most politically important thing a President can do these days. Rather, the most important thing is to be seen trying to "relate" to "average Americans."

In 1976, Americans found that side of Carter very fetching. "Many a man in love with a dimple makes the mistake of marrying the whole girl," wrote Stephen Leacock. But Americans may marry Carter again, because he satisfies the Silverware Criterion.

Many Americans believe, wrongly but firmly, that no President can govern effectively. And they also have come to the quite correct conclusion that Carter at least will not steal the White House silverware. They feel about Carter the way Jefferson felt about Washington: "He errs, as other men do, but he errs with integrity." And today, when people expect from a President little but error, they hope for little but integrity.

The public virtues, such as the ability to lead, and the ability to formulate and administer policies that address the great issues of the day, are considered beyond the reach of today's political class. So the electorate evaluates candidates less in terms of the public virtues and more in terms of private virtues, such as piety, sincerity, earnestness, self-deprecation.

Here, then, is the great paradox of today's politics. For the candidate who campaigned in 1976 on the slogan "Why not the best?," the best reelection strategy is to count on the electorate's radically lowered expectations, for which he is partly responsible.

July 22, 1979

Showboat

August is the Middle West's month. April in Paris and autumn in New York, but August is the month in the Mississippi Valley. Some people say August is hot, dusty and glamourless, and is tinged with melancholy because it brings us to the brink of school, another football season and other unpleasantnesses. But those of us reared in The Great State (Illinois), and those from the lesser but still grand states of the region, know the charms of August. The afternoon sky is luminous and peculiarly flat, like the prairie that stretches, gold and green and black, to the horizon. The night air is saturated with sounds of life, like cicadas, and corn growing (real Middle Westerners can hear that).

In August, the Mississippi River, like the states that prosper along it, is generally placid without being dull. Jimmy Carter came to the Father of Waters as the faithful go to the waters of Lourdes, seeking miraculous recovery from ailments that seem beyond the reach of orthodox treatment. Life, wrote Baudelaire, is a hospital in which each patient believes he will recover if he is moved to another bed. Carter moved his ailing Presidency to the *Delta Queen*, seeking politeness that would at least have the appearance of political support.

He came trailing clouds of glory, or at least such glory as still attaches to political office. In one of the novels by my hero Peter De Vries, a healthy man visits Lourdes and falls deathly ill. Carter's river trip, like almost everything else recently, may have made matters worse for him.

When things are going badly, politicians, like other people, enjoy the turning to places where things went well. The *Delta Queen* repeatedly nuzzled up to Iowa, scene of Carter's first victory in 1976. But when politicians' troubles are as manifold as Carter's are, it seems impossible for them to move without bumping painfully into some sharp edge of reality. Even so, it was awfully rum luck for Carter to cruise past Iowa just as the state's AFL-CIO was expressing its uncontainable desire to replace Carter with Kennedy. The national press, which was following, somewhat less than deferentially, in the wake of Carter's progress, tumbled ashore higgledy-piggledy to report that the grass roots are (if I may mangle a metaphor) up in arms.

Carter is becoming a bit testy about journalists and their works. Like tart apples, they set his famous teeth on edge. And truth be told, it was churlish of editorialists to say that he should get off the boat and get back to work. It is true that his trip coincided with yet another embarrassment along the Potomac. But there is no unembarrassing way to get caught practicing appeasement of the murderous Palestine Liberation Organization. While he was doing his darnedest to focus attention on the *Delta Queen*, and on the agreeableness of the natives wherever it docked, the public's attention, or at least that sliver of it which can be captured in August, was being drawn to this fact: Carter's policy, Andrew Young's dishonesty and the Administration's disharmony have produced, within the ragtag remnants of the civil-rights movement, a constituency for a terrorist organization.

Nevertheless, those who said that Carter should get off the boat and back to his job should consider what Carter thinks his job is. The word that recurs in Washington conversations about Carter is "irrelevant." What is meant is that his policies and passions seem almost impotent; he leaves only a faint impress on events. But perhaps he is more interested in being shaped than in shaping.

While Carter was rolling on the river, using a steamboat to

capture the attention of an inattentive nation, I came upon a little
book about William Gladstone, written by James Bryce in 1898,
the year Gladstone died. Gladstone sat in Parliament for sixty-two
years. At the beginning, he opposed men old enough to be his
grandfather; at the end, he was opposed by men young enough to
be his grandchildren. He is a hero of democracy, not just because
of his longevity but because of his power to cause people to follow
the chariot of his rhetoric. Standing on a stump, not a steamboat,
he could attract a crowd, hold it for four hours and send it away
transformed.

In his day, of course, people had few competing entertainments
and longer attention spans. But Gladstone's rhetoric did have what
Bryce called "elevation," the "power of ennobling ordinary things
by showing their relation to great things." For many reasons, including the nature of contemporary education and the practice of
politics in the era of TV, such rhetoric is even rarer today than it
was then. But Gladstone's famous successes at mass persuasion
also presupposed a particular understanding of his job. As Bryce
wrote, "It was the masses who took their views from him, not he
who took his mandate from the masses."

That idea offends today's democratic sensibility. Public opinion
is thought of as a given; it is supposed to form itself spontaneously,
and well up vigorously to control government. There is, today, a
clamor for "leadership," but the prevailing theory of democracy
virtually precludes real leadership. The theory, to which Carter
seems to subscribe, is that the politician's job is a modest, even
humble one. His job is to establish intimacy with the masses in
order to open himself to their sentiments. This theory encourages
politicians to duck the difficult and perilous task of doing what
Gladstone did. Gladstone, wrote Bryce, "evoked new sentiments
and turned sentiments into new channels."

The public cannot have it both ways—demanding leadership
while subscribing to a theory of democracy that requires ostenta-
tious humility from politicians. Politicians cannot be commanding
figures and also commodities merchandised conspicuously.

By sallying forth like Howard Keel in *Showboat*, Carter may
have been indulging in the sort of show business needed to arrest

the interest of Americans in August. But he has relied so much on merchandising novelties that he has devalued the theatrical dimension of politics. If my memory serves me (and I often wish it wouldn't), last August also found Carter on a river, on a raft in Idaho. That trip was considered the stylistic debut of Gerald Rafshoon, the advertising man, in his role as official curator of the Presidential image. Rafshoon's remarkably conspicuous White House role is part of the degradation of the art of politics into the "science" of packaging. It is somehow satisfying that Rafshoon's tenure has coincided with a collapse of confidence in his client.

The lesson, I hope, is this: If you want to move pickles or radial tires, a Rafshoon may be useful. But if you want to move the nation, you had better not be quite so conspicuously concerned with your "image." It is bad for your image.

September 3, 1979

For Muscular Politics, Not Metaphorical Wars

In his speech last Sunday, the President asked each of us to say something good about America. So I say: America is not as sick as you might gather from what the President said about it last Sunday. Taken separately, both halves of his speech would have been interesting; taken together, they were strange.

The first decried the "crisis" of "heart and soul and spirit," the "longing for meaning" that (says Carter) grips America, the "emptiness" of American lives that have no "purpose," the definition of "human identity" in terms of "what one owns," and so on. The President's suggestion that everyone say something good about America came in the second half, after his description of the desolateness of American life.

The second half concerned petroleum and related matters. In

the first half Carter had said he greatly regrets the importance of the "isolated" Washington "island." But in the second half he proposed another new energy policy, this one involving vast centralization of power in the "island."

He implied that the energy policy will somehow help assuage America's emptiness, purposelessness, and so on. The first half of the speech deplored American materialism. The second half concerned how to provide the energy needed to keep America's industrial system humming.

For generations, people have been worrying about what would happen to the American spirit if the nation ran up against limits. Frederick Jackson Turner, the historian, thought a turning point was reached in the 1890s, with the closing of the frontier. Perhaps he was right. Certainly a constant theme of modern American politics is the search for "new frontiers" to provide an outlet for American dynamism.

Carter yearns, as Presidents frequently do, not for war but for one of war's social effects, the submergence of America's dynamic and unruly "interests" in a common enterprise. War is the politician's great simplifier, the giver of a "sense of purpose." It is not good enough just to attempt to alleviate poverty; there must be a "war on poverty."

Carter, who longs for wartime unity, is repelled by the sight of Congress "twisted and pulled" by "special interests." But what repels him is the essence of politics in a free, commercial, continental nation. James Madison explained this in the two most important newspaper columns ever written, *Federalist Papers* 10 and 51.

The American contribution to democratic theory was the idea that democracy does best in a large, not a small, society. A "multiplicity" of factions prevents a single, stable, tyrannical majority, the form of tyranny to which democracy is prey. "Extend the sphere," urged Madison, "and you take in a greater variety of parties and interests. . . ." Indeed, "the first object of government" is the protection of the "different and unequal faculties of acquiring property," which produces "a division of society into different interests and parties."

Madison's attitude about factions was, approximately: the more the merrier. The politician's task is to cope with them, to broker them, not to sermonize against them.

Carter, in his 55th year, still seems surprised by the nature of this nation, and offended by its political task. But American politics in 1979 is just Madisonian politics of 1787 writ large.

This is a big, muscular nation, full of muscular "factions," and the nation cannot be governed by other than muscular politicians. It can't be governed by someone who is not good at—let us use the honorable phrase—"wheeling and dealing." And over the long haul of a Presidency, no one can do that well who despises it, who doesn't actively enjoy it, even relish it.

Carter has not been notably successful and has not seemed to be truly at ease since early 1976, since the intimate politics of the church basements of Iowa and the living rooms of New Hampshire. That was the politics of small, tidy, docile, homogeneous groups, of soft talk and soft promises amid the soft clatter of teacups.

But this nation is no living room. Its many "interests" have to be dealt with, not just deplored; and they won't stand at attention and salute just because a President announces yet another metaphorical war. What Speaker Sam Rayburn said of President Eisenhower was wrong about Eisenhower but fits Carter: "Good man, wrong job."

July 19, 1979

A New "Party of the People"?

The second-funniest phrase I know is in a Ring Lardner short story: " 'Shut up,' he explained." The funniest is the title of a book written in the late 1960s: *The Emerging Republican Majority*. The 1960s are just a bleak memory; the 1970s have come and gone, rich in marvels; yet another decade has dawned, but that Republican majority has not yet got around to emerging. The birth of this majority is so delayed that some skeptics are beginning to doubt that the country is pregnant.

But in Arlington, Virginia, in the Reagan-Bush headquarters, Republican obstetricians are preparing to induce labor. In the next few days five million pieces of mail will flood out, five hundred thousand volunteers will be set in motion, daily polls will be taken in critical states, "rifle-shot" advertising will be directed to trouble spots and phone banks will be humming. In the autumnal beauty of America, nothing is more beautiful, to a politician, than a phone bank. Elections are, in the end, exercises in locating and turning out one's own voters.

That task is especially complicated this year because of the high number of undecided voters (who may not, this year, be voters). The Democratic Party, for example, claims to have registered two hundred thousand Hispanics in Texas this year. On November 4, the party will summon these spirits from the vasty Texas deep. But will they come? Nationally, Republicans are more apt to vote than Democrats, and what little enthusiasm there is this year is among Reagan supporters. So perhaps the shrewdest expenditure of the Reagan campaign's last dollars would be in rainmaking— seeding the clouds, coast to coast. On November 4 there will be "Republican weather" wherever there is driving rain and wailing winds.

Gadzooks! If a Republican majority emerges, it may do so wearing galoshes. That is not chic and should not be necessary if the GOP future is as potentially sunny as some suggest. My friend James Q. Wilson, a Harvard political scientist, is so alarmingly sensible he may cause Harvard and political science to seem more sensible than they are. Writing in *Commentary*, Wilson, an independent, notes that for perhaps the first time since Teddy Roosevelt, the GOP is the party of change, whereas "Democrats are simultaneously bereft of new ideas and forced to take responsibility for old ones." In the 1920s, the GOP was the party of "normalcy"; in the 1930s and 1940s, of resistance to F.D.R. (and of halfhearted "me-too-ism"); in the 1950s, of national unity behind a hero. But in the 1960s, it began to have something new: ideas.

In 1967, after Reagan won his first election, Wilson wrote (in *Commentary*) that Reaganism should be taken seriously because "it will be with us a long time." In 1980, Wilson says, Reaganism has an "issue constituency" opposed to "those who believe in the unrestrained right of personal self-expression and the need for government to rationalize all other aspects of human affairs by rule and procedure." The Democratic Party may still be (although less than before) the intellectuals' party, but it no longer is the intellectually interesting party. Indeed, Wilson says, "the Democratic Party resembles nothing so much as the old Republican Party in the era of Robert Taft and Thomas E. Dewey." It possesses stale, and to some extent discredited, views about what American government and society should be like.

Wilson is too sensible to suggest that anything like the emergence of a Republican majority is inevitable. So are my friends Richard Scammon and Ben Wattenberg, the Butch Cassidy and Sundance Kid of electoral analysis, the fastest draws in the West when drawing correct conclusions from complex data. Writing in *Public Opinion* magazine, they say, categorically, that the day of old-style liberalism "is over," and they insist that "politics in a democracy is the ultimate Darwinian activity: adapt or die." But Democrats, who are no longer confident enough to be complacent, and who are not weighed down by a heavy ballast of certainties, may adapt, and by doing so retain their majority.

The Democrats' problem is that the nation's political center has wandered over to the Republican positions on two great issues. The center insists on the Federal Government's culpability for inflation and rejects the weakness of recent foreign policy. Because the Democratic Party has such incompatible factions, Carter's Presidency has been what Butch and Sundance call a "Chinese-menu Presidency": take one policy from column A, another from column B, a third from column C. "Soft on Russia—no, tough on Russia. Don't deregulate oil—no, do deregulate oil. More programs for poor people and blacks—no, austerity. Most important politically: big spending one year, old-time religion the next, yielding some of the economic problems that are at the root of Carter's 'incompetent, indecisive image.' "

The party's most conspicuous faction, say the authors, earns its livelihood dispensing, receiving or promoting government services. This faction, for all its claim to be a champion against old special interests (big business, and so on), is seen as a champion for new special interests. Government itself has become an interest group, and the Democratic Party is its party. Still, the party can salvage itself by acknowledging that "a humane welfare state cannot be funded without a vigorous private sector," by latching on to what has become the GOP issue of "growth economics" and by advocating "a guns-and-margarine position on defense—until we can afford butter again." As the authors say, "When you hear Democrats, in private, practicing to say the words 'capital formation,' you know the process is well under way."

Those authors—both Democrats—say, correctly, that big, broad political realignments are produced by big, broad ideas, such as F.D.R.'s "We are the party of the people." Today the Republicans have such an idea. It is *"We* are the party of the people." That contested idea lacks a certain Hegelian chewiness, but a mushroom can understand it, so it is suitable for politics.

Will it work for the Republicans? A friend at Reagan-Bush headquarters explains, with impressive data and logic, that it will. And the explanation if it doesn't? "Shut up," he will explain.

October 27, 1980

The Perpetual Campaign

The nation's quadrennial bludgeoning is over, and you will be forgiven for feeling like Evelyn Waugh's fictional Gilbert Pinfold: "There was a phrase in the thirties: 'It is later than you think,' which was designed to cause uneasiness. It was never later than Mr. Pinfold thought. At intervals during the day and night he would look at his watch and learn always with disappointment how little of his life was past, how much there was still ahead of him." But cheer up. If there is God's will in the fall of a sparrow, there must be a bushel and a peck of God's will in these interminable Presidential campaigns that involve candidates bouncing around the continent like popcorn in a skillet.

The 1984 campaign is under way. The two mastiffs in the liberal kennel, Walter Mondale and Edward Kennedy, are hard at it. On the Republican side, a covey of chaps are positioning themselves to win the (if you'll pardon the expression) hearts and minds of the conservative base on which Republican nominees stand.

Political campaigns have always been steamy stews of public issues and private egotisms, often conducted in the spirit of cheerful irresponsibility expressed by Thomas Gray: "As to posterity, I may ask what has it ever done for us?" In the bad old days, before the full flowering of democracy—before television and the League of Women Voters—Presidential candidates were inconspicuous to the point of invisibility. Writing in *American Heritage*, Louis Koenig notes that until 1896, campaigning of any sort by a Presidential candidate was considered bad form.

All Jefferson consented to do in his own behalf was correct a biographical pamphlet. Jackson, who was not long on decorum, nevertheless refused to travel outside Tennessee or even attend public dinners, and he boasted, "I have not gone into the highways and marketplaces to proclaim my opinions." Lincoln, leaning an elbow on his mantel, received visitors in Springfield, but made almost no speeches. In 1876, Rutherford B. Hayes, although Governor of Ohio as well as Republican Presidential nominee, doubted the propriety of attending Ohio Day at the Philadelphia Centennial.

In 1896, William McKinley, emulating Benjamin Harrison's 1888 style, conducted a "front porch" campaign. Railroads that understood the beauty of GOP philosophy offered dirt-cheap excursion fares to his front yard, which soon looked "as if a herd of buffalo had passed that way." But his 36-year-old opponent managed, as creative losers often do, to effect a fundamental change.

William Jennings Bryan raced and raged across the country, arousing "the people" against their enemies. Koenig writes:

> To reach crowds of forty thousand in a day innocent of voice amplifiers, and to keep pace with the resulting enormous demands on his physique, Bryan developed a monstrous appetite, consuming platterfuls of food, and demanding for his breakfast double or triple servings of what ordinary people expected for their dinner. His orgiastic consumption and his rushed schedule demolished his table manners, sometimes nauseating those who watched him eat. Bryan favored radishes above all foods, and thoughtful hostesses provided them by the bagful, to be munched on as he pushed through his hyperactive day.

Bryan's wardrobe reflected his manic single-mindedness. Most shoes then had pointed toes, but he adopted square-toed shoes that made him less apt to stumble as he leaped aboard moving trains.

Vachel Lindsay satirized Bryan's prairie populism in a marvelously funny poem about "Smashing Plymouth Rock with his boulders from the West," and avenging the "defeat of wheat" by thrashing plutocrats with "spats on their feet." The boys in spats fought back. According to Koenig, "depositors were informed that if Bryan won, their banks would fail, insurance companies advised policyholders that they would be unable to fulfill their obligations, and investment houses predicted a shattering collapse in the value of securities."

Ah, those were the days. Wicked bosses acted wickedly, and populists gorged themselves on radishes, as it somehow seems right for populists to do. By comparison, today's slick campaigns seem like "light" beer—perhaps better for us, but beer just isn't supposed to be "light."

Today's campaigns may lack colorful coarseness, to say nothing of depth, but by cracky, they are long on, well, length. Why? Perhaps modern campaigns are among the afflictions that God sends to test us and make us more spiritual. As Evelyn Waugh knew, the path toward perfection is paved with ordeals. To a friend who visited him after an operation for hemorrhoids, Waugh said that the treatment was very painful and had not been really necessary.

Why then, asked his friend, had he undergone it? "Perfectionism," Waugh explained.

But now, for the first time in this week's column and for the last time in this year's campaign, I shall lapse into complete seriousness.

I do not think our campaigns are too long. And they are a lot longer than most people know. You can't even measure their length: they have obvious endings, but they have hazy, indiscernible beginnings. The 1988 and 1992 campaigns have begun in the tentative thoughts and actions of a few men and women, including those who will win. The Presidential season, the process of generating Presidents, never ends; nor should it. Presidential campaigns overlap, and each is a melding of many individual careers, each with its own life cycle, all making up, together, an important part of our country's continuous conversation with itself.

As much as I pity those people who have never known democracy, I pity Americans whose souls are dead to the poetry of our politics, the generally civilized and civilizing churning of a great nation. However much our campaigns may at times seem to trivialize politics, they have an essential dignity, inherent and indestructible, because through them a great people conducts the peaceful disposition not just of power but of authority—legitimacy. That act, viewed against the tapestry of history, is a social miracle, nothing less.

November 10, 1980

The Awesome Shudder

An awesome shudder went through the Republic, as through a stately sailing ship that is altering course in heavy seas. The electorate meted out punishment to many people it considered guilty of embracing ideas that have been refuted by events. It was a brutal exercise in assigning political responsibility, an affirmation that ideas have consequences and that politicians must be held responsible for their ideas.

There may be more poetry than justice in poetic justice, but there was enough of both in the fact that the latest Iranian impudence was the catalyst of President Carter's downfall. Considering that he had ridden the crisis to great heights, and that it had dominated more than a quarter of his Presidency, and that the first three-quarters of his Presidency helped precipitate it—all things considered, it was an appropriate catalyst.

But this was a rebuke to a party as well as a repudiation of a President. The party that is widely thought to have been too complacent about cultural change, too sanguine about a dangerous world and too negligent about the material base of the nation's welfare has paid dearly.

Events cast their shadows forward, and the nation has just stepped out of the shadows of Vietnam and Watergate. Those episodes made possible the Carter Presidency, which, in turn, made a Reagan Presidency necessary. It is said that the "lessons" we choose to learn from our calamities are often calamitous. The "lesson" of Vietnam was, for many people, that the nation had been suffering an "inordinate," not to say neurotic, fear of Communism; that America had been provocative and overbearing in the postwar world; that America had relied excessively on traditional forms of power and insufficiently on the power of moral persuasion.

For many people, often the same people, the "lesson" of Watergate was that public officials should be judged primarily by "private" criteria—that the most important characteristic in a President is personal "goodness," manifested in moralizing. The election results indicate that the lessons are being unlearned.

You are doubtless feeling about campaigning the way a Randall Jarrell character felt about conversation: "People say conversation is a lost art: how often I have wished it were." But believe it or not, this campaign was educative, in the broad-brush way that campaigns must be. The wax of the public mind is soft, but not so soft that it cannot take an impression, and the yearlong argument has impressed upon it this truth: The nation is not as productive at home or strong abroad as it must be.

President Carter's campaigning was ineffective, at best, but it was his governing that doomed him. "Difficulty," said Edward R. Murrow, "is the one excuse that history never accepts." Americans are more forgiving than history, but they draw the line somewhere, and they drew it well this side of Carter's performance.

When Cicero spoke, listeners said, "How well he speaks"; but when Demosthenes spoke, his listeners said, "Let us march!" Neither candidate this year stirred in the masses an unmanageable urge to march, but there was ample passion abroad in the land, and Reagan and others running beneath him on state ballots became vessels for that passion.

Reagan, who has always suffered the derision of cultured despisers, won not because he inherited with the nomination a coalition of interests, but because, over a decade of patient politics, he creatively assembled a potent constellation of ideas. With a large assist from events, but with remarkable reliance on his own personality and persuasiveness, Reagan has cobbled together an "issue constituency."

When the Republicans adopted a platform emphasizing cultural conservatism, it was widely disparaged as evidence of their preference for being right-minded rather than effective. But they were realists, sensing the seething determination of many millions of Americans to find a political voice for their cultural anxieties.

It is, however, radically wrong to regard Reagan's inner compass as pointing backward, or to regard his mood as nostalgic. He does not want to return to the past; he wants to return to the past's way of facing the future.

Most societies have had a vision of a golden age, and most have located it in the distant past. Americans have always located it in the future. Reagan rejects, viscerally, the notion that the trajectory of American history has passed its apogee. Reagan is an unusual kind of conservative restorer, seeking not to restore traditional social structures but rather to restore belief in progressive change.

This year he described where he wants to take us. "Political ability," Churchill said, "is the ability to foretell what is going to happen tomorrow, next week, next month and next year. And to have the ability afterward to explain why it didn't happen." Ronald Reagan has several years to polish that last part.

November 6, 1980

An Un-American Election

A century ago, German philosophers announced that if we could but pierce the veil of appearances, we would see that History is intelligible, logical and progressive. Now a Californian has vindicated those Germans.

In 1964, when Barry Goldwater's candidacy was the occasion for the political debut of a providential force named Ronald Reagan, Goldwater cleverly contrived to get so decisively shellacked that he took down to defeat a raft of Republican congressmen and senators. He thereby shattered the moderate conservative legislating majority that had existed since 1938 (the election that turned, in part, on F.D.R.'s "court-packing" plan).

Suddenly Congress had a liberal majority, and there was a President eager to use it. Rarely has History played such a scurvy trick on the unsuspecting: It afflicted Democrats with the curse of great opportunity. They began building the "Great Society," promising much more ("model cities" and the like) than they could reasonably expect to deliver, thereby accelerating the erosion of confidence in the competence of government.

In foreign policy too the Democratic Administration had a misplaced confidence in its ablity to operate with surgical precision on societies. It believed in "nation-building" in South Vietnam, and in using finely calibrated bombing to send subtle, not to say unintelligible, "signals" to North Vietnam. Those policies flowed from a mentality not unlike the one that led to the pursuit of "racial balance" and other abstract equities at home.

The two most important political developments of the past twenty years were, initially, intellectual developments.

One was the acceptance by many Democrats, radicalized by a Democratic Administration's policy toward Vietnam, of the "revisionist" interpretation of the Cold War. That interpretation turns on the judgment that the United States was at least partly, and perhaps primarily, culpable for the Cold War. The interpretation devalues the record of the United States, and of the Democratic Party, in the postwar containment of Communism.

The other development was the emergence of an articulate conservative intellectual movement. It derived primarily from reflection about recent demonstrations that societies are less mechanical and more organic than liberal policies have assumed, less amenable to "social engineering." It also was a reaction to the cultural dissolution that has been aggravated by liberal policies.

Until relatively recently, too many American conservatives were content to be rear-guard skirmishers, rarely rising to the dignity of political philosophy, rarely experiencing, or even desiring, the enlarging discipline of political responsibility. Instead, they adhered to an anti-political economic doctrine (severe *laissez-faire*).

Today, thanks in part to a reaction against forces let loose by the anti-Goldwater landslide, there is a deeper, richer conservative movement. Its major theme is what Robert Nisbet rightly identifies as the major theme of Western conservatism: the defense of society against the political state; the preservation, to the extent feasible, of the autonomy of social groups against politicized control.

An irony of last week's electoral upheaval is that an authentic nationalist won a somewhat "un-American" election. It was a "European" election because, to an unusual and healthy extent, voters treated it as a nationwide contest between parties, not just a series of utterly unrelated contests between individuals.

It is an axiom—a somewhat battered axiom—that all American elections are local elections, meaning that parochial concerns and perceptions, rather than national issues and passions, predominate in contests for House and Senate seats. The results of this election suggest a continental judgment about the parties. A century ago, Lord Bryce said that America's parties are like two bottles with different labels and nothing inside. It was not very true then, and is even less true today.

Goldwater's 1964 loss was, perhaps, less consequential than his conquest of the GOP, a conquest that sealed the conservatives' victory in the Republican civil war that had simmered and occasionally raged since the 1912 split between President Taft and former President Roosevelt. That is one reason that conservatism mellowed and matured: it turned away from internecine struggles.

Today the question about the Democratic Party is: Was McGovern's shellacking in the 1972 election less important than the McGovernite conquest of the party that year? Twice now Americans have said, emphatically, that they do not want a McGovernite President. They said it in 1972, and in 1980, when they had learned that they had one in office.

Republicans may hope that Democrats will never learn and McGovernites will never lose control of the party, but that is unlikely. History can be funny, but rarely is it sustained slapstick.

November 13, 1980

No Panic in the Oval Office

On the afternoon of his second full day on the job, his desk (the one under which "John-John" Kennedy played hide-and-seek) still uncluttered, Ronald Reagan is quietly explaining his confidence when suddenly Secret Service agents burst through the door from the garden, exclaiming, "Is everything all right, sir?" Now, "all right" hardly does justice to how everything is for Ronald Reagan after working twelve years to get to this oval room. He asks, equably, why they are in such a lather, and they say the Oval Office "panic alarm" has gone off.

Gadzooks! Is there a panic detector, akin to a smoke detector, that sniffs anxiety in the air? And has it sniffed it so soon? No, someone has accidentally bumped an alarm button. That's the way it is for a few days when the White House gets a new crew. If there really were a "nuclear button," someone would long since have set a cup of coffee down on it.

He is wearing a suit of blue plaid that probably is funereal by Pacific Palisades standards, but is bold enough by Washington standards to set off an alarm. However, watch for Washington to break out in plaids. Washington takes cues. Up to a point.

In his inaugural address, Reagan said "there will be no compromise" about such priorities as tax cuts, and minutes later Speaker "Tip" O'Neill, looking uncommonly scowly, was on TV pointedly intoning that politics is the art of the possible. When Reagan is told that O'Neill seemed a tad grumpy, his face registers real concern. He had not meant to be belligerent; he meant, he says, only that certain principles would be his lodestar.

O'Neill, a Democrat down to his chromosomes, is the highest-ranking Democrat Reagan must deal with. In November, after Reagan visited O'Neill, he was asked what O'Neill had said. "He said," Reagan replied drily, "I was in the big leagues now." Pause. Then softly: "I'd gathered that already." Today, Reagan admits his reply was tinged with qualities he keeps hidden. There was drollness and light sarcasm, evidence of sharp edges beneath the smooth surface of a proud man who, having carried forty-four states, notices when he is being patronized. Many Americans might enjoy seeing more of those edges, more signs that beneath his preternatural affability there is some acid and steel.

A President's power over the bureaucracy depends, in part, on respect born of fear; during the first term it depends, in part, on the idea that a President may run again. Asked about this, Reagan smiles at the impertinence of asking, implicitly, about a second term with 1,459 days to go in this one. All he says is "Well"—

nod—"you know, I never could have achieved welfare reform in California without a second term." He is too clever not to know he is being tantalizing.

He drove even some of his campaign aides batty by running over and over that "Hey, I was Governor of California" commercial, but his point, then and now, is that he is not a rookie. He has done this before, this Chief Executive role. Kennedy assessed the Presidency this way: "The pay is pretty good and you can walk home to lunch." "Oh?" Reagan says. "I've been here two days and I've had lunch both days in this office." But he, like Kennedy, is distinctly un-bowled over. Can he already sense what will be the rhythm of his White House life? He says he knows what it will be because enough of his senior staffers have done this before, and know his needs. We—and he—shall see, when he is standing watch at Chrysler's deathbed or worrying about our hostages in Lower Slobbovia.

His evident assumption is that the Presidency is a governorship writ large. But what of the President's isolation from "the people"? Can he, for example, sense the surging anger about Iran? Yes, he says, at each inaugural ball, "I didn't refer to them as hostages but as prisoners of war, and there was always a roar"— he raises a clenched fist—"of anger." Furthermore, he says, one thing you learn in the entertainment business—about which he is never apologetic—is "sensitivity to what people want." Every good politician puts it his own way, but it always comes down to this: trained intuition.

Right now, some of "the people"—fifty thousand of them— have him almost surrounded. The annual Right to Life march began on the Ellipse, due south of his office window, and is snaking past his front porch. In a few hours he will receive the leaders of the march. But meeting with Right to Lifers is, for him, like an inaugural ball: friendly faces. Soon he plans to address a joint session of Congress, and then, perhaps, the kissing will stop. Of the current euphoria, Reagan, who has an actor's sense of the perishableness of moods, says simply, "That can't go on."

As we talk, his Butch Cassidy and his Sundance Kid are in the antechamber, spinning the cylinders of their six-guns, waiting for permission to shoot up the town. They will get it. David Stockman is budget czar and Martin Anderson is domestic adviser. Given their druthers, these hell-for-leather free-marketeers might sell the Post Office. Reagan's druthers, though different, are going to raise dust. He vehemently disagrees with those who say Americans must permanently and generally lower their expectations, but he probably must soon say that some expectations must be lowered, and some gains must be given back.

Already the Chrysler cliff-hanger has involved a union voting to yield some gains won in collective bargaining. And the logic of what Butch, Sundance and their boss say is that the government must take back some promises made in entitlement programs. "We may have to take a little medicine—all of us," he says blandly, as though Dr. Congress were accustomed to administering castor oil. His emphasis is on the last three words—"all of us"—because he knows that misery loves company: pain is more acceptable when thy neighbor is hurting too.

One way to democratize discomfort is to cut the indexing of benefits. Perhaps 40 percent of federal spending is directly or indirectly indexed to inflation. Every percentage-point increase in inflation increases indexed programs $2.2 billion. Direct indexing alone may cost $23 billion in 1981. If indexing were cut just to 85 percent of current levels, the saving through 1985 would be $50 billion. Reagan says, "I separate Social Security from the general economic program." But the direction in which he must go is pointed by arithmetic others got wrong when they created or enriched (through indexing or expanded eligibility and benefits) many programs. When disability insurance was added to Social Security in 1956, the estimate was that it would cost $860 million by 1980. Actually, it cost $17 billion. In 1965, when federal spending on health was less than $1 billion, Congress enacted Medicare and, almost casually, Medicaid. No one foresaw that these would cost $53 billion in 1981.

More than any other postwar President, Reagan is interested in economics. (Kennedy said he had difficulty remembering the difference between fiscal and monetary policy unless he thought:

William McChesney Martin is head of the Fed, and his name begins with "M," so monetary policy is the Fed's business.) But Stockman expresses the prevailing disenchantment with economic analysis in a joke about the politician and the economist who fall into a deep pit with steep walls. The politician asks if the economist has a plan for getting out, and the economist says, "Sure. First, we assume a ladder."

Usually if a President gets half of what he seeks he should be content. But if Reagan gets just half, the result could be scary. He wants substantial tax cuts, and substantial cuts in spending through 1985. But if he just gets half, guess which half it will be? If, with another big deficit impending, he gets much more than half of his tax cuts, and much less than half of his spending cuts, the result could be awful. But so could the result of tentativeness.

Can Reagan confound the conventional wisdom about Congress? The success of Reagan's Presidency, and much else (such as the currency), depends on his ability to enlarge Washington's sense of the possible. To that end, Representative Jack Kemp recently sent Reagan a memo noting the following: Before General Douglas MacArthur's masterstroke, the landing at Inchon, MacArthur's advisers, and emissaries sent from Washington, said it could not be done. The harbor, the weather, the ships, the tides—everything was wrong. Recalling MacArthur's peroration that carried the crucial meeting, a witness said, "If MacArthur had gone on the stage, you never would have heard of John Barrymore." After all the skeptics spoke, MacArthur rose. In his memoirs he wrote, "I could almost hear my father's voice telling me as he had so many years before, 'Doug, councils of war breed timidity and defeatism.' " All councils do. There never was a bold committee. Boldness is individual.

Reagan the actor never made anyone forget Barrymore, but Reagan the President, serenely confident and not apt to panic, is going to try to make Washington forget where others found the limits of the possible.

February 2, 1981

Journalism and Friendship

Billy Loes, the patron saint of columnists, was a pitcher, mostly for the Brooklyn Dodgers. He was not, shall we say, all polish. He once lost a ground ball in the sun. He committed a memorable balk in a World Series game. (The ball squirted from his hand at the start of his windup. "Too much spit on it," he explained.) But he was a deep social thinker. ("The [1962] Mets is a very good thing. They give everybody a job. Just like the WPA.") And he was a major-league complainer. That quality inspired a poem, whose full text is "This is the trouble with Billy Loes,/ He don't like it wherever he goes." This week's column is about writing columns, which is in part, but only in part, the art of complaining usefully.

Fearful rumors are afoot that I may abandon the columnist's basic stance of thorough disapproval of all conduct but his own. Readers by the millions—well, okay, a couple of you, your eyes wet with unshed tears—are worried that on January 20 I shall succumb to conviviality, my captious spirit will vanish and I shall commence to carol like a lark. Caroling is fine from larks, but boring from columnists. Worriers note that last autumn I was not your basic undecided voter, and (believe it or not) they worry because the Reagans came to the Wills' for dinner. The latter was a small matter, but large enough to fill to overflowing the minds of some people.

The financial markets are gyrating, the budget is hemorrhaging, the currency is evaporating and the Russians are practically in Duluth, so there are questions more urgent than the following: Is journalistic duty compatible with feelings of friendship between journalists and those political people who do the work of democracy? And will this columnist be as critical of Reagan's Administration as he was of Carter's?

The answer are: yep, and I certainly hope not. I am moved to expand upon these answers only because journalism (like public service, with its "conflict of interest" phonetics) is now infested with persons who are little "moral thermometers," dashing about taking other persons' temperatures, spreading, as confused moralists will, a silly scrupulosity and other confusions.

We all have our peculiar tastes. Some people like Popsicles. Others like gothic novels. I like politicians. A journalist once said that the only way for a journalist to look at a politician is down. That is unpleasantly self-congratulatory. A journalist's duty is to see politicians steadily and see them whole. To have intelligent sympathy for them, it helps to know a few as friends. Most that I know are overworked and underpaid persons whose characters can stand comparison with the characters of the people they represent, and of journalists.

Friendship between journalists and politicians offends persons who consider a mean edge the only proof of "candor" in writing about politicians. ("To be candid, in Middlemarch phraseology, meant," George Eliot wrote, "to use an early opportunity of letting your friends know that you did not take a cheerful view of their capacity, their conduct, or their position . . .") But friendship, including relaxation in social settings, reduces the journalist's tendency to regard politicians as mere embodiments of ideas or causes, as simple abstractions rather than complicated human beings. The leavening of friendship may take some of the entertaining savagery from our politics, but then, politics has not recently suffered from an excess of civility.

The idea that only an "adversary relationship" with government is proper for journalists pleases some journalists because it seems hairy-chested, and because it spares them the tortures of thought. Continual thought about what to publish, and how to adapt to the nuances in a political city, is necessary for journalists who believe that they are citizens first. They have particular professional duties, but they and politicians are part of the same process, the quest for the public good.

John Kennedy showed a draft of his inaugural address to Walter Lippmann, who suggested a change (to refer to a hostile nation as an "adversary," not an "enemy"), which Kennedy made. On inauguration night Kennedy went to the home of Joseph Alsop, the columnist. He went for the best of reasons: friendship. Lippmann helped draft Woodrow Wilson's "fourteen points" (then became an astringent critic of Wilson and the Versailles Treaty). For five decades he preached detachment but practiced a decorous, public-spirited involvement.

Shortly after the Second World War, Senator Arthur Vandenberg asked Scotty Reston to read a speech about relations with Russia. Scotty did, considered it unfortunately negative and made a suggestion (that Vandenberg, formerly a leading isolationist, signal a turn toward internationalism), and the speech became a significant event. Lippmann was, Reston is, a citizen too: a citizen first.

Today good citizens ache for a chance to applaud the reasonably graceful exercise of power. I am hopeful; I am not *quite* of Evelyn Waugh's persuasion ("I have never voted in a general election as I have never found a Tory stern enough to command my respect"), and I do not covet the Billy Loes trophy for most incessant complaining. But . . .

The columnists I most admire, from Samuel Johnson to G. K. Chesterton to Murray Kempton today, have written about the "inside" of public matters: not what is secret, but what is latent, the kernel of principle and other significance that exists, recognized or not, "inside" events, policies and manners. Following, in my dim way, their luminous example, my columns are meditations on various principles. And in behalf of my own principles, which, I suspect, will not be fully and perfectly worshiped within the Reagan Administration. And unless there is unflagging worship at the altar of Will's creed, Will will emulate the great complainer, the sainted Billy Loes.

The most useful complaints are couched as arguments, and make a case for better ways, finer things. Often, the most useful arguments are the civil but spirited ones we have with friends. Invariably, it is this for which I write: the joy, than which there is nothing purer, of an argument firmly made, like a nail straightly driven, its head flush to the plank.

January 19, 1981

Part Five

"GOVERNING"

Suffocating in the Open Air

The gasoline riots in Levittown, Pennsylvania, began at an intersection mournfully adorned by four gas stations. Rampaging suburbanites smashed windows and watermelons. And a stereotype. Social disorder in Levittown? The postwar era really has ended.

Some people say Levittown *is* a social disorder. "Levittown" once was a synonym for "suburbia." The first of three Levittowns sprouted in the potato fields of Long Island, New York, in 1946, when Long Island was empty and Americans were bursting with pent-up appetites. The Depression and the war compelled Americans to do something un-American: to defer gratifying their desires, especially for single-family housing. When the shooting stopped, the consuming began, with a boost from the GI housing bill and from highways built for commuters. The rush was on for low-density communities and a long drive from city congestion. Levitt & Sons' housing was mass-produced and prefabricated, not long on variety, but ready *right now*.

Writers plumbed the shallows of surburban life, in books like *The Crack in the Picture Window* and, yes, *Levittowners*. Suburbs, Daniel Boorstin says, are for folks moving "rapidly about the country and up the ladder of consumption." Today, such movement is more problematic. Suburbia's symbol, the cul-de-sac, expresses America's mood on the eve of the 1980s. A cul-de-sac is, after all, just a fancy dead end.

Americans feel they are suffocating in the open air. Inflation is devaluing savings from the past, poisoning the present and clouding the future. OPEC, with the help of the Department of Energy's allocation fiasco, is causing Americans to worry about life's little things, like license-plate numbers, and whether to drive to the

213

drugstore. It's summertime, and the living is supposed to be easy, but events are winding tight the springs of tension.

The understandable urge to drop something heavy on OPEC from a great height has produced a jolly idea: let's haul OPEC into court on antitrust charges. Americans increasingly live by a child-like faith in the power of judges to make the world "fair." Many who complain about OPEC resemble the lady who complained she did not like the night air. "Madam," said her doctor, "during certain hours of the twenty-four, night air is the only air there is."

OPEC has oil. The West needs it. *Some* of it. Thus far, OPEC has not pushed up prices; they have been pulled up by the suction of Western, and especially American, carburetors. Before 1973, oil-exporting nations, many of them poor, charged much less than their national interest required, and much less than the market would bear. When they quadrupled the price of their non-renewable asset, American demand for it continued to rise. Six years later, the U.S. Government is subsidizing the consumption of imported oil: directly through subsidies for oil imports, indirectly through price controls on gasoline and domestic crude.

OPEC provides Americans with a scapegoat for inflation. The real cause is closer to home. Since 1967, the U.S. money supply has grown nearly three times as fast as the supply of U.S. goods and services that money can buy. Americans have not allowed their negligible productivity growth to interfere with the fun of climbing the ladder of consumption. They have sustained their climb by scanting investment. The consumption explosion that began in 1945 went on too long, and the price is being paid in wretched productivity and ruinous inflation.

It may be that since 1973, OPEC has done to the United States what Egypt did to Britain in 1956. OPEC may have demonstrated the fragility of U.S. power. It certainly has demonstrated that economic forces are primary, diplomatic maneuvers are secondary. The year after Nixon and Kissinger clinked glasses with Mao and Chou, some less famous men changed the price of oil. By doing so, they changed the world far more than those who clinked glasses changed it.

Changes in the world since 1945 are maddeningly clear. When

the first Levittown was planted in potato fields, America was unchallengeable. Since then, it has been frustrated in war by two half-nations, North Korea and North Vietnam. At the Vienna summit, Carter was reduced to asking Brezhnev to give permission for U.S. reconnaissance aircraft to use the airspace of an American ally, Turkey.

At the Tokyo summit, an assistant Secretary of State, who opposed America's use of force against Hanoi, said that Hanoi's viciousness toward the boat people was "intolerable" and "must stop." Brave talk, that, but a bit late. The United States had a chance to confine Hanoi's viciousness, and failed. For the United States, the price of that failure is to lament "intolerable" things it has no choice but to tolerate. For the boat people, the price is higher.

In domestic policy too, pains are multiplying. Fifteen years ago, it seemed that henceforth the political task would be to allocate abundance. Management of the economy had been perfected; growth would be uninterrupted and would produce, at constant tax rates, a "fiscal dividend" of surplus revenues. Now it seems that in the 1980s politics will be about the allocation of scarcity.

Even clean air will be rationed. At the dawn of this decade, in 1970, the word "ecology" suddenly was on millions of lips. Environmental legislation flowed from Congress. All of it had calculable costs that now, in a changed social climate, are actually being calculated. A chastened nation realizes it is not rich enough to have all the environmental rules it has and all the economic efficiency it wants. The last two decades of the American century may be tiresome, and not just for snail darters.

Damn it, where *have* you gone, Joe DiMaggio? What ever happened to the fun in our future? What happened to 1945's sense of a fresh start. What happened to Levittown's tranquillity? Never mind. Those who are nostalgic for the good old days of urban living before automobiles and energy problems should read Otto Bettmann:

Of the 3 million horses in American cities at the beginning of the twentieth century, New York had some 150,000, the healthier ones each producing between 20 and 25 pounds of manure a day. These dumplings were numerous on every street, attracting swarms of flies and radiating a powerful stench. The ambiance was further debased by the presence on almost every block of stables filled with urine-saturated hay. During dry spells the pounding traffic refined the manure to dust, which [a New Yorker] remembered blew "from the pavement as a sharp, piercing powder, to cover our clothes, ruin our furniture and blow up into our nostrils."

Life in Levittown can be trying, but the view from the picture window could be worse. Not long ago, "suffocation in the open air" was more than a metaphor.

July 9, 1979

Good Grief

In 1895, there were only two cars in Ohio, and they collided. That confirmed Murphy's Law ("If anything can go wrong, it will") and the buttered-side-down law: "The chance of the bread's falling buttered-side down is directly proportional to the cost of the carpet." Such proverbs for pessimists may come to Jimmy Carter's mind as he pledges to put the federal budget through a wringer. He may soon see the truth of another proverb: "Friends may come and go, but enemies accumulate."

On a recent Saturday, he vetoed three bills. One authorized $200 million for nurses' training, and someone from the nurses' lobby hinted darkly that the veto had something to do with "the fact that nursing is predominantly a woman's profession." A cattlemen's group lamented the veto of a bill that would have revoked the Presidential power to expand meat imports, and a spokesman for the textile industry expressed "grave disappointment" about the veto of a bill that would have forbidden reductions of textile tariffs. The nurses' bill authorized ten times as much money as the Administration had requested. The meat and textile vetoes merely preserve the President's right to take actions that might be anti-inflationary, but that he might not take. So as episodes in the war on inflation, Carter's vetoes called to mind the communiqué issued during the Spanish Civil War: "The advance was continued all day without any ground being lost."

But Hamilton Jordan, Carter's principal political adviser, insists no program is safe from Carter's zeal to "cut back to the bone." In the words of Dickens' Coachman (in *The Pickwick Papers*), "That remark's political, or what is much the same, it ain't true." But Jordan, who is notoriously frisky and informal, has been appearing in a dark blue suit, which is a harbinger of tomorrow's mood of Democratic liberals.

Recent history has been hard on common preconceptions about American politics. Under two conservative Republican Presidents, defense spending declined as a percentage of GNP and of federal outlays for eight straight years, and that part of the federal budget (now 43 percent) which consists of payments to individuals expanded more rapidly than before. Today Carter feels compelled to make conservative gestures in defense and to administer conservative economic medicine. Indeed, conservatives consider today's Washington a place where people are hectically inventing the wheel, lighting upon the obvious with a sense of real discovery.

People are discovering that, yes, minimum-wage increases (another is due on January 1) have inflationary consequences. An ambitious ($77 million over ten years) research project about welfare has discovered that . . . well, let the *Washington Post* headline proclaim it:

STUDY SAYS PEOPLE WORK LESS WHEN GUARANTEED AN INCOME

Some hardworking Americans are the town fathers of Warsaw, Indiana, a community with an unemployment rate of just 1.5 percent. It is trying to get workers to move there. Nevertheless, it has received federal funds under the Comprehensive Employment and Training Act for the hard-core unemployed. Says Warsaw's plucky mayor: "We had a heck of a time trying to find someone to put on that program. We finally came up with eight or nine fellows." Carter's seriousness about austerity may be more believable if programs like CETA are passed through the metaphorical wringer. The only thing CETA has passed through recently is Congress.

"Frankly," said a democratic leader as devout and intense as Carter, "I am not satisfied with the state of the public expenditures and the rapid rate of its growth. I trust, therefore, that we mean in a great degree to retrace our steps." So said William Gladstone when he was Britain's Chancellor of the Exchequer in 1860. Of course, nations never retrace their steps. But if Carter and his aides mean what they are suddenly saying about the stark choice facing the nation—austerity or calamity—Americans are at least going to see how far they have gone, step by step, toward the kind of state that exists today in Britain and most other nations with a strong tradition of democratic socialism.

In 1949, *Collier's* magazine reported that when five thousand Americans were asked what was traded on the stock exchange, 64 percent said "livestock." Today's economic confusions are different, but equally startling. Library shelves groan beneath the weight of books and learned journals explaining why America has never developed an appetite for socialism. Someday the scholars will emerge from their studies, blinking, and look around. They will discover that moderate socialism—what Europeans call "social democracy"—is an accomplished fact.

Not for years have sensible socialists believed that the achievement of their objectives depended upon (in the classic formulation) "public ownership of the means of production, distribution and exchange." Public ownership is largely irrelevant to the goal of permeating economic life with public policy. That goal can be achieved by the regulatory instruments of the activist, interventionist state that has supplanted the minimalist "night-watchman state" idealized in the nineteenth century. The importance of political choices relative to market choices has been expanding for generations, and whatever selective "deregulation" occurs will not "retrace our steps" to the night-watchman state.

The exhaustion of political categories, the depletion of realism and the sterility of argument are apparent in the attempt to clarify politics by distinguishing between proponents and opponents of Big Government. One working American in six works for the government; nearly one American in three receives income from government; the biggest government program of all, Social Security, is the most sacrosanct. The state dispenses so many payments, entitlements, tariffs and other protections and subsidies that it would be hard to assemble a roomful of people who do not receive some particular benefit.

That explains much of Carter's problem. And this explains more: an awkward fact about a political tent as large as the Democratic Party is that almost every economic interest is in some sense inside it. Wherever Carter applies his pruning shears to the budget, he will cut something valued by a Democratic constituency. But perhaps the way to persuade an interest group that it does not have a special grievance is to generalize grief. People mind social pain less than they mind the idea that other people are not in similar pain, so the way to ease the sting of particular disappointments is to democratize disappointment. If the disappointed nursing, meat and textile interests are 3 of, say, 10,000 clamorous interests, then perhaps Carter's strategy should be to disappoint the other 9,997.

November 27, 1978

The FTC as Federal Nanny

A walk past the cereal shelves in a supermarket is a walk on the wild side, past boxes of Count Chocula and Frankenberry—chocolate- and strawberry-flavored cereals, with marshmallow bits. Now the Federal Trade Commission may move to protect children from acquiring appetites for such stuff.

A staff study suggests banning all advertising directed at "very young" children; or banning all advertising of "sugared products" directed at audiences containing a "significant" proportion of children; or requiring that advertisements of such products be "balanced" by messages urging good nutritional habits.

Michael Pertschuk, FTC chairman, has looked upon the staff report and found it "monumental." Pertschuk, who speaks Bureaucratic Baroque, worries about "distortions of the child's information environment." But plainly, the issue is: Granted that too few parents are autocrats at the breakfast table, should government intervene to compensate for parental inadequacies?

This is a nation in which a family is more apt to have a television set than indoor plumbing, and in which *The New York Times* rightly considered it newsworthy when some Manhattan children forswore television *for a whole week.* In 1977, the average child between ages 2 and 11 watched three hours and forty minutes of television a day, and saw twenty thousand commercials during the year. There is evidence that Ronald McDonald, the hamburger corporation's clown, is the second-most-recognized figure (Santa is first) among children.

Dr. Jean Mayer, the nutritionist, is probably right when he says that a rough rule of thumb is that the nutritional value of a food varies inversely with the amount spent to advertise it. The largest volume of advertising directed at children is for food with a high sugar content. The advertising is effective.

Anyone with a small child feels as Cardinal Wolsey felt about Henry VIII: "Be well advised and assured what you put in his head, for ye shall never pull it out again." The aim of advertising directed at children, especially on Saturday morning, is not just to set visions of sweets dancing in small heads. The aim also is to make children even less like angels than it is their natural inclination to be. The aim, a candid assessment has said, is to turn them into "very successful naggers."

Conclusive evidence that advertising achieves this aim is the hundreds of millions of dollars spent each year on such advertising. Advertisers are not fools; they would not spend so much if they did not have hard evidence that it pays to bombard little people, even though little people have no money. Little people successfully belabor big people.

The FTC staff says advertising aimed at children exploits "disparities in knowledge and power between buyer and seller." But children are only naggers, not buyers. The people with the money are called "parents."

Certainly, children can manipulate parents. A study indicates that two-thirds of all mothers sometimes take their small children to the supermarket, and one-third *always* take their children. Supermarkets are increasingly places for impulse buying—for purchases people did not plan in advance. When a child in a supermarket cart is being beastly, there is a powerful impulse to silence him by giving him something beastly, like a box of Count Chocula.

Such parental surrenders are bad for children's teeth and, more important, their souls. It gives children the wrong idea—or, perhaps, the right idea—as to who is in charge. But is this the FTC's business?

You bet, says the FTC staff. Disputes about Count Chocula "will be resolved by some sort of negotiation between the parent and child, which is often a continuing source of tension. . . ." God forbid there should be tension between parent and child, so a primary aim of the FTC is to prevent some tension-producing negotiations.

The FTC's staff says that the child nags "until he breaks down the sales resistance of his parent" and "this takes a toll on the parent–child relationship." An alarmed psychiatrist says this "encourage[s] confrontation and alienation on the part of children toward their parents and undermine[s] the parents' child rearing responsibilities."

Actually, the average child is much improved by occasional confrontation and alienation. And speaking of child-rearing responsibilities, the FTC has none.

Regarding television, diet and many other matters, the principal hazard to children is foolish parents. The FTC has made the empirical argument that children's teeth suffer because many parents' dietary decisions are influenced by children who have been influenced by television. But cavities are less harmful to the nation than is the FTC's premise, which is the "helplessness" of parents.

March 9, 1978

The Politics of Sentimentality

With the exquisite timing Chicago Cubs fans develop from watching their heroes, I recently offered here a defense of nuclear power. You will admit it was grand of me to start you thinking about the issue before Three Mile Island made it fascinating. I will pass over the possibility that I caused this, but I recall Stephen Leacock's words: "When I state that my lectures were followed almost immediately by the union of South Africa, the banana riots in Trinidad and the Turco-Italian war, I think the reader can form some opinion of their importance." Now, coming briskly to the point, I say:

Events have not contradicted most of what was said here about nuclear safety. The nuclear industry, as quoted here, was much too blasé about its ability to anticipate and contain malfunctions. But the record of commercial reactors remains what it was: no one has been killed and public-health damage, if any, is unmeasured. After the hydrogen bubble began dissolving, one network still referred to the Harrisburg "calamity." What language does that network reserve for events that kill people?

Actually, people who have read Genesis should not be surprised when new knowledge brings difficulties. And people who have read history know that most new technologies fail, often, and are improved by trials and errors. The blueprints of industrial society, its dams and bridges and transportation, were drawn in blood.

Think of the ships that broke up or blew up before maritime engineering matured; ships that collided before sea-lanes were organized; ships that foundered before Samuel Plimsoll's "line" on hulls limited loads. Think of railroad and airplane accidents during the infancy of those technologies.

Now consider the safety record of commercial reactors, including the fact that defense in depth did not fail at Three Mile Island and will be refined in light of that experience. The more damage that can result from a single failure, the more skepticism is justified regarding the particular technology. Nuclear power warrants unsleeping scrutiny of its operations and redoubled concern about its wastes. But policy must turn on probabilities, not possibilities. And today, as two weeks ago, nuclear power has a safety record remarkable among new technologies of the industrial age.

Society must become more conscious of the logical and psychological complexities of risk analysis. As Cyril Comar of Cornell University writes, "It is human nature to be concerned primarily with effects on our own person and family and secondarily with effects on the population at large. Unfortunately, although we can predict statistical effects on populations, there is no way to predict effects on individuals. This is why fortune tellers never become as rich as insurance companies."

About 350,000 deaths this year will be related to smoking, but some newspapers carrying cigarette ads worry more about the risks of nuclear power. Over the roar of rushing traffic that will kill more Americans this year than were killed in Vietnam, drivers listen to broadcasts about the "unacceptable risks" of nuclear power. The biggest public-health hazard is the public's behavior when eating, drinking, smoking and not exercising. The second-biggest hazard is in your garage, gentle reader. Many of this year's 50,000 traffic deaths and 2 million disabling injuries would be prevented by the prohibition of left turns. All in favor say "aye."

You are considerably safer living near a properly functioning nuclear power plant than near a coal-burning plant. (By the way, coal contains radioactive elements, and many coal plants emit more radioactivity than nuclear plants are allowed to emit.) Nuclear plants, like everything else, can malfunction and become hazardous. Coal plants are hazardous when functioning normally.

But as *The Washington Post* says:

> Americans are highly selective in their perceptions of risk . . . Though [coal's] costs to human life are large, they are familiar. Coal became part of our lives when people were poorer and life was cheaper. The usage established then still seems to influence attitudes today. It surprises no one that from time to time a mine should collapse and men die. Nor does it surprise anyone that, after ugly accidents, mines should reopen . . . But, in terms of health hazards, mining coal is less dangerous than burning it. There have been many studies [comparing nuclear and coal plants] and . . . they demonstrate clearly that coal imposes a much greater cost to human health, perhaps 100 times as high—measured in terms of premature deaths.

Actually, the costs of coal are not familiar to most people. The costs of burning it are cumulative and long-term. They are not the stuff of spine-tingling journalism or other entertainments. The costs of mining coal are paid by a working class that is, to most Americans, as foreign as Mongolia.

Many opponents of nuclear power flinch from endorsing coal. So they speak of "alternative life-styles," meaning less economic growth, fewer comforts. Such talk issues from people comfortably supplied with the fruits of economic growth. Many of these people see themselves as in the governing class; their largest disappointment with America is the weakness of the redistributionist impulse in politics. For them, a slow growth is not a problem, it is a political program, a way of shifting society's attention from creating wealth to redistributing it. The impact of slow growth is regressive. Those at the bottom have most to gain from economic dynamism, and will lose much, including hope, if dynamism declines. But for a governing class, the supreme power and pleasure is to allocate hope.

In a flight of unconscious self-satire, *The New York Times* asks that nuclear power be assessed by a commission equipped with "a poet." Certainly, physicians and physicists should be heard concerning health hazards and technical feasibilities, but the issue is, at bottom, political: it is about the allocation of social values. "Everything," Einstein said, "should be made as simple as possible, but not simpler." Alas, terrible simplifiers are proclaiming easy choices, and playing to today's sentimentality. By sentimentality I mean a willed ignorance of the costs of basics, from electricity to liberty. I mean the belief that nature benevolently ordains that in any situation, the best choice is necessarily a good choice.

Those who think abandonment of nuclear energy is an obviously good choice should curl up with a good book, the National Academy of Sciences study *Energy and Climate* (soon, perhaps, to be a Jane Fonda film). The study says the long-term effects of the release of carbon dioxide (sulfur and particulates are other problems) from fossil fuels might include temperature increases that would have incalculable, probably dreadful, effects on precipitation, photosynthesis, agriculture, sea levels and aquatic life. Call it "The CO_2 Syndrome."

April 16, 1979

Candor, Commerce and the Skeptical Child

I am staring, raptly, at a headline: "TV ADS ARE SAID TO BENEFIT CHILD BY DEVELOPING SKEPTICISM." An advertising executive says children "must learn the marketplace" and: "Even if a child is deceived by an ad at age 4, what harm is done? He is in the process of learning to make his own decisions."

When a kindergarten class, told not to squeeze a turtle, names it "Charmin," or half a class of third-graders, asked to spell "relief," write "R-o-l-a-i-d-s," alarmists cite the power of advertising. I merely admire the wittiness of American youth.

But the theory that being deceived improves children is alarming. The problem with routine public deceit is not just that children are indeed harmed, but that the culture is as well. The "skepticism" instilled is really cynicism that seeps like a stain across society.

Recently, an Army doctor claimed that his enlistment contract was void because the Army had used misleading advertising to recruit doctors. An Army lawyer responded that the advertisement's promises of modern equipment and other benefits were acceptable "puffery," just "a commercial thing," and "simply bragging on the part of the government." Casualness about deceit in commerce leads to casually deceitful government.

There will always be dumb demands for advertising "reforms." Recently, militant homosexuals demanded that advertising be less heterosexual: "We would like to see two women or two men discussing a product at the breakfast table. There could be some affection shown, such as one saying, 'Honey, pass the Aunt Jemima pancakes.'"

But advertisers should forestall dumb regulations by combating deceit rather than rationalizing acceptance of it. So it is important, if only symbolically, that advertisers are no longer permitted to use actors dressed as doctors for medicine commercials. Actors must refrain from looking "too pained," before taking an over-the-counter medicine, lest the commercial exaggerate the relief the product delivers. No longer is whipped cream used in shaving-cream commercials. No longer are marbles put in soup bowls to suggest that the soup is crammed with vegetables. It matters, if only as a gesture, that the FTC wants celebrities to make "reasonable inquiries" into the claims they make for products. (By the way, the first celebrity brought to heel was—I'm not making this up—Pat Boone, in connection with his inordinate praise of an acne medicine.)

Language offers ample opportunities for shading the truth. In *Murder Must Advertise*, published in 1933, Dorothy Sayers' detective, Lord Peter Wimsey, says:

Of course there is some truth in advertising. There's yeast in bread, but you can't make bread with yeast alone. [Consider] the delicate and important distinction between the words "with" and "from." Suppose you are advertising . . . perry. If you say, "Our perry is made from fresh-plucked pears only," then it's got to be made from pears only, or the statement is actionable. If you just say it is made "from pears," without the "only," the betting is that it is made chiefly from pears. But if you say, "made with pears," you generally mean that you use a peck of pears to a ton of turnips, and the law cannot touch you. Such are the niceties of our English tongue."

Michael Pertschuk, chairman of the Federal Trade Commission, sometimes seems to think that the FTC should see that no advertising is "withholding essential information from consumers." But the FTC would have to define "essential" information regarding every product, and so determine the content of all advertising. Besides, informing and enticing often are two different processes, and both are legitimate uses of advertising.

Let the record show that *American Banker* magazine recently carried an advertisement of ruthless candor. Someone was trying to sell a bank in Mount Prospect, Illinois:

> We have a very small bank for sale. The total purchase price: $232,500 for 100 percent. The population of the town is negligible and the building is very old. . . . . But for a banker willing to move to town and run this bank on a day-to-day basis it is an excellent first bank. . . . The price to pay is the willingness and ability to move to a dreary little town.

Except for the patent (and hence harmless) falsehood about an Illinois town's being dreary, that is a sterling example of candor in commerce.

January 28, 1979

Doctors, Lawyers and the Politics of Resentment

Oil companies, doctors and lawyers all are grist for President Carter's mill. For parlor populists, it is always open season on oil companies. But Carter's attacks on the medical and legal professions indicate an unusual flair for discerning and exploiting resentments.

Unlike other groups (bankers, Wall Street, munitions makers) that have been tempting targets for politicians, doctors and lawyers are resented less for what they are than for what they do. What Carter is fanning is less class-resentment than function-resentment.

Doctors and lawyers are symbols and custodians of vexing complexities of modern life. They create in people a sense of dependency. Although people often are deferential toward elites that are presumed to possess special wisdom, doctors and lawyers are elites less because of their wisdom than because of their mastery of particular techniques.

Seventy years ago, when a visit to a doctor was still as likely to do harm as to do good, doctors nevertheless were respected for the wisdom they had acquired during long practice, and for their bedside manner. And even today the image of the ideal doctor is television's Dr. Welby, who dispensed more homilies than medicine. But the increase in group practice, and the technological intensity of modern medicine, mean that to be in a doctor's "care" is often to feel oneself to be under an impersonal power.

Doctors and lawyers are two groups with which contact is apt to be involuntary and unpleasant. They are people to whom a person is most apt to turn when having difficulties, so they seem to profit from misfortune.

Furthermore, doctors and lawyers are more vulnerable than, say, corporate executives to the charge of crassness. All groups have their share of public-spirited people. But doctors and lawyers have well-elaborated standards of professional education and ethics that commit them to the pursuit of ends (health and justice) larger than personal gain.

That is, doctors and lawyers are elites defined not just by what they are capable of doing, but also by what is impermissible for them to do and be. They are elites defined by technical proficiencies, but they are supposed to have moral virtues commensurate with the nobility of the ends that those proficiencies serve.

Law has the trappings of a science (complexities expressed in a specialized vocabulary) and the subjectivity of an art. Hence it has an aura of limitlessness, of acknowledging no restrictions on its competence. It is no coincidence that the most "limitless" form of health care, psychiatry, is the form most distrusted.

Lawyers are even more vulnerable to resentments than doctors are. However complicated medicine becomes, its ends are clear: the cure or amelioration of illness. But lawyering often seems to offend against the most basic American value—productivity—because much lawyering seems like make-work.

Sinclair Lewis described Babbitt as someone who "made nothing in particular, neither butter nor shoes nor poetry, but was nimble in the calling of selling houses for more than people could afford to pay." Americans know that America was built by people who made steel and electricity and new strains of wheat, and although a minority of Americans today are horny-handed sons of toil, they are ready to regard lawyers as people who are nimble and nothing more. This is in part because Americans believe that the law is less and less the codification of custom and common sense, and more and more the creation of functions for a technical guild.

Carter invites people to be indignant because "90 percent of our lawyers serve 10 percent of our people." It is unclear (not least to Carter) what Carter means. Does he think a lawyer serving AT&T or GM is serving one client, or a vast number of stockholders? Surely he does not think that any 10 percent of the population has to consume 10 percent of the lawyering. The criminal class must use more than its "share." So must the business community as it struggles to cope with the kind of government that Carter favors.

Carter has a penchant for attitudinizing, and he is essentially an opposition figure who last was effective when campaigning against an incumbent President. As his frustrations increase, Carter may lengthen his list of groups to attack. Perhaps utilities and insurance companies will be next. They are large, indispensable, and charge for their services, three sins a populist can have a jolly time denouncing.

May 11, 1978

The Testy West

Somebody's comin', Pa.
Well, let 'em come.

So spoke the wide-eyed boy and his pa, the sodbuster, in the opening frames of *Shane*. That movie, made in the shadow of the Grand Tetons, is chock-full of the beautiful clichés of the Western and the beauty of the Mountain West. Today, folks out there think somebody's comin', and they are becoming testy.

They think the rest of the nation has designs on their land, minerals, oil, coal, timber and water. But there is a problem with the pronoun "their." Whose resources are those, really? And just who does the Mountain West think it is, anyway, trying to take life on its own terms, long after other regions have come to terms with the homogenizing forces and economic imperatives of modern America?

The Mountain West's sense of being surrounded and set upon was acute even before the nation began casting covetous glances at the region's energy resources. And by now it has replaced the

Deep South as the region with the strongest senses of distinctiveness and grievance.

In 1879, the area between California and the first tier of states west of the Mississippi—a third of the country—had just half a dozen towns with more than five thousand people. In 1979, it is still the most unformed region. Fly over the Middle West and Plains States and you see geometric orderliness imposed by the hand of man. Then come the mountains, and Nature again is boss. It is no reflection on people there to say that humanity is more marginal in the Mountain West than elsewhere. Even the cities, Denver and Salt Lake, are diminished by the nearness of the mountains.

The Mountain West is the region most nearly invisible to the rest of the nation. No Faulkner or Sinclair Lewis has done for it what they did for—or, if you prefer, did to—the South and the Middle West. It has not yet produced a President. (It did contribute Senator Key Pittman to the gaiety of nations. At the 1933 monetary conference in London, the Nevada Democrat scampered down the corridors of Claridge's, stark naked and brandishing a Bowie knife, in pursuit of an economist whose views about silver did not square with Pittman's.) To most people, the Mountain West still seems like a place between more substantial places. Yet no other region feels such certitude that it is God's own country within God's own country.

There is something quaint about the Westerner's insistence that he built the place all by his lonesome, with no help from God or the socialistic East. In fact, the West came nicely endowed with empty space and lots of grass. There were steers grazing all over that space before there was much law about such niceties as who owned the land and water on which everything depended.

The West cherishes a myth about life before the law got there, when the West was in a state of nature. Never mind that it was nature red in tooth and claw; never mind that around unfenced range and disputed water, life often was nasty, brutish and short. The myth is that men were brave, women were fair and life was sweet before the tea-sipping, paper-pushing dudes from Washington started butting in. Then came regulations about not being beastly to coyotes, and about everything from grazing to clear-cutting.

At the risk of being deemed a governmentsymp (one soft on government), I must note that even before meat-import quotas, the West had its uses for Washington. The West is the only region that feels entitled to, and often has custody of, a Cabinet department. The Interior Department was founded in 1849, and its first job was to administer President Polk's acquisitions, which included much of the West. Acquiring the West was not private enterprise, it was Army enterprise. Before the Union Pacific could reach Promontory, Utah, government in the form of the U.S. Cavalry had to persuade the Indians that iron horses and white people were the wave of the future. Government dispensed rights-of-way to railroads and homesteads to settlers. The productivity of the modern West depends on water, which means government reclamation projects. In short, Westerners have never been bashful about wringing benefits from Washington.

Today, almost everyone is bullish about the economic future of the Mountain West. But Westerners should pause to consider the cautionary tale of Nevada's Comstock Lode. Silver was discovered in 1859. Before it was gone in the 1880s, it made handsome profits, but primarily for businessmen elsewhere. Then (I am simplifying a bit), Nevada had to wait for the invention of air conditioning, which made possible an economy based on gambling and Wayne Newton. The moral of the story is that Westerners are right to keep a jaundiced eye on the boom that is bearing down on them.

Already the Mountain West is waist-deep in progress. Fertilized by energy money, skyscrapers are sprouting like dandelions in downtown Denver, soaring into the most polluted air between the coasts. The Mountain West has always attracted some singularly determined people, such as trappers and Mormons. Now it may attract all kinds of people, in job lots. The President's oil-shale program probably would quintuple the population of northwest Colorado. Sensible Westerners are of at least two minds about the transformation of their region. Some are flatly opposed; all want whatever comes to come on their own state's terms. It's their oil shale (and coal, minerals, timber, land, air, water), isn't it?

Well, no, actually it isn't. Much of that stuff is controlled by the Federal Government, or by people or corporations that wouldn't know aspen from aspirin. And after two hundred years of erosion of property rights and states' rights, there is a stir-fried jumble of competing claims and responsibilities. The basic fact is that America is a continental market and there are national imperatives behind the decisions that will determine the future of the region and probably will make it more like everywhere else.

That's a pity. I am glad that postwar Europe, although a somewhat homogenized consumer society, still shows that people can look like one another without really liking one another. You can't have the old, enriching differences without some of the old prejudices. So if the Mountain West is testy these days, think of that as the enriching period it is.

Alas, if there is a Jeremiah Johnson (the romantically solitary mountain man played by Robert Redford) in the Mountain West now, he probably has a battery-operated Sony in his recreation vehicle, and when the sun sets over Rifle, Colorado, he is looking at what folks are looking at in the Bronx. If we really want to preserve regional identities (and even if we don't), we should make it a crime to broadcast *Three's Company* across state lines. But it is a bit late for that. The modern world is closing in on the Mountain West. As the boy said, "Somebody's comin', Pa."

September 17, 1979

No "Right" to Health

Human beings, unlike oysters, frequently reveal their emotions. And they are prolific at discovering new "rights." Today they speak often, and crossly, about their "right" to health. They are paying a lot for medicine and are not getting all that they think they are paying for, a guarantee of endless betterment. Their disappointment is rooted in mistaken inferences from a few spectacular medical achievements.

Twenty-five summers ago, many children were kept home from theaters that were packed with peers watching Randolph Scott cowboy movies. Many parents were afraid, and rightly so, of polio. The Salk vaccine made summers safer, but that achievement has given rise to unreasonable expectation based on the "polio paradigm." Many people assume that advances in public health have generally resulted from a conquest of a disease by a new technology. This is a misunderstanding of the social history of health.

When Shakespeare, Coke, Bacon and Drake were advancing drama and poetry, jurisprudence, experimental science, navigation and exploration, John Donne, who was doing as much for poetry and preaching, was being treated for fever by doctors who placed a dead pigeon at his feet to draw "vapours" from his brain. Until this century, medicine developed slowly, in a social setting in which infant mortality was high, life expectancy was low even for those who survived childhood, and diagnostic and therapeutic skills were few. The sudden development of sophisticated medicine has coincided, in fortunate societies, with sharp improvements in infant survival and life expectancy, and undreamed-of freedom from many diseases. As a result, medicine has been given undue credit for mankind's betterment.

Many people believe that society's level of health depends primarily on medical treatment of the sick. But the relationship between increased investment in medicine and improvements in health is tenuous. Behavior usually has more to do with how long and healthily people live than does the soaring investment in medical treatments to restore health, or to slow its decline. Leon Kass of the University of Chicago notes that other animals "instinctively eat the right foods (when available) and act in such a way as to maintain their naturally given state of health and vigor. Other animals do not overeat, undersleep, knowingly ingest toxic substances, or permit their bodies to fall into disuse through sloth, watching television and riding in automobiles, transacting business or writing articles about health." For humans, health must be nurtured by "taming and moderating the admirable yet dangerous human desire to live better than sows and squirrels." So in one way, it makes little more sense to claim a right to health than to claim a right to wisdom or courage.

As Kass says, in an age that has cracked the genetic code, built kidney machines and performed organ transplants, the idea that prudence is the path to health seems banal. But there is much to be learned about the sociology of health, such as why some subgroups of the population are especially healthy. "If the incidence of each kind of cancer could be reduced to the level at which it occurs in the population in which its incidence is lowest, there would be 90 percent less cancer. Recent studies show that cancers of all sorts— not only cancers clearly correlated with smoking and drinking— occur less frequently among the clean-living Mormons and Seventh-day Adventists."

Recent history illustrates the secondary importance of clinical medicine in improving public health. Eric Cassell of Cornell Medical College notes that in 1900 the death rate from tuberculosis was 200 per 100,000, and the rate declined to 20 per 100,000 by the 1950s, when the first effective anti-TB drugs became available. The decline was due primarily to better nutrition and less crowding. Typhoid became rare before effective drugs were available, thanks to chlorination of water and better sanitation and personal hygiene.

The decline of infant mortality occurred because of reduction of the diarrhea-pneumonia complex. This too was a result of social changes, not of preventive or therapeutic medications. Modern food packaging and distribution has done more than medicine against food-borne diseases. The swift decline of a soup company after reports of botulism demonstrated how much the mass media can do for public health. In the last five years, the death rate in the United States has undergone the sharpest decline since the advent of penicillin, primarily because of a reduction in heart diseases, owing to individual efforts at health maintenance.

A British writer, Robin Bates, contends that streptomycin may have accounted for only 3 percent of the reduction in tuberculosis deaths, and that medicine always concentrates on such a "3 percent solution." That is an understandable concentration for clinical medicine, but it is an unwise concentration for public policy, given the evidence that medical intervention has not been primarily responsible for the most substantial improvements in public health. But in an age when people are inventive and clamorous about "rights" and deny duties, they do not want to be told that health is primarily their duty, not medicine's or the government's responsibility.

Such an age is ripe for socialized medicine, which broadens access to what Kass calls "hospital-centered, highly technological, disease-oriented, therapy-centered medical care." Recently a Carter Administration spokesman, advocating national health insurance, declared: "The highest priority must be to guarantee to all the American people a quality of health care and a standard of health that our worldwide lead in medicine currently guarantees only to an affluent minority . . ." Confused thinking promotes dubious policy: health is the product of medicine, so by controlling the distribution of medicine, government can "guarantee" a "standard of health" commensurate with the sophistication of medical technology.

But national health insurance might do harm by reinforcing public acceptance of the "no-fault principle" that discounts personal responsibility for health. A better way to begin improving health insurance might be to institutionalize inducements to prudence. Payments for treatment of particular diseases could be reduced when patients discontinue behavior causatively linked to the diseases.

Human beings, unlike oysters, are organisms that make choices. Today, much illness is willful, in the sense that it results from foolish living habits of people who have a duty to know better. And today, insurance plans spread the burden of paying for illness: the prudent and dutiful are paying heavily for the irresponsible. That is a wrong which should preoccupy people who are eager to establish "rights" where health is concerned.

August 7, 1978

Unpadding the "Padded Society"

The "science" of economics increasingly resembles a branch of psychology, nervously invoking such concepts as "confidence" and "spirit." Keynes considered society's "animal spirits" a crucial variable, and in this regard, at least, President Reagan is a Keynesian. He speaks of America's "spirit" being "ready to blaze into life" if we "stimulate our economy." But MIT's Emma Rothschild, who is descended from some spirited capitalists, asks: can the capitalist spirit blaze, now that America's employment structure has shifted further than any other large industrial nation's from manufacturing and toward labor-intensive, low-productivity services and trade sectors?

Reagan's promise to "put America to work" came at the end of a decade in which Americans went to work in record numbers. Even in the "stagflation" years, 1973–1979, while total employment held steady in France and Britain and declined in West Germany, the U.S. private sector created almost eleven million new jobs. As Rothschild says, it is as though Canada's entire labor force moved south and found employment. Actually, the most important factor was that women, driven by economic necessity, moved out of the home, creating a supply of labor with a low level of experience, and hence low productivity. More than 70 percent of the new jobs were in services and retail trade. By 1979, 43 percent of all Americans in nonagricultural jobs were in those two fields.

Rothschild says that the *increase* in employment in eating and drinking places since 1973 is greater than *total* employment in the auto and steel industries *combined*. Three service industries—eating and drinking places, health, and business services (mailing, janitorial, and the like)—each produced more than one million new jobs in the 1973–1979 period and now have a larger combined employment than "total employment in an entire range of basic productive industries: construction, all machinery, all electric and electronic equipment, motor vehicles, aircraft, shipbuilding, all chemicals and products, and all scientific and other instruments."

Last week Reagan referred to America as "this once great industrial giant." Two days earlier General Motors, the dominant corporation in America's emblematic industry, had announced that in 1980, for the first time since 1921, it had lost money. Chrysler probably now has more debts than assets: a negative net worth. Reagan also referred to the second symbol of American industralism: steel. But golden arches, not blast furnaces, are becoming the symbols of American enterprise. Today McDonald's has more employees than U.S. Steel. Our "once great industrial giant" used to make big locomotives, big Buicks. Now it makes Big Macs.

And litigation.

Here are the percentage increases in practicing engineers and lawyers: 1940s, engineers 83, lawyers 0; 1950s, engineers 59, lawyers 19; 1960s, engineers 40, lawyers 25; 1970s engineers 15, lawyers 83.

Furthermore, America has become, for the majority, what Felix Rohatyn calls a "padded society"—padded with cost-of-living allowances, automatic wage increases regardless of productivity, stock options and other benefits for executives regardless of performance, constantly increasing unemployment compensation and pensions. Padding? In the 1920–21 slump, the factory-wage level fell about 2 percent. In the 1980 recession, it rose 11 percent. The biggest padding is the biggest middle- and high-income subsidy: the deductibility of mortgage-interest payments.

That makes many Americans winners from inflation, and contributes to large capital gains for homeowners. Also, it diverts excessive credit resources. More savings are expended on mortgages than on any other use, to the detriment of capital formation and job creation in basic industries. The nation will really be serious about fighting inflation and about reindustrializing when such interest deductibility is at least limited. But don't hold your breath.

As Robert Samuelson of *The National Journal* says, "the essence of the orthodoxy inherited from the Depression" is that government must temper the rigors of the free market. Thus the proliferation of groups demanding "protection from normal economic change and chance." But today the question is: what do Americans consider "normal" change and chance?

Risk, an indispensable facet of capitalism, has been plentiful for smaller businesses. One study estimates that a firm in business in the mid-1960s had a more-than-50-percent chance of being out of business by the mid-1970s. But the government keeps coming to the aid of large economic entities: Lockheed, Penn Central, Franklin National, New York City, Chrysler. Even when those two Texas cutups, the Hunt boys (who do not have a large constituency), got into hot water, federal authorities encouraged banks to aid the boys' creditors. As Alfred Malabre says, "After so many years of governmental flinching," one task for inflation fighters is "the introduction of a believable element of risk into the economic environment."

There is going to be abundant risk in the political environment. Capitalists believe in the division of labor, and Reagan reportedly has told his aides, "You worry about the fiscal side and I'll worry about the political side." His aides should worry, because the budget is a President's only substantial instrument for influencing the economy, but there is not substantial certainty about how the budget can be used to do that. Reagan's "political side" involves asking Congress to pull a bit of padding from the "padded society," which means in large measure from the middle class.

Government generally is a servant of the strong. In this middle-class nation, middle-class representatives generally legislate comforts for the comfortable, for those persons educated, leisured, organized, articulate and confident enough to master the art of complaining. The middle class is the padded class. So in the long, hot summer of 1981, as Washington simmers in humidity and Congress shivers in fear, we may see confirmation of Rohatyn's rule: this country cannot muster a majority for anything but complaint.

February 16, 1981

Heroes Are Heroes, Valets Are Valets

"Did anybody ever see Washington nude?" asked Nathaniel Hawthorne. "It is inconceivable . . . he was born with his clothes on, and his hair powdered, and made a stately bow on his first appearance in the world." To understand what has happened to heroism in our time, it helps to begin at the beginning, with America's first hero, and with what aroused Hawthorne's irony, the apotheosis of George Washington by biographers like Parson Weems. Published in 1800, Weems's biography was, shall we say, approving:

> "George," said his father, "do you know who killed that beautiful little cherry tree yonder in the garden?" This was a tough question; and George staggered under it for a moment; but quickly recovered himself: and looking at his father, with the sweet face of youth brightened with the inexpressible charm of all conquering truth, he bravely cried out, "I can't tell a lie, Pa; you know I can't tell a lie. I did cut it with my hatchet." "Run to my arms, you dearest boy," cried his father in transports, "run to my arms; glad am I, George, that you killed my tree; for you have paid me for it a thousand fold. Such an act of heroism in my son is more worth than a thousand trees, though blossomed with silver and their fruits of purest gold."

Weems could tell a lie. Well, not a lie, exactly. His was, the subtitle said, a biography "enriched with a number of very curious anecdotes, perfectly in character." It sold like hot cakes through eighty editions.

An age reveals its values in its choice of heroes. In the nineteenth century, the Republic thought of itself as a frail bark on uncharted oceans, a daring experiment in self-government that could be ruined by insufficient self-control. James Russell Lowell celebrated Washington as a paragon of the "balanced soul":

How grand this quiet is, how nobly stern
the discipline that wrought through
*   lifelong throes*
that energetic passion of repose.

By the time Teddy Roosevelt exploded across the landscape, Americans had had enough quiet and repose, thank you. They were full of beans and bravado, and ready for a splendid little war and other enjoyments of animal vigor. T.R. was an incarnation of the nation's bumptiousness. As a young man he was described as muscular Christianity without Christianity, and he got livelier as he got older.

T.R.'s cousin became President and then became a hero, first as "Mr. Fix-It," then as "Mr. Win-the-War." Ike became a hero, and then became a distinctly, even studiously unheroic President. But fashions in heroes change and are, like all fashions, fleeting. The deviousness of Nixon helped to turn "plain-speaking" Truman into a folk hero. When the first serious biography of Lyndon Johnson appears, I hope and expect he will become, at least briefly, a bit of a hero: the man who was right about Hanoi before the boat people proved his point; the man who was more right than anyone since Lincoln on the permanent American problem, race; the Washington politician who enjoyed Washington politics.

Meanwhile, where have all the heroes gone? Historians long ago discovered the common people, who make shoes and steel and soldiers and history. Biographies of great men no longer seem to be the heart of history. And one reason that even many heroes of the past no longer seem quite so heroic is that the art of biography has changed for the better.

Like a lot of other biographers back then, Weems was more interested in improving than in accurately informing his readers. Well into the nineteenth century, many biographies were written primarily to edify, to explain the awful lessons of a bad life or the uplifting lessons of a good one. The "very curious anecdotes, perfectly in character" that Weems fabricated about Washington were designed to be (in another phrase from Weems's rambling subtitle) "exemplary to his young countrymen." But modern standards of scholarship, and the sophistication of the reading public, have made biography a generally austere art.

Writing a biography of a political person is a political act; it shapes the appraisal of the past, and the perception of possibility. One task of the biographer of political people is to show that they were more complicated than they contrived to appear. As George Orwell said, every life, viewed from within, is a series of defeats. A conscientious biographer tries to get "within" the life that is his subject. The result is apt to be a rounded portrait of the person's ambiguities, doubts and defects. This does not mean that the person does not deserve to be thought of as heroic. It does mean that those people who want to have heroes must outgrow the desire for cartoon characters, or monumental bronze statues.

Some say that people should outgrow desire for, or belief in, heroes. They say that only an unhappy nation needs heroes. But only an unusually fortunate nation can do without them. No democracy, least of all a diverse, continental democracy, should want to do without those rare figures who capture and condense in their personalities a moment, a movement, an idea.

The idea of heroes does make democracies uneasy. Democracies want to disperse credit for achievement. They want to believe that virtue and vision well up spontaneously from the common people. So democracies are ambivalent even about the idea of leadership. Today, Americans are clamoring for leadership, but thirty-three months ago they chose a President who ran an anti-heroic campaign (golly, he carried his own garment bag) against Gerald Ford, who established his anti-heroic credentials by calling in the television cameras so he could assure the country that he buttered his own English muffins. Carter's theme was that the leader's task is just to get government to mirror the marvelousness of the citizenry ("A government as good as the people"). That was before he discovered that the people lead wasteful, self-indulgent, purposeless, meaningless lives.

Like modern historiography, biography and democratic theory, modern journalism makes it harder for people to have heroes.

People are given disenthralling glimpses of political mechanics and theater, of the dealing and contrived drama that are facets of democracy. Still, even unenthralled democracies can and should have heroes. Democracy has its own homey but demanding heroism. For example, study L.B.J.'s achievement of the 1964 Civil Rights Act.

One of the least attractive aspects of the present is the absence of affection and respect for the people who struggled with the problems of the recent past. There is something awfully small about someone who cannot admit that anyone else is exceptionally large. As has been said, if no man is a hero to his valet, that is not because no men are heroes, but because all valets are valets.

August 6, 1979

Sexism in the Car Pool: DOT Rides to the Rescue

In the beginning, before God created heaven and earth, He probably created the press release. That is the natural order of things. So before the Department of Transportation's conference on Women's Travel Issues, a press release there was. It announced, inauspiciously, that the questions to be discussed would include "Do men and women react differently to riding in autos, airplanes, buses and trains?" Perhaps this question was addressed in the paper titled "Gender Differences in Reaction to Vehicle Environments." In his opening remarks, a DOT official made the obligatory observation that "transportation has long been a male-dominated field," and he mentioned various "inequities," such as the fact that "in car pools women tend overwhelmingly to be passengers rather than drivers."

Academics are inclined to begin, relentlessly, at the beginning.

"The paper," commented one academic participant in the conference about someone else's paper, "conceives the world as composed of individuals and groups who distribute choices over available alternatives . . ." Research has revealed that men are "more positively disposed toward freeways than women." (Well, you know what was meant.) Research has revealed that full-time workers may be tired and hence reluctant to walk "when faster modes are available," and "have less positive feelings about the walk mode than part-time workers/students."

Some participants had a quite exquisite regard for "gender" sensitivities. Several researchers reported that they encountered difficulties in "eliciting personal feelings and desires from male participants" in a survey, but that "this problem may disappear as men redefine their role and move away from stereotypes." The same researchers suggested that, "due to socialized perceptions of themselves as weaker and more vulnerable to attack than males, females would perceive all modes of transportation to be less safe than would males." That forced, touchy reference to "socialized perceptions" revealed an almost heroic determination to deny sexual differences.

"Another role which the focus-group interviews indicate may influence transportation decision-making is whether or not the individual has the role of spouse or roommate. Specifically, the interdependency inherent in living with another person is likely to impact transportation decisions." There was a dreadful clanging and clanking and grinding as jargon lumbered toward the expression of a "possibility." It is, reported a researcher, "quite possible that the space-time constraints of a suburban middle-class housewife with children under 5 and no car are such that for many hours of the day she has only one or no acceptable alternative within any choice set for travel . . ."

The more lumpish the vocabulary and syntax, the more portentous the conclusion can seem, at least until the verbal dust settles, revealing a banality. What most social scientists do constitutes a triumph of form over substance. The elaboration of "models" and algebraic formulas is less to demonstrate something that could not otherwise be demonstrated than it is to prove that models or algebraic formulas can express what can be expressed better in common language.

There are, of course, interesting things to be known about almost everything, and there are things the government needs to know about women's changing needs for transportation. Women compose a growing portion of the labor force, and especially of the part-time force. Because women fill a disproportionate share of low-paying jobs, they are less likely to be able to own (or park) an automobile. It is reasonable for DOT to wonder whether transportation policy is taking sufficient account of women's needs. But worse even than the empty pretentiousness of much research that government solicits is the government's own rhetoric.

The DOT official who opened the conference needed no research to tell him this: "In the end the issue is equality—equality of opportunities, of choices, and of rewards." Actually, DOT's proper concern is transportation, not social transformation. Each government department likes to believe that its specialty is a lever than can move the world, and perhaps bureaucrats need, periodically, to pretend that they are at the barricades of a revolution. But government is mostly talk, and confused talk makes for confused government.

A government department that proclaims in noisy self-reproach that a field of policy has been "male-dominated" is a department ready, even eager, to believe the worst about itself. It is open to the accusation that as regards the "impact" of any program, a disparity between the sexes constitutes an "inequity." Indeed, one paper at the conference pointedly asked if the transportation-planning process has "neutral underlying assumptions." And it asked, "are analytic techniques neutral?"

But it is unclear what "neutrality" can mean in such contexts. Transportation resources, like everything else, are finite, so transportation policy must prefer some uses to others. Frequently, resources have been invested in expanding transportation capacity in congested areas, with the primary purpose of facilitating travel to and from work. Most of those trips are taken by men. Is this inequality an "inequity"?

Any social policy affects various groups in unequal ways. Citing evidence that more men than women use automobiles as opposed to public transit to get to work, two researchers said "it is not coincidental" that transportation policy has emphasized reducing automobile congestion. All right, it is not a "coincidence." Neither is it, necessarily, an inequity against women.

To govern is to choose, and government has chosen, for political and economic reasons, to devote substantial resources to expediting automobile traffic to and from work places.

But transportation policy did not cause men to compose a substantial majority of the commuting work force. Transportation policy can do little about the composition of that work force, and there is no mandate from Congress or heaven for DOT to try. The idea of a transportation policy, or any other policy, that "impacts" all subgroups of the population equally is unintelligible

The staring fact is this: if the disparate "impacts" of a policy upon men and women are considered "inequities," and if every government department feels entitled or obligated to shape policies to redress whatever "inequities" it discerns, then government is becoming frantic. After the DOT official proclaimed that "the issue is equality—equality of opportunities, of choices, and of rewards," after he was back beneath the cold fluorescent lights at DOT he must have remembered that his job concerns the movement of people and goods, not of the social order.

October 16, 1978

Part Six ᠈ᡃ

LIVES, PRIVATE AND
PUBLIC

Lech Walesa: Seizing History by the Lapels

The man of the year bears a disconcerting resemblance to a clerk in a health-food store. With his droopy mustache and hint of impishness, Lech Walesa, Poland's world-shaking pixie, calls to mind a description of E. M. Forster, the novelist: "He looked like a whim." Walesa is a political Bing Crosby, as natural as a yawn. But his task is to be the Enrico Fermi of twentieth-century politics. Fermi conducted the first controlled nuclear reaction. Walesa is struggling to control the release of the crackling energy of the Polish people.

This century's two most dreadful inventions are nuclear weapons and totalitarianism. In the physics and politics of these, a crucial concept is "critical mass." It can be the key to huge explosions. The cardinal tenet of totalitarianism is that the masses must not be allowed to mass. Totalitarianism is a mortar and pestle, grinding society to dust, atomizing individuals and assembling them only into compounds controlled by the state. But somehow the strength of the Poles has survived the grinding and has generated social cohesion sufficient to threaten the regime.

This century's art, literature and morals reflect pervasive anxiety about impermanence: everything from empires to atoms has been shattered. Yet amidst all the disorienting flux, totalitarianism has suggested the possibility of awful permanence. Armed with modern communications and other technologies of social control, totalitarians have tried to immunize themselves against internal change that would challenge the state's total sovereignty over society. Thus only someone dead to the central drama of the century

249

can fail to see that Poland is in the throes of the most important struggle of the postwar era. Watching the Iranian revolution on TV gave a sense of what viewers would have seen had there been cameras at the Bastille in 1789. But no similar comparison comes to mind regarding pictures from Poland. There's no precedent for this internal challenge to totalitarianism.

Like the Roman Empire, Russia shows signs of crumbling at the periphery. As Oxford historian Leszek Kolakowski says, the signs refute a rationalization of appeasement, the idea that all change in Russia's empire must be directed from Moscow. Communism is crumbling in Poland because protest is aimed not at the periphery but at the heart of the fraud. Communism, like feudalism, assumes "a place for everyone, and everyone in his place." The party's monopoly of power is rationalized because the Party is the "vanguard of the proletariat," and the workers are the progressive force in history. But Poland's opposition springs from the workers, so by just existing it puts an ax to the roots of the regime's claim to legitimacy.

This is the second straight year in which a Pole has been the great newsmaker by shaking Eastern Europe. In 1979 the Pope's nine-day homecoming demonstrated the futility of the Communists' thirty-five-year struggle for legitimacy, not only in Poland, but from the Baltic to the Adriatic.

Poland has constantly been pulled between Russia and the Europe to the west. At times it has been pulled asunder: between 1795 and 1918, Poland was partitioned among Austria, Prussia and Russia. History has taught Poles to draw a sharp distinction between the real nation and the state, between the nation and whatever regime is imposing itself at a particular moment. Communism, the doctrine of permanent revolution, has encountered in Poland a nation of permanent opposition. In Walesa, Poland has found a leader worthy of Lippmann's description of great leaders like De Gaulle: it is as though their countries were inside them, not just that they are operating within their countries.

The last two hundred years have been strewn with promising moments, and promise lost: the French Revolution gone rancid;

Lincoln's healing spirit snuffed out when most needed; the Romanovs replaced not by reformers but by Bolsheviks; the dreams of Versailles and Weimar dissolved into the nightmare rise of the dictators. And Eastern Europe "delivered" from Hitler by Hitler's accomplice in launching the war.

Perhaps in each case the promise was a chimera. Perhaps France was incapable of making a moderate revolution; perhaps not even Lincoln's magnanimity could have contained the passions aroused by fratricide; perhaps only dictatorship could have grown in Russia's social soil in 1917; perhaps after Europe gnawed on itself between 1914 and 1918, virulent political infections were inevitable. And perhaps it was inevitable that Eastern Europe pass from Hitler's shadow to Russia's.

Mankind has been so schooled in skepticism about "promising moments" that we assume Poland is poised on the edge of tragedy. The logic of totalitarianism reinforces the Russian mentality and produces a powerful impulse to invade and suppress. When the United States was young, George Bancroft, the historian, said, "the wrecks of the past were America's warnings." Poland's warnings were in Eastern Europe's wrecks, Hungary in 1956 and Czechoslovakia in 1968. But Russia too has had a warning: the sight of Poland's workers "on their knees before God and on their feet before tyrants." Walesa, according to an ally, is working to increase freedom "up to the limits set by Soviet tanks." But no one knows those limits. The tank commanders in the Kremlin today know fear: in the long run, their tanks may be as impotent against Poland's "critical mass" as they would be against Fermi's.

It is said that *fin-de-siecle* Vienna, the city of Freud and Wittgenstein, of new ideas and new wrappings for an old one (anti-Semitism), was "the little world in which the big world has its rehearsals." Perhaps Lech Walesa's Poland is that today. Whatever the outcome, he has given the world an unforgettable moment. Actors come and go on the world's stage; they play their parts and depart. Usually (in the words of Dwight Eisenhower), "things are more the way they were than they have ever been before." But things will never be the same in Eastern Europe, or wherever bravery echoes, now that Lech Walesa, incarnating an indomitable nation, has vindicated faith in the ability of individuals to seize history by the lapels and shake it.

December 8, 1980

John Wayne: Doing Himself

For those of us who became sentient, more or less, in the late 1940s or early 1950s, the flavor of our awakening was the flavor of Jujy-fruits. This candy, sold at the movie theaters where we spent Saturday afternoons, had (and for all I know still has) the texture of asphalt and the taste of dime-store perfume. It was a fine condiment for the Westerns we paid nine cents to see.

Even those who hated Jujyfruits ate them, just as people who dislike champagne drink it at weddings. Central Illinois nine-year-olds had a noble sense of ceremony, and Jujyfruits were part of Saturday afternoon. When we swaggered, blinking, into the sunlight, mounted balloon-tire Schwinns and rode off, we were experiencing (or so we are now assured, by very assured people) the joys of "male bonding."

The art of the Western movie has fallen upon hard times, and so has the Western world—a correlation that may be a coincidence, although I doubt it. Yet the decline of Westerns did not harm the career of John Wayne, the last cowboy.

At those hearings where congressmen pretended it was an open question whether they would vote Wayne a medal, folks testified that Wayne "symbolized" this or that, usually America. But a symbol takes its significance from its relation to something else. Wayne's significance was that he was Wayne, whether playing the lean Ringo Kid when he was lean and young, or old Rooster Cogburn when no longer young.

After about 1950, people paid the price of admission to see that walk, the heavy heaving of a barge on a rolling ocean swell. Or to hear that voice, an instrument designed by God for the purpose of saying, "I wouldn't reach for that six-shooter if I were you, pilgrim."

Wayne is not the only star who wound up playing his own persona. In *Anatomy of a Murder*, Jimmy Stewart plays Jimmy Stewart playing a small-town lawyer. And Stewart has raised self-caricature to an art in his Firestone Tire commercials.

Stewart's voice is like a Holiday Inn sign, or golden arches, or any other famous trademark. It is something by which fast-moving people in a fast-changing, continental nation get their bearings. Whether you think the thing to which the trademark is attached is good, bad or indifferent, at least it is a bit of America that is holding still. It promises the same experience you had a few days ago, or a few thousand miles ago.

McDonald's current slogan is "Nobody can do it like McDonald's can." The pronoun "it" means "be McDonald's." Coca-Cola says, "It's the real thing." That is, Coca-Cola is Coca-Cola. And say what you will, Jujyfruits are the real thing, the best Jujyfruits money can buy.

Nightclub impressionists "do" John Wayne, trying to counterfeit the real thing. They do not "do" Robert De Niro. As an actor, De Niro is a rich sundae of possibilities. But his persona is just vanilla ice cream. He can be a fine actor because his persona does not overpower his roles.

In the end, no one cared a fig what role John Wayne filled. Most Wayne movies were shot somewhere gorgeous, like Monument Valley, Utah, and most of the movies called to mind Alexander Woollcott's review of a play: "The scenery in the play was beautiful, but the actors got in front of it." Wayne did not spoil the view; he was part of it, a great slab of scenery, like some of those rock formations in Monument Valley, and sometimes about as expressive and predictable.

When Joan Didion, the writer, first met Wayne she was startled to realize that his face was, in a sense, more familiar to her than her husband's face. The fame conferred by movies and television often is odd. First, and briefly, a person may be famous for doing something—for flying in space, or anchoring the evening newscast, or whatever. But soon he or she may be famous for being: for being famous.

Think about it: What does Walter Cronkite do? Yes, of course, he does the news nicely. But primarily he "does" Walter Cronkite: the punctuating eyebrows, the inflections of a very papal Pope, the slightly lurching cadence of an engine with a cold carburetor. He does it brilliantly: it's the real thing.

John Wayne was an unmistakably nice man who, like many nice men, knew exactly what he was and liked it a lot. And he did the best John Wayne anyone ever saw.

June 17, 1979

Father Herbert A. Ward: Saving One Child at a Time

I am aware of, and share, the conviction of many readers that their daily diet of news is unnecessarily dismal because good works are not frequently enough considered newsworthy. That is why I came here to a stony bluff on the Mojave Desert, just over the horizon from the glare of Las Vegas, to Saint Jude's Ranch for Children. It is a home—often the first real home—for abused children.

The sufferings that bring children here are—I was about to say—indescribable. Actually, they can be described easily, as case histories do, in a flat narrative, whose very tonelessness somehow magnifies the horror.

I won't describe them because newspapers are wrenching enough these days, and because I feel—I'm not sure why, but I'm sure I'm right—that to retell these children's stories is somehow to compound their hurts by violating their privacy. Suffice it to say that one of the invaluable volunteers assisting Saint Jude's is Dr. Joseph Ferreria, a plastic surgeon from California who helps repair physical damage that has been done to the children. An even bigger challenge is repairing the psychological damage done to children like the one who said, "I'm lucky, Father, 'cause my little brother was smeared all over the kitchen wall and he's dead now."

Father Herbert A. Ward is a gray-haired, but otherwise young-looking, 42-year-old Episcopal priest. A fifth-generation Mississippian, he left a splendid job as a parish priest and headmaster of a fine school in New Orleans to come here to manage a struggling little institution named for the patron saint of lost causes. Here, he and a few aides shepherd the children—the youngest is 6—through adolescence and into the world.

When physical injuries have healed, there often remain broken spirits in children who cringe beneath the gentlest touch. An abused child is apt to have a horrid self-image and no self-confidence. Children are all too ready to feel guilt, and often are oppressed by a vague sense that they must somehow have deserved what befell them.

During the most formative years of these children's lives they have been told, verbally and violently, that they are worthless. Father Ward and his three nuns (salary: $10 a month) tell them otherwise.

Undoing what sick or evil adults have done is urgent, not only so that the children may blossom, but also for the sake of the children's children. Child abuse can be a communicable disease: a battered child is particularly susceptible to becoming a battering parent.

For four years Father Ward was, from his own modest salary, the largest donor to Saint Jude's. The ranch still operates on a thin and frayed shoestring, and might not operate at all if Las Vegas stars did not help every year with a big fund-raising bash. The operating budget this year ($265,000) is much less than a big casino rakes in on a weekend.

There are 24 children here now. When a new dormitory is completed, there will be 36. In fourteen years, Saint Jude's has served

177 children. These are small numbers; the ranch is a small sponge in what is, nationally, a sea of problems involving child abuse. But when an institution's task is to administer intensive care to small souls, small is not just beautiful, it is efficient, even essential.

Asked why he left a region and a city and a job he enjoyed to come here for what was a precarious undertaking, Father Ward answers with a directness that neither invites nor permits further inquiry. He says he was called by the trustees to see Saint Jude's, and when he saw it, he was called by a Higher Authority to serve it. "It is," he says with Saint Paul, "a fearful thing to fall into the hands of the living God."

There is really nothing strange about this healing enterprise in the desert. It is as American as the "errand into the wilderness" undertaken by the first Americans, the pilgrims who pushed inland for their own purposes, and explained their purposes the way Father Ward explains his.

It is in America's genetic code, this tendency for devout people to go off to unlikely places and start practicing what they are then almost too busy to preach. That is why the American landscape is flecked with little platoons like Saint Jude's, hard at the business of making the world better in the best way, one person at a time.

January 20, 1980

Sir Thomas More: The Limits of Accommodation

In the nation's capital, which is not famous for martyrs to conscience, scholars have gathered to commemorate the five hundredth anniversary of the birth of Thomas More, whose life blended action and contemplation, and whose death—"I die the King's good servant, but God's first"—was noble.

More, the "layman's Saint," was at home in the world, and unblinkingly realistic. When More's son-in-law was impressed that Henry VIII walked with an arm draped around More's neck, More reminded him that "If my head could win him a castle in France, it should not fail to go."

Professor Charles Trinkaus of the University of Michigan believes that people today see in More something they wish they had. But it is not his political philosophy, which few of his modern admirers know or would approve.

There was continuity between the quarrels that cost the lives of Thomas à Becket and More. Neither asserted the sovereignty of private conscience; both defended the Church's claim against secular government's claim to administer belief.

Henry VIII impoverished More's family to teach families not to have fathers like More. The King gave More's property to the King's little girl, who eventually became Elizabeth I and proclaimed that she would not "make windows into men's souls." More made windows. As Lord Chancellor he was a vigorous prosecutor of heretics, whose books, he thought, killed souls as surely as brigands killed bodies.

His most famous work, *Utopia*, was a prescription for gentlemanly totalitarianism. And as one More scholar, Germain Marc'hador, says: "The book denounced individualism while it was still in its cradle."

The most inspiring martyrdoms are of people, like More, who love life, not those who crave burning. More was a rarity, a martyr to intellect, who died not for a feeling but for a precise distinction. Wordsworth called him the "unbending More," but in fact he bent like a sapling in the gale the King turned upon him.

He was a brilliant lawyer who struggled to find a semantic loophole that would enable him to endorse Henry's change of wives and succession plans without having to swear that he believed Henry, rather than the Pope, to be spiritually preeminent as head of the Church in England. He found no loophole, so the executioner's ax fell upon the neck around which Henry had once draped the arm of friendship.

More's reputation in our time derives primarily from Robert

Bolt's play *A Man for All Seasons*, in which More says to his daughter, "When a man takes an oath, Meg, he's holding his own self in his own hands, like water, and if he opens his fingers *then*— he needn't hope to find himself again." And in his argument with the pliable Duke of Norfolk, More says:

"I will not give in because I oppose it—*I* do—not my pride, not my spleen, nor any other of my appetites but *I* do—*I!*" (More then grabs Norfolk in various places, testingly, as he would grab livestock.) "Is there no single sinew in the midst of this that serves no appetite of Norfolk's but is, just, Norfolk?"

In the preface to the play, Bolt says of More:

> He knew where he began and left off, what area of himself he could yield to the encroachments of his enemies, and what to the encroachments of those he loved. . . . But at length he was asked to retreat from that final area where he located himself.
>
> And there this supple, humorous, unassuming and sophisticated person set like metal, was overtaken by an absolutely primitive rigour, and could no more be budged than a cliff.

Perhaps that—"that final area where he located himself"—is what More's modern admirers find missing in themselves. As Bolt says: "We feel—we know—the self to be an equivocal commodity. There are fewer and fewer things which, as they say, we 'cannot bring ourselves' to do."

We try, says Bolt, to "assure ourselves that from the outside at least we do have a definite outline. But socially and individually it is with us as it is with our cities—an accelerating flight to the periphery, leaving a center which is empty when the hours of business are over." More's sense of self was not equivocal, and his modern admirers must ask whether his enviable sense of "where he began and left off" derived from convictions that the modern world is pleased to consider superstitions.

June 22, 1978

Hubert Humphrey: Without Tears

The enduring memory of a great politician's life should be of his voice, an echo of exhortations in the nation's ear. For most Americans, and especially for the postwar generation that has not known politics without him, the chorus of public life henceforth will seem incomplete without Hubert Humphrey's voice. It was a voice as flat as the prairie, flat as the political landscape seems with him cut down. But it was a carrying voice, vibrant with the energy of a man happy in his work.

Today it is difficult to summon a sense of Adlai Stevenson or Dwight Eisenhower addressing a crowd. But twenty years from now, those who heard Humphrey in full flight will remember his delight. It was the sense of his overflowing affection for his audience, not just the pleasure most political men derive from seeing themselves reflected in an audience's eyes. Perhaps Humphrey exhausted more people than he persuaded, but in politics the effect can be the same. More notable than the amount of talking he did was the Gatling-gun pace at which he did it. He talked so fast he did not seem to be a calculating man, which warmed audiences. But he also did not seem to weigh his works, and friends urged him to affect a halting graveness. He refused. He could be quick without being rash because his purposes were fixed and clear and he saw no conflicts between them. He was, as someone said of Voltaire, a chaos of clear ideas.

Postwar politics has been a long lesson in the incompatibility of many of the worthy goals of Minnesota liberalism. Minnesota is a green and pleasant paradox, a liberal state full of conservative people. It believes in bread-and-butter liberalism. Its Scandinavian and rural elements, and perhaps its severe winters, incline it to a political ethic of collective provision, and in Humphrey it produced this century's only Presidential nominee who had been mayor of a large American city.

Bread-and-butter liberalism was Social Security, TVA, rural electrification and scores of similar, if not similarly successful, programs of material amelioration. The decline of liberalism in Humphrey's lifetime is less the result of the excesses of such politics than of the transformation of liberalism into a doctrine of "administered enlightenment." The old liberalism delivered material advantages that were intended to enable people to live the lives they had chosen. The new liberalism, typified by forced busing and affirmative action and the explosive growth of regulation, administers "remedies" to what society's supervisors consider defects in the way people live.

Humphrey was very much the son of a small-town druggist in the Midwest. Years ago the pharmacist, second only to the doctor, represented the practical use of knowledge against the distress of life. For Humphrey, politics was pharmacy practiced on society. The liberal temperament is exasperating because of its expansive belief in social pharmacy: there are no disagreeable conditions that must be endured, only problems that must be solved. In today's climate of disappointment with government, it is easy to caricature Humphrey's penchant for prescribing elixirs, and his inability to give *anything* his undivided neglect. But at the end of his life, he had the compensating certainty that he had fought on the winning side. When he entered politics it was an open question whether the United States would embrace welfare-state practices. Today that question is closed. Few persons see most of their youthful opinions become policy; fewer still see that without a trace of embarrassment or regret. Humphrey did. In his party he was more than a political leader; he was a climate of opinion.

An extraordinary politician usually embodies a characteristic value of his culture. And Humphrey embodied the belief that to persist is to triumph. Yet he drank a full draft of defeat. In 1956, he was one of the first and most forceful supporters of Adlai Stevenson's renomination, and he wanted to be Stevenson's running mate. But Stevenson let the convention choose, and it chose Estes Kefauver. And John Kennedy, not Humphrey, was second. In the 1960 West Virginia primary, Humphrey, the least synthetic of men, was beaten by Kennedy, the first thoroughly packaged candidate. At the 1968 convention, when he should have been able to savor a fulfillment long delayed, the smell of tear gas drifted into his room overlooking Chicago's Grant Park. That autumn, his personality energized a dramatic home-stretch drive, and at the end, votes were shifting his way so fast that if the election had been twelve hours later, he probably would have won.

In 1972, when he was considered worn goods, he came close to stopping George McGovern's drive for the nomination. In 1976, when he was beginning to be regarded as a classic deserving a comeback, like *South Pacific*, he was too spent to face another disappointment.

Like Moses, Humphrey was discovered young, at the 1948 convention, and like Moses, he was always a bundle of opinions. He rose fast enough and lived long enough to see five men succeed to the Presidency after he first sought it in 1960, and he believed that he could have done the job better than each of them. Because he was cherubic, not lean, it was easy to underestimate how hungry he was, first for acceptance in the Senate, then for the great prize of American politics. Because he lost so many of life's close calls, and because liberalism often is a form of sentimentality, there is a tendency to patronize Humphrey while praising him. He did lack the *necessary* coldness of a national leader. A friendship tended to be a lifetime contract, so as he rolled through life he acquired a soiled snowball of political associates. Rarely does a man have such extraordinary dynamism and lack an instinct for the jugular.

But Humphrey also had a guileful side, as you would expect of one who learned about national political realities from the likes of Oklahoma's Senator Robert Kerr, a sort of *rough* Lyndon Johnson whose ability to bend nature can be seen in the fact that Tulsa is a seaport. For thirty years, Humphrey was a professional. More than any other man of his generation, he lived the political life as Plutarch described it:

> They are wrong who think that politics is like an ocean voyage or a military campaign, something to be done with some particular end in view, something which leaves off as soon as that end is reached. It is not a public chore, to be got over with. It is a way of life. It is the life of a domesticated political and social creature who is born with a love for public life, with a desire for honor, with a feeling for his fellows . . .

During the 1964 campaign, the paths of Barry Goldwater and Hubert Humphrey crossed in an airport, and they paused to chat. As they parted, one professional said to the other, "Well, keep punching, Hubert." He did.

January 23, 1978

The Little Brothers of the Poor: Charity with a Human Face

There is winter, and then there is winter in Chicago. Under skies of gunmetal gray, the wind whips off Lake Michigan charged with chilling dampness and pours inland like a torrent of broken glass. In winter in Chicago, life's edges seem jagged, and even the young feel brittle. But in the city of the broad shoulders, the Little Brothers of the Poor temper the wind for a few people who are in the winter of their lives.

The Little Brothers began in Paris in 1946, Catholic laymen serving the elderly poor. In 1959, Michael Salmon came from France to plant the Little Brothers' seed in Chicago's concrete. His wife, Lilo, met him here in 1967, when she came from Berlin to pitch in. About half of the small staff (it is now nondenominational and includes women) live in the group's building and are paid a pittance. The Little Brothers shop for the poor, deliver meals, drive the ailing to clinics, find housing and fill out society's endless, intimidating forms for people whose hands shake and whose eyes are weak. Most important, the Little Brothers come calling, for no reason but friendship.

Their motto, "Flowers before bread," is very French. The French can be confusing as philosophers and tiresome as allies, but they have an instinct for civilizing amenities. The idea of "Flowers before bread" is that the poor too—actually, the poor especially— should have some small luxuries, like coffee, sugar, candy, an occasional movie, even a few days in the country at a vacation house. (The Little Brothers' budget comes from private sources and would not keep a government agency in paper clips.) One of the Little Brothers' approximately four hundred volunteers takes elderly friends to lunch at the Drake Hotel. The Little Brothers are avid party givers, and are passionately, you might say religiously, opposed to paper plates at their parties.

De Gaulle, who navigated it well, said old age is a "shipwreck." It isn't always a sad or disagreeable season, of course, but it is for the elderly who are alone and infirm in cities. It is said that for anyone over 80, all contemporaries are friends. But there are few contemporaries to be friendly with when they live—when they are warehoused—in small rooms in run-down residential hotels. (Hotels with mockingly grand names, like "The Consulate" and "The Riviera.") Americans have a *Little House on the Prairie* idea of neighborliness. Somehow neighborliness seemed more natural when neighbors were miles apart rather than two doors down the block, or the hall.

A cause of depression for the elderly is the sense of superfluousness. That is what turns three elderly men into rookie bank robbers in the splendid movie *Going in Style*. Jean de La Bruyère said, "The young can bear solitude better than the old, for their passions occupy their thoughts." For many elderly people, ailments and anxieties have replaced passions as the only relief from the melancholy that often accompanies a retrospective cast of mind. As a sign in the Little Brothers office says: "Old trees grow stronger, old rivers grow wider, but old people just grow lonesome."

Consider Helen, who is in her 90th year. She has no family. The husband in her faded snapshots died forty years ago. She has lived for twenty-one years in a hotel on Chicago's North Side, in a room so small there is barely space to walk between the bed and the jumbled leftovers of life that are piled along the walls. The glare of two naked light bulbs falls on walls with huge water stains. Plaster is falling onto the rug that squishes underfoot from a radiator leak. Helen can't cook (hot plates are banned because too many drunken residents of the hotel started fires), so the Little Brothers bring her many meals.

To get to her room ($110 a month, and many pay more) she must use an elevator with a door so heavy she can barely budge it. Such impediments, invisible to most of us, are strewn through the lives of the elderly, and can imprison them. The Little Brothers could find Helen better housing, but she wants to stay near the elderly man down the hall, who has cancer. Besides, home is home. And many elderly people are terrified that if they move, their mail—public-assistance checks, the Medicaid "green card"—will not catch up with them.

Many elderly people are afraid to venture forth, afraid of crime, afraid of icy pavement. Helen was found on the pavement in December. "I fall down," she says, obviously thinking that statement exhausts the subject. "I can't see or hear or walk so well. I'm what you call a handicapped," she says, and laughs loudly. A wilting poinsettia, a souvenir of her hospital stay, is the only patch of color in her room. But a cloth flower flies like a defiant flag from her wool-knit cap as she heads for a long sit in the "lobby," a barely furnished and unspeakably drab and drafty place where two cops have just quieted a drunk woman. But Helen is uncomplaining, as people are who have much dignity and no illusions, who only dimly remember when things were better and who can't imagine things getting better.

An elderly woman once said, "Since Penelope Noakes of Duppas Hill is gone, there is no one who will ever call me Nellie again." The Little Brothers exist so that Nellies will always have someone to call them Nellie. Operating from a storefront,* the Little Brothers do a kind of good that cannot be done from the gray stone pentagons of public assistance. The welfare state does not make groups like the Little Brothers dispensable. The welfare state is society's safety net, but its mesh will never be so fine that no one falls through. Besides, as society's compassionate impulses become bureaucratized, society needs to nurture the little platoons that practice "charitableness with a human face."

Platoons like the Little Brothers serve as society's softeners—softening the lives of people like Helen, and softening, by the reproach of their example, society's hardness of heart. They incarnate a value that, in the mean streets of a modern city, must struggle against strangulation, like a flower pushing through a crack in the concrete. The value is neighborliness. That is the business of the Little Brothers and countless similar groups that honeycomb America with unseen and unsung networks of kindness.

March 3, 1980

John Paul II: A Pope with Authority

John Paul II is described increasingly, and with an insistent undertone of disapproval, as the "paradoxical" Pope. Many people find it inexplicable, or at least inconsistent, that the man who in Poland was a tenacious adversary of an overbearing state is in

*At 1658 West Belmont Avenue, Chicago, Ill. 60657, for those who would like to send some support.

Rome a vigorous enforcer of orthodoxy. The misperception of paradox is related to the modern chafing against all claims to authority in matters of the mind. John Paul II does indeed bristle with judgments, about women in the priesthood and priests in politics, about liturgical innovations and theological speculations. Critics ask, with mounting impatience, "Just who does he think he is?"

And there, to begin with, is the rub. He knows exactly who he is, which makes him something of an oddity and, to some people, a kind of reproachful example. Not for him the "identity crisis" so much in fashion. The Church's explanation of the Pope's—any Pope's—identity is clear even to those who are, as I am, outside the Church and perhaps sunk in what the Church calls, splendidly, "invincible ignorance." The doctrine is that Christ, who left behind no writings, left instead a tradition, and a teaching body, the Church. It is authoritative by virtue of Him who made it custodian of the tradition that it believes is mankind's most precious treasure.

Papal supremacy is a stumbling block to ecumenicism, but Protestant denominations have been bedeviled (just the right word, don't you think?) by the inescapable problem of authority. To locate it in Scripture merely recasts the question: who is to construe Scripture authoritatively? The Roman Catholic Church's claim that its teaching in matters of faith and morals is Providentially guaranteed against error is not new and is not really what rankles many people about today's Pope. The reason this Pope stirs uneasiness, and the reason his example is of political as well as theological interest, is that he makes vivid a timeless and awkward truth about communities, political or religious. That truth is that any community must have a core of settled convictions, and any community determined to endure must charge some authority with the task of nurturing, defending and transmitting those convictions.

Consider the Vatican's action against Hans Küng. At issue is not Küng's right to teach, but only his right to present himself as transmitting Catholic teachings. Few argue that Rome has misunderstood Küng. Rather, Rome has agreed with Küng's reiterated contention that, on some important matters, including the Church's teaching authority, his position is not the Church's position. (Pope Paul VI reportedly enjoyed this joke: the Vatican, determined to resolve the dispute, offered Küng the papacy, but was told, "No, thanks, I'd rather remain infallible.")

Tension between theologians and church authorities is inevitable. But authority is subject to this law: use it or lose it. Whether the Vatican drew the line at the right point is beyond my poor power to know. But surely there must be points at which private judgment by any member of a community is circumscribed by institutional judgment. And some person or body—a Pope, a Parliament, a Supreme Court—must decide where those points are.

Reluctance to accept authority that is rooted in tradition often reflects the pridefulness of people who assume that they have nothing to learn from any prior human experience or consensus. The sin of pride derives from belief in the inevitability of progress in all things, and hence belief that mankind must be wiser today than yesterday.

But rejection of authority can also involve what I nominate as the eighth deadly sin: a perverse kind of mental modesty. It derives from the philosophical judgment that all human judgments are idiosyncratic, or from historical disillusionment with institutions as being too irrational, or at any rate too changeable, to reach trustworthy conclusions about anything. As Chesterton said, we are becoming too mentally modest to believe in the multiplication table.

Fifty years ago, Ronald Knox, Catholic chaplain at Oxford, noted that in this century, for perhaps the first time, this is thought to be true: "You do not believe what your grandfathers believed, and have no reason to hope that your grandsons will believe what you do." No community can accept that proposition unless it is reconciled to passing away, or—which is much the same—being transformed beyond recognition in every generation. John Paul II is unreconciled. He believes that the Church can become so distracted by political involvements and temporal causes that it becomes just another social-welfare organization. And as Knox said,

"The pilots of our storm-tossed denominations have lost no opportunity of lightening ship by jettisoning every point of doctrine that seemed questionable." Yet "Dogmas may fly out at the window but congregations do not come in at the door."

A diluted faith cannot compete with the distractions of the modern world. Knox believed that "the modern facilities for pleasurable enjoyment have killed, in great part, the relish for eternity . . . And the same causes which have multiplied pleasure have multiplied preoccupation. A rush age cannot be a reflective age." Or as Kin Hubbard put it, with Midwestern concision: "Mrs. Lafe Bud's gran'father passed away yisterday. He had long been prominent in th' business life o' th' community an' was a constant churchgoer till he got a car."

The decades immediately after the Depression and Second World War were characterized by relentless materialism, the pursuit of gratifications long deferred. Now there is a quickening sense that mankind is made for something finer, and needs fixity in fundamental beliefs. As the West sleepwalks into a decade in which moral confidence and steadfastness will be increasingly needed and decreasingly found, and as a cry for "leadership" issues from millions who probably would not recognize it if they saw it, and probably reject it if they did, John Paul II becomes more fascinating. It has been noted that although his wardrobe reflects his personal tastes hardly at all, and is indeed like what Popes have worn for centuries, a fashion organization recently voted him "world's best-dressed statesman." Do clothes make the man? Not that man.

June 23, 1980

John Paul II: The Cross and the Red Star

Igor Stravinsky, speaking with a Russian's stoicism about Poland's predicament, said that if you pitch your tent in the middle of Fifth Avenue you are going to be hit by a bus. For centuries, Poland was beset by Austria and Prussia and Russia. In this century, it has been pinioned between Germany and the Soviet Union. As much as any nation, Poland is owed compensation for the calamities of modern history.

Poland even more than Czechoslovakia was the victim of Munich, which guaranteed that Poland would be Hitler's next meal. Appeasement at least preserved Prague; Warsaw was more destroyed than any other European capital, including Berlin. The Nazi-Soviet pact was about the dismemberment of Poland, and it was at Poland's expense that Germany first demonstrated *Blitzkrieg*. Britain's decision to honor its alliance with Poland transformed Poland's crisis into a world war. Warsaw resisted—"magnificent and forlorn," in Winston Churchill's words—and John Lukacs writes: "Years had to pass until such bravery was shown in the face of Germans by European soldiers during this war."

Russia's Katyn Forest was the site of a massacre of Polish officers by Germany's Soviet allies. Auschwitz is near Cracow, in what is today the diocese just left by Pope John Paul II. The revolt of the Warsaw ghetto in 1943 was heroism without hope. When the Polish home army rose against the Germans in August, 1944, it hoped Russian help would arrive. But Stalin halted his troops in order to give the Germans time to save him the trouble of massacring Poland's resisters. He even denied U.S. and British planes the right to land at Soviet bases after dropping supplies over Warsaw. After the war, he used Poland to demonstrate that Yalta would not inconvenience the imposition of Stalinism.

The world has been transformed by two world wars, yet it is neglectful of Eastern Europe, where both wars began. But the elevation of Cardinal Wojtyla to Pope draws attention to the unity of European culture, and underscores the brutality of all attempts to impose Communism on ancient nations. Poland, especially, illustrates the truth that a state is not a nation. The Polish nation is a people united by culture. Through the centuries, the nation has been forced to render unto many Caesars. But today in Poland, more than elsewhere in Europe, the people inhibit the state. They do so because of the Church Militant, the resilient institution that is as old as the idea of Europe. The church pulpit is, as a Polish exile group says, "unique as a source of the uncensored word." A Politburo member says, with fear and loathing, that the Church is the only opposition that "has at its disposal a coherent philosophy, a strong organizational base and numerous cadres."

In the intensity of its Catholicism, Poland resembles Ireland, but in Poland even more than in Ireland patriotism and religion are entwined. That is why the Communists have so completely failed to graft their police state onto the Polish nation. When asked whether the new Pope speaks Russian, an aide cryptically replied, "No Pole speaks Russian, but everyone understands it." When Cardinal Wyszynski declared, "After God one must above all remain faithful to our homeland, to the Polish national culture," he implied the illegitimacy of the regime which is utterly alien to that culture.

The Church in Poland is a serious force. Churches in the West are, increasingly, "relevant," which is different. In a biting article in the current *Harper's* magazine, Paul Seabury says the Episcopal Church attitude is "trendier than thou." The revision (Seabury would say desecration) of the Book of Common Prayer illustrates the desire "to make the church, its language, and its practices conform to contemporary values." The boredom of directionless churches produces compulsive tinkering with liturgies. Elsewhere, Seabury notes, churches have more pressing preoccupations: "A missionary society in England recently asked a bishop in Uganda, 'What can we send your people? You are being persecuted. Your archbishop has been martyred. What can we send you?' The answer came back: not food, not medicine; 250 clerical collars. This was the explanation . . . 'You must understand, when our people are being rounded up to be shot, they must be able to spot their priests.' "

Oppression concentrates the mind on essentials. John Paul II is a formidable philosopher who understands, as a result of hard thinking and hard living, the great struggle of the century, the struggle between the totalitarian state and all rival allegiances. The time is ripe for such a toughened intellectual as Pope. Secular enthusiasms have lost their allure. No one still believes that "the death of God" would mean the birth of an age of reason. Only the willfully ignorant believe that a "new man" is being shaped in Russia or China or Cuba. And the papacy, the oldest Western institution, is more likely than any secular regime to last another 2,000 years.

Rome grew from a fort on a Tiber Riber crossing to the capital of an empire to the seat of a universal Church. Then in 1517, Luther nailed his ninety-five theses to a church door in Wittenberg, and in 1522, Rome elected its last non-Italian Pope for 456 years. The Church relied on its Italian foundation to withstand the Reformation and support the Counter-Reformation. The Vatican's splendor, much of which dates from the sixteenth and seventeenth centuries, was produced as a defiant assertion of permanence. Napoleon and Italian nationalism cost the papacy its lands and reduced it to a menaced Italian power. But the selection of a Pontiff from Cracow continues the Church's twentieth-century reassertion of its universality.

Men of political action are proudly "practical," and tend to discount the history-shaping force of such ideas. Communists are, in theory, materialists who deny that ideas are a primary force in history. But Étienne Gilson, the eminent student of medieval philosophy who died last month at 94, correctly compared the triumph of Thomas Aquinas' philosophy over Arab philosophies to the military triumph of Charles Martel over Arab armies at Tours in 732, which halted the Moorish conquest of Europe. And Kant in his study at Königsberg had a deeper impact on the world than did his energetic contemporary Napoleon.

In 1935, Stalin, who was to become the architect of the modern Polish state, said to Pierre Laval, "The Pope! How many divisions has he got?" Stalin spoke rhetorically and contemptuously. But Poland's Stalinist regime has learned the truth expressed in one of G. K. Chesterton's Father Brown stories: " 'I'm afraid I'm a practical man,' said the doctor with gruff humor, 'and I don't bother much about religion and philosophy.' 'You'll never be a practical man till you do,' said Father Brown."

October 30, 1978

John Paul II: The Subversive Pope

Nothing is as distinctively modern, and as demoralizing, as the sense that nothing lasts, that everything changes and that change is autonomous. People are plied with theories purporting to show that vast impersonal forces rule the world. Thus nothing is such fun as a demonstration that a solitary figure can make a difference; that history is a realm of surprise, not necessity. Surprise? The most fascinating figure on the world stage today traces his authority to the most potent figure in history, a Palestinian who during his ministry never traveled more than a hundred miles from his birthplace, never wrote a book and died at 33.

John Paul II has come and gone, leaving a glow of warmth "like a spark sheltered under the skin of our days." (Those words are drawn from his poetry.) The meaning of his astonishing reception here is unclear. He is, of course, a gifted public performer, and this Republic always is starved for public ceremony. And although he ignited and fanned many flames, it is the nature of fires to burn themselves out. Still, consider the curiousness of it all.

The occupant of the West's oldest office has cut a swath through the New World. In the last quarter of this secularizing century, the world's most galvanizing man works at an altar. Today power is associated with prosaic men governing great states, all of whom must envy the power of the poet whose "state" is a Rome neighborhood. We marvel at the importance in history of some small states: ancient Israel, Athens, Florence and Elizabethan England. John Paul II's Vatican City may one day be added to the list. Two centuries ago Daniel Defoe said a hundred thousand Englishmen were ready to fight to the death against popery without knowing whether popery was a man or a horse. Today the Pope is cheered by millions who know next to nothing about him, only that his gravity and serenity are enchanting. So you well may wonder: What, in the name of God, is going on?

Begin with the obvious: What is going on is going on in the name of God. There is a religious revival, or at least a quickening of sympathy for religious impulses. One drop from a lake of evidence is the remarkable demand for books by and about C. S. Lewis, perhaps this century's foremost author of Christian apologetics. There also is a surge of interest in science: science journalism is proliferating, and two science books are best-sellers. Science and religion seem, to many, less competitive than complementary because science deepens, rather than diminishes, the sense of life's mysteriousness, and religion speaks to anxieties science stirs.

Modern science is about the strangeness of things: solid objects are mostly space; the experience of time is a function of speed; gravity bends light. The human mind no longer seems to be a sovereign "ghost in the machine"; it seems tied in unexplained ways to our physical selves, and to nature. The philosopher's question ("I can do what I want, but can I want what I want?") has become a general anxiety. We are born without intending to be, we die without intending to and perhaps our intentions don't matter much in between. If neither reason nor passion makes the world go round, what does? And what has become of the idea of one's "self"? There are numerous disconcerting theories purporting to explain why one's "self" (sometimes called "consciousness") is not really one's own. It is said that one's self is a mere reflection

of external events (sometimes called History), or it is a kind of
fractious committee composed of Id, Ego and Superego (today
known as "hang-ups") and other sovereign members.

John Paul II's message to Americans and other comfortable
people is that "being one's self" is problematic. Not long ago
America's social ideal was the "well-adjusted" person. But Christianity is a religion of unadjusted people whose obligation is to
adjust to something that transcends the culture of the day, any day.
That is why, seventy years ago, Charles Péguy said that this century's real revolutionaries would be the parents of Christian families.

It is fitting that the Pope's pilgrimage to America gathered
steam in Ireland. There, during the Dark Ages, Christianity gathered steam for the conquest of Europe. Today Ireland, plagued by
religious strife, could use a bit of amnesia. America has insufficient
memory of its spiritual origins. But John Paul II's spark has fallen
on dry tinder because, to many people, contemporary society is arid.

Since 1945 the standard of living in the North Atlantic community has risen more than it did between the French Revolution and
1945. This has happened because, after the deprivations of Depression and war, people were so single-minded about the pursuit
of prosperity. Now John Paul II believes he hears the clanking of
invisible but real shackles, the chains on people enslaved by appetites.

He could not avoid a dramatic reproach to the regimes of Eastern Europe. His challenge to free and prosperous people is option-
al and subtle, but perhaps no less subversive of the established
order. This traveling Pope is a bit like a modern John Wesley,
who said, "I look upon all the world as my parish" and traveled
250,000 miles on horseback in his evangelizing. When the poor
gathered in huge throngs to hear Wesley preach, the ruling classes
said he was threatening the social order. Indeed he was—not because he had a political message, but just because he treated the
lower classes as human. The Pope's exhortation to the West, calling it to a life less partial and distorting than the pursuit of pleasure, would, if taken to heart, shake the foundations of the affluent
societies he passes through. But he does pass through, and away, as

Wesley did. And hardened hearts are not so quickly softened—at least not lastingly.

It is said that in the eighteenth century, when every sixth house in London was selling spirits, Wesley did more than any other single person to keep the British faithful. Then the effects of Wesley and others wore off. As Charles Williams wrote, "The middle class in England did not wholly lose the habit of going to church until they acquired motor cars—so negligible in the end is intellect itself." This Pope says:

> *A flame rescued from dry wood*
> *has no weight in its luminous flight*
> *yet lifts the heavy lid of night.*

He knows the strength of weightless things, like ideas, but he may not know the weight of the lid he wants to lift, the materialism that, he says, stunts the spirits of consumer societies.

A Pope today does not need to weigh his words as carefully as Popes once did. (A few centuries ago, Chesterton noted, a carelessly phrased sentence about what is acceptable religious symbolism might have shattered all the best statues in Europe.) Today when the Pope speaks to the nations he is more apt, but alas not very apt, to shatter their delusions of adequacy.

October 15, 1979

John Bunyan: Preacher at the Crossroads

John Bunyan was a common man lumpy with talent, and he believed that talent is a gift from God to be used for Godly purposes. So three hundred years ago this spring he published *Pilgrim's Progress*. No book since the Bible has had a circulation comparable to Bunyan's novel about Christian's adventures in the Slough of Despond, Vanity Fair, and Doubting Castle (inhabited by Giant Despair and his wife, Diffidence) and with the likes of Messrs. Hate-light, Live-loose, and Worldly-wiseman from the town of Carnal Policy.

There was no mass market or distribution system for books then, but a hundred thousand copies were sold by the time Bunyan died in 1688. It has been translated into more than a hundred languages and dialects, often for missionaries. It has followed the Bible "from land to land as the singing bird follows the dawn."

Bunyan was in English prisons on and off for twelve years, and wrote *Pilgrim's Progress* while serving a sentence for unlicensed preaching. The book was a continuation of his offense by other means.

He was opinionated, uncompromising and articulate. He would have been at home among the Protestant pilgrims in Massachusetts. Indeed, just three years after his book was published in England an edition appeared in New England.

The novel was part of Lincoln's formative reading. Huckleberry Finn noted the books on a table in a house he visited: "One was a big family Bible full of pictures. One was 'Pilgrim's Progress,' about a man that left his family, it didn't say why. I read considerable in it now and then. The statements was interesting, but tough."

No book other than the Bible did more to shape the American sensibility; no book better expressed the national idea of mission, a rage to journey toward the perfection of a City on a Hill.

Pilgrim's Progress has been called the last book written without a thought for the reviewers. It was written in the plainest English ever used by a writer of the first rank, and it heralded the dawn of a day when books would be written for persons other than scholars.

Its popularity waned in the eighteenth century; it was not an Age of Reason book. It is rarely read today: all is slackness and *laissez-faire* in matters of morals, so there is little interest in a book written to lead the erring to righteousness.

There is a whininess to much modern literature, which (a critic has said) portrays man as more a prisoner than a pilgrim, a passive victim of "society" or "history" or other vast, impersonal forces. But Bunyan insisted that life is a succession of free choices, and that the stakes in the choices are, literally, infinite.

No other novel is so determinedly didactic, or has been read so often by people who came to it for entertainment rather than instruction. Its rival for the rank of greatest English allegory is George Orwell's *Animal Farm*. The seventeenth century's most compelling anxieties concerned religion; the twentieth century's concern politics, and especially the totalitarian temptation to treat politics as a religion.

The word "improvement" is too mushy to express what Bunyan had hoped his book would help readers achieve. The correct word is "salvation." But *Pilgrim's Progress* was, in a sense, a precursor of today's "self-improvement" books. Today millions seek serious guidance from *I'm OK, You're OK* and *Your Erroneous Zones* and *Looking Out for No. 1* and *Winning Through Intimidation*. You should tremble for your country when you see how the times, and ideas of seriousness and improvement, have changed.

Bunyan penetrated the husk of manners to describe man's inner life. Christian abandoned his family to seek the Celestial City, and his story expresses a psychological insight recently reacquired with much fanfare: Many of life's most unsettling "passages" occur in the middle of life.

Many people do not believe that either trumpets or flames are at the end of each human journey. But they can share this much of Bunyan's vision, as C. S. Lewis expressed it: "The choice of ways at any crossroad may be more important than we think and . . . shortcuts may lead to very nasty places." *Pilgrim's Progress* has endured for the best of reasons: it is true.

April 27, 1978

Josef Stalin: History's Ice Ax

This century's most prolific killer, and one of its greatest achievers, has been dead twenty-five years. The Bolshevik state was provisional when Lenin died in 1924, but it was a colossus when Stalin died March 5, 1953. It still reeks of Stalin's spirit.

In the battle for Lenin's mantle, Leon Trotsky, orator of the Revolution and creator of the Red Army, was beaten by the consummate conspirator. Stalin pioneered a new form of tyranny by making the police the central institution of society—police whose primary purpose was not combating crime but arresting people designated by the regime.

Hitler said he had "unqualified respect" only for "Stalin the genius," and Stalin trusted only Hitler. But unlike Hitler, who used radio and pageantry to make government resemble a Black Mass, Stalin's regime of random terror had a gray face. In Hitler's Reich, most people were safe, if they were docile. In Stalin's Russia, insecurity was pandemic.

Stalin's chosen name meant "steel." His closest collaborator was Molotov ("Hammer"). Together they pounded a population to dust, atomizing it in order to turn it into concrete, inert and weighty. Stalin created the industrial sinews for a modern military machine. It absorbed perhaps the greatest miscalculation in history—Hitler's invasion of Russia—in June, 1941.

British intelligence thought Russia could resist for ten days; U.S. intelligence said three months. German soldiers carried no winter clothes. But by December the Wehrmacht, which had anticipated fighting fewer than 200 Soviet divisions, had identified 360 enemy divisions. When Eisenhower was saying that the invasion of Sicily would fail if opposed by 2 German divisions, Stalin was fighting 185 German divisions.

Stalin won the most savage battle in history at a city that bore his name: Stalingrad. He won the Second World War, and that is why, when he died, the western border of the Russian empire was where Marx, a century earlier, had predicted that someday it would be, extending from Stettin on the Baltic to Trieste on the Adriatic.

When Hitler struck, Stalin came unglued for ten days. Then he made his first radio speech to his people. The nation was startled by his thick Georgian accent.

Many men who have regarded themselves as fulfillers of their nations' destinies—Napoleon, Pilsudski, Ataturk, Hitler (who became a German citizen just fifteen months before becoming Chancellor)—were born outside those nations, or near frontiers. Stalin was another semi-outsider.

Hannah Arendt notes that when Stalin decided to rewrite the history of the Russian Revolution, he did not just destroy the old books; he destroyed their authors and readers—the intellectuals. Stalin believed that Pavlov had found the key to man in the conditioned reflex: people could be manipulated by verbal stimuli. According to Professor Robert Tucker, Stalin's theory was that "of all monopolies enjoyed by the Soviet state, none would be so crucial as its monopoly on the definition of words. The ultimate weapon of political control would be the dictionary."

Stalin ("How many divisions does the Pope have?") had little respect for intangibles. Yet his regime, although ideologically materialist, was obsessed with manufacturing definitions and revising dictionaries, an obsession that George Orwell captured in *1984*. Khrushchev's horror of West Berlin and Brezhnev's horror of Solzhenitsyn reflected, in part, a Stalinist obsession with the state's monopoly of concepts. And Brezhnev's use of "mental hospitals" and "psychology" as instruments of torture is, in part, a continuation of Stalin's faith in absurd notions of human nature.

In Stalin's mild moments his anti-Semitism, like Brezhnev's, was just a continuation of old Russian policies. But Stalin's more ferocious anti-Semitic moods expressed his seething resentment of Trotsky and some other Jews among the early Bolsheviks, whose brilliance accentuated Stalin's crudeness.

While in exile in Venice, Paolo Sarpi, a seventeenth-century critic of the papacy, was attacked by papal agents who hacked him fiercely and left him for dead. When the surgeon dressing his wounds commented on the crudeness of his attackers, Sarpi said: *"Agnosco stylum Curiae Romanae"*—"One sees the style of the Roman Curia."

Similarly, the assassination of Trotsky in exile expressed the nature of the Soviet regime, then and now: patient, implacable, cruel and brutal. Stalin, who was delicate only in stalking, surely found it amusing that in Mexico, of all places, Trotsky died with an ice ax in his skull.

March 2, 1978

Alger Hiss: The Persistent Lie

Alger Hiss has waged a thirty-year war against truth, promoting historical amnesia. Now he and his allies are about to suffer. Professor Allen Weinstein, a historian at Smith College, began his research believing Hiss innocent. But Weinstein's book *Perjury: The Hiss-Chambers Case* demonstrates that Hiss was guilty of perjury, and hence of espionage. Occasionally a work of history is a historic event. This is one such. It is stunningly meticulous, and a monument to the intellectual ideal of truth stalked to its hiding place. It also is a substantial public service. It comes as Hiss is attempting to get his conviction expunged as a miscarriage of justice, and when anti-Communism is in season. It is based on forty thousand pages of previously classified material, and meetings with forty people involved but never before interviewed, including retired Soviet agents who confirm Whittaker Chambers' testimony. The myth of Hiss's innocence suffers the death of a thousand cuts, delicate destruction by a scholar's scalpel.

On August 3, 1948, Chambers, a former Communist undercover agent, testified that he had known Hiss as a secret Communist in government in the 1930s. Hiss, an eminent former State Department official, then head of the Carnegie Endowment, immediately denied that he had ever been a Communist or known Chambers. Chambers' knowledge of details of Hiss's private life soon forced Hiss to say he had known Chambers slightly, but had not met him since mid-1936. Hiss felt forced to file a slander suit, and Chambers, who until then had not mentioned espionage, responded by revealing documents stolen in 1938, most of them typed on a typewriter Hiss had owned but discarded.

Weinstein demonstrates that Hiss lied about the transfer of his car to Communists; lied when he said he had received a gift rug from Chambers in 1935 rather than 1937; lied when he said he did not remember how he had disposed of the typewriter; lied by omitting from a list of former maids the name of the one to whose family he gave the typewriter. For as long as possible, Hiss hid even from his attorneys the fact that he had located the typewriter. A spare recitation of the documented lies would fill pages. For thirty years, Hiss's allies have swept evidence beneath the rug, no matter how lumpy the rug has become. But no rug is large enough to cover Weinstein's mountain of incriminating evidence. A friend of Hiss's says, "Alger would not have put his friends and others through what they went through for him if he was guilty." Yet he did. Why? Weinstein quotes the following from Rebecca West's classic study of traitors:

> In [July] 1948, in a Philadelphia bar during the Progressive Party convention which adopted Henry Wallace as a Presidential candidate, a Russian forgot and talked. He said: "In England . . . persons detected in espionage on behalf of the Soviet Union are instructed by whichever of our organizations it is which has been using them, to plead guilty . . . In the United States, where legal proceedings are likely to be prolonged and confused, and all sorts of considerations may prevent the truth from appearing, it is worthwhile putting up a plea of not guilty, no matter how absurd this may be in view of the real facts."

Hiss spent forty-four months in prison, convicted of perjury for swearing he had not met or passed documents to Chambers in 1938. Weinstein does not say Hiss committed espionage after

1938, but he notes that in 1945, Hiss made a sweeping request to the Office of Strategic Services (predecessor of the CIA) for highly sensitive information unrelated to his duties. In 1945, Soviet Ambassador Andrei Gromyko urged that Hiss be made temporary Secretary-General of the United Nations. But Igor Gouzenko, the Russian who defected in Canada in 1945, said there was an agent close to Secretary of State Edward Stettinius, and U.S. officials believed Gouzenko meant Hiss. In 1946, Hiss was isolated from sensitive materials and eased out of government to avoid scandal.

Hiss says he was "radicalized" by the 1960s, when he was an ornament to "peace" rallies. He has benefited from "revisionist" history, which argues that U.S. paranoia caused the Cold War. And since Watergate, the fact that Congressman Nixon was involved in the case has helped the campaign to sanitize Hiss. In 1975, Hiss became the first person ever readmitted to the Massachusetts bar after a major criminal conviction. One judge emphasized that Hiss "believes" he was wronged and has done nothing *since* prison that supports "the thesis" that he was guilty. In 1975, Hiss examined microfilm Chambers had hidden in a pumpkin, and told the press easily refutable lies, including that he had not previously known the contents of the film. (He knew the contents at his 1949 trial.) The press was a passive conduit for his lies. Hiss, 73, thinks he will be "venerated" by the time he is 80.

At his trials (the first jury split 8–4 for conviction), his principal defense was an attack on Chambers' homosexual and conspiratorial past. In 1967, a pro-Hiss psychologist published a "psychobiography" of Chambers, whom he had never met. He ignored inconvenient evidence, distorted sources, repeated well-refuted lies and "proved" that, *somehow,* the suicide of Chambers' brother in 1926 had made Chambers frame Hiss, *somehow.* The psychiatrist detected "saintliness" in Hiss.

Hiss recently was defended by Lillian Hellman. She has defended Stalin's purge trials, attacked those who organized relief for Finnish victims of Soviet aggression, and neither the Stalin-Hitler pact nor the Soviet overthrow of Czechoslovakia's democracy prevented her from being a fixture in front groups. In her most recent book, a celebration (and misrepresentation) of herself and her politics, she asserts Hiss's innocence, citing as facts elementary falsehoods about the case that suggest, at best, indifference to truth.

Anyone who had defended Hitler's tyranny for fifteen days the way Hellman defended Stalin's tyranny for fifteen years would be indelibly stigmatized as a scoundrel. But for several years, as Diana Trilling says, many intellectuals measured their liberalism "by their sympathy with, or at least silence about, Soviet dictatorship." Now the scabrous careers of Joseph McCarthy and Nixon, and the pain of Vietnam, have resuscitated anti-anti-Communism.

Last week was the thirtieth anniversary of the murder of the Czech Foreign Minister Jan Masaryk in the Communist seizure of power. Last week, President Carter, who has chided Americans for their "inordinate" fear of Communism, toasted Marshal Tito, the Communist dictator of Yugoslavia, as "a man who believes in human rights" and has "protected" the "freedom" of his people. This week the French go to the polls, having been asked to take seriously U.S. warnings against entrusting their freedom to Communists.

March 20, 1978

Adam Smith: The Impoverishment of Politics

A reader, who may think I would write more sensibly if I dressed more ideologically, has given me one of those neckties now fashionable in Washington: one embellished with little profiles of the man on whose tombstone in a British churchyard is inscribed the information that here lies the author of *The Wealth of Nations*.

Fewer people in Washington have read Adam Smith's book than are wearing Adam Smith neckties. The book was launched the year this Republic was launched, 1776, and the Republic's current problems are related to the sort of ideas expressed in that book.

Frequently, a new fashion in economics derives from a new book, such as Keynes's *General Theory* forty years ago. There is no new text explaining "supply-side" economics, which may be one reason there are so many more people who say they are "supply-siders" than there are people who say precisely what they mean. Adam Smith is revered by the people struggling with the nation's problems. He also may be a source of its problems.

Smith was an absentminded professor (he once stepped into his garden wearing only a dressing gown, began daydreaming and walked fifteen miles away). He helped make the modern world. He lectured on "moral philosophy," of which economics was then understood to be a facet. He is famous as the philosopher of *laissez-faire,* and deserves the gratitude of subsequent generations for illuminating the merits of free markets as allocators of society's resources.

But he also was among the first modern political philosophers; he assumed that the aim of social life is to increase the consumption of goods and services. Furthermore, he argued that individual self-interestedness, when given ample scope, can produce this result and guarantee social harmony.

To an age fascinated by physics and the "laws of motion" in planets and other bodies, Smith announced that men, and hence the body politic, obey "laws of motion." He discovered orderliness beneath the turmoil of society—predictability based on the simplicity of man's unchanging desires and self-interestedness. The uncoerced cooperation of people pursuing their private interests produces, through the mechanism of free markets, social betterment. This result is unplanned; indeed, no one aims to better society's condition: each man aims to better only himself. It is, Smith said, as though a "hidden hand" guided the process whereby the public good, although unintended, results from the pursuit of private goals.

Unfortunately, implicit in Smith's theory is a sharp distinction between society and government, and the seeds of hostility toward government. The theory makes government seem merely coercive and barely necessary: Society is essentially independent of, and morally superior to, political institutions. Society is natural, spontaneous, cooperative and productive. Government is of marginal importance and negligible dignity.

This devaluing of government radically lowered the stature of the political vocation. Political philosophy was eclipsed by an economic theory which described society as a system of forces able to function well in equilibrium without the help of politics.

Before the modern age, of which Smith was a herald, political philosophers disagreed as to what constituted the public good, but agreed that the public good was to be discovered by reason: the reasoning of the wisest. Modern political philosophy holds that the public good is rooted in, and produced by, the desires of the many—including desires (for wealth, acquisition, consumption) generally considered low. The assumption is that the public good (defined by Smith and other moderns as increased consumption) is produced by the unfettered pursuit of private goals.

Today in Washington, people wearing the Adam Smith neckties are grappling with some problems made, and made more difficult to solve, by the sort of ideas Smith helped make prevalent.

How did we get today's misshapen government? The problem is not so much that the government is "too big" as it is that the government is considered a low and hostile thing. Thus it is an entity factions may compete at capturing, for the purpose of increasing their consumption. People feel no compunction about bending public power to private purposes when the public good is complacently defined as whatever results from the pursuit of private interest.

Given that definition, the concept of "public-spiritedness" evaporates. The rhetoric of modern politics is such a watery soup of "interests" and "rights" and "entitlements" that the Reagan Administration finds itself appealing for sacrifices with the strained argument that all sacrifices are really in everyone's personal "interest."

Adam Smith was among the makers of the modern mind, with its impoverished sense of politics. That is why I find the Adam Smith necktie lovelier than his philosophy.

March 22, 1981

Joe Louis: Win, but Never Smile

The world into which Lillie Barrow, 28, brought her seventh child, an eleven-pound boy, in May, 1914, was unpromising. But Joseph Louis Barrow was destined for a career open to his incomparable talents.

Louis tells only a bit of his story in his new autobiography. Considering his life, it is a remarkably uncomplaining testament.

Gerald Aster, a biographer of Louis, notes that in 1914, Booker T. Washington said, "I have never seen the colored people so discouraged and bitter. . . ." President Wilson was segregating many hitherto integrated government agencies, and the lives of white sports fans were blighted because Jack Johnson, a black man, was heavyweight champion.

Johnson's marriage to a white woman caused uproar, and the nation so yearned for a "white hope" that nineteen deaths were attributed to the riots when he beat Jim Jeffries in 1910. A congressman, one of many who introduced bills to ban mixed marriages, proclaimed:

> No brutality, no infamy, no degradation in all the years of southern slavery, possessed such villainous character and such atrocious qualities as the state laws which allow the marriage of the Negro Jack Johnson to a woman of the Caucasian strain.

When Henry Ford decided to replace the Model T (born, like Louis, in 1914) with the Model A, Louis' family, eighteen strong (his mother had had another child, and had married a widower with eight children), joined the migration of Southern blacks to booming Detroit. There, in 1932, Louis first entered a ring, and was so soundly thrashed and poorly paid ($7) that he too went to work for Ford.

Then he tried again, with a prudent manager who warned: "For God's sake, after you beat a white opponent, don't smile!" Another warning was "Above all, never have your picture taken with a white woman."

Jimmy Carter recalls black neighbors listening on the Carters' radio as Louis whipped a white opponent:

> There was no sound from anyone . . . except a polite, "Thank you, Mister Earl," offered to my father. Then, our several dozen visitors filed across the dirt road . . . and quietly entered a house about a hundred yards away. . . . At that point Pandemonium broke loose. . . . But all the curious, accepted proprieties of a racially segregated society had been carefully observed.

The Nazis had "explained" Jesse Owens' victories at the 1936 Berlin Olympics in terms of "African heelbones" that enabled blacks to outrun members of the Master Race. When, in 1938, Louis destroyed Max Schmeling in 124 seconds, the Nazis edited the film to suggest that Louis had won on a foul.

This was the world as Louis knew it:

A black professor had worried that if Louis beat Italy's Primo Carnera, Mussolini would "annihilate Abyssinia." New York's police commissioner said a Louis fight would not cause disorder in Harlem because "the American Negro is by nature . . . happy and fun-loving." A quite ordinary newspaper story described Louis as "an ordinary colored boy, slow thinking and emotionless." When war came, a journalist urged Louis to join the Air Corps because "colored men can see much better at night than whites." Louis was pelted with such advice about how to "deserve" the words that arena announcers routinely spoke: "Joe Louis, heavyweight champion—and a credit to his race."

It has been said that the succession of heavyweight champions from Louis to Sonny Liston to Muhammad Ali is a rough measure of black emancipation. Louis established the right of a black to be quiet and talented. Liston, a convict, established the right to be mean and talented. Ali established the right to be obnoxious and talented.

Until the sharp tooth of time took his skills, Louis was a model of implacable concision. He won 68 of 71 fights, 54 by knockouts. But most of his earnings slipped through his amazing hands. He wound up doing degrading "wrestling" exhibitions while the Internal Revenue Service pursued him for $1 million in back taxes.

Recently he has been a "greeter" at Caesar's Palace in Las Vegas, paid to loiter around the casino. That is no place for a champion from the sport in which luck matters least.

August 7, 1978

Strom Thurmond: The Great Nay-Sayer

Sixty-eight years ago, John Thurmond packed his 6-year-old son, Strom, into a buggy for a trip to see Senator "Pitchfork" Ben Tillman, a somewhat crusty statesman who once proposed sticking a pitchfork into President Cleveland. Strom stuck out his hand to the great man, who grasped it roughly and demanded roughly, "Well, what do you want?" Strom: "To shake your hand." Tillman: "Well, why the hell don't you shake?"

"I've been shaking hands ever since," says South Carolina's senior senator. And not infrequently he has been shaking a clenched fist, too.

South Carolina was the first state to sign the Declaration of Independence, and in 1860 it was the first to secede. At about that time a native declared that South Carolina was too large to be an insane asylum and too small to be a nation, and after the unpleasantness at Fort Sumter, a lot of non-natives agreed. The state motto, woven into a rug in Thurmond's office, is *Dum Spiro, Spero*— "While I Breathe, I Hope." That expresses the defiance of people who are not strangers to defeat. It also expresses Thurmond, who is full of vinegar and spoiling for a fight.

Thurmond sits at his desk like a pilot at the controls of a bomber, erect, alert, both hands busy. Riffling through his ammunition, a file of papers pertaining to the Panama Canal, he plucks a document explaining the sorry state of liberty in Panama. It is unthinkable, he says solemnly, that we could turn the canal over to a country that is unsound on *civil rights*. Thurmond does not have a sense of irony.

He has Daniel Webster's eyebrows, and eyes like tarnished dimes. He has the large hands and wrists of a man built for seizing and subduing things, as a senator learned when he and Thurmond settled a parliamentary point with a wrestling match. Thurmond's general demeanor calls to mind Ray Nitschke, a Green Bay Packers linebacker who looked like a grandfather and played like the Godfather. Thurmond has not been characterized by a cold, donnish aloofness from the turmoils of his time, and the idea of ceding control of the Panama Canal has made him somewhat fractious.

A friend of mine, a Catholic priest full of the ecumenical spirit, once asked a bishop for his views on cooperating with Protestants. The bishop explained: "We're right and they're wrong and they've got to admit it." The answer, although a bit elementary, was admirably direct. Directness is the defining trait of Thurmond, who feels more strongly about almost everything than most senators feel about anything. He often expresses himself with what colleagues consider unnecessary strength. He has always compensated with energy for what he lacks in finesse, and will do so again to fight the Panama Canal treaty.

In *The Last Hurrah*, Edwin O'Connor's novel about Boston politics, Mayor Frank Skeffington cheerfully says that man's best friend is the compromise. Thurmond doesn't think so. He practices the politics of Pickett's Charge, marching into the enemy's guns. He has achieved Pickett's results. He has planted himself in front of the galloping horse of history and cried "Halt!" and has been trampled in the dust time and again. No senator fought more raucously or with less effect against the Senate's finest acts, the civil-rights laws. The reward for failure has been seniority.

In 1948, while a Democratic governor, he ran for President as a Dixiecrat. In 1954, he took on South Carolina's Democratic hierarchy and became the only U.S. senator ever elected by a write-in vote. He became a Republican in 1964. In 1968, Thurmond's support of Richard Nixon's Southern strategy was so crucial to Nixon's nomination and election that the White House was supposed to become "Uncle Strom's Cabin." But Thurmond knows a dangerous gang when he sees one and soon denounced Nixon's "ultraliberal advisers."

Until Jimmy Carter, it was said that a Deep South politician is a wine that will not travel. But today Thurmond is traveling hard, rallying his infantry for a charge against the treaty. Recently he was in Minneapolis swapping expressions of esteem with the national convention of the Veterans of Foreign Wars. His exercise in preaching to the choir was crowned with success when the veterans voted overwhelmingly to oppose the canal treaty.

While in Minneapolis he went to Hubert Humphrey's bedside, a visit by the bitter-ender to the Happy Warrior. Their careers ignited simultaneously at the Democratic Convention in 1948, when Humphrey, the mayor of Minneapolis, led the fight for a civil-rights plank that provoked Thurmond's Dixiecrat candidacy. Thurmond, the champion filibusterer (24 hours 18 minutes), and Humphrey, the great exhorter, have been the Senate's famous talkers. Humphrey, the enthusiast, has shaped the nation; Thurmond, the nay-sayer, has not. But the struggle over ratification of the treaty will put Thurmond in the limelight for the first time since the civil-rights showdown, and he could win, for a change. If thirty-three senators join with him, the treaty will die, and if the vote were today, at least that many would.

Popularly elected legislatures are happiest when saying "Yes" to constituents. But variety is the spice of life, and merely saying "Yes" can come to seem servile, so it is pleasant to have opportunities for saying "No." It is especially pleasant for the Senate to enhance its institutional pride by saying "No" to the Executive Branch. In recent years, the Senate has done so regarding Justice Abe Fortas, Judge Clement Haynsworth, Judge Harrold Carswell, the SST, Cambodian bombing, aid to Angola.

Many conservatives are as happy as clams that the treaty, product of thirteen years of negotiations, and of principles formulated in 1974, has fallen into President Carter's lap. It is a chance for a dramatic confrontation with a President who has been a frustrating target. It is odd that persons who fancy themselves conservatives look for leadership to Thurmond, who for decades, on the issue (civil rights) that most engaged his passions, compiled a record almost unblemished by realism. After all, the foremost conservative virtue is prudence, which involves facing facts, facts like Panamanian nationalism and the reluctance of Americans to pay the cost of opposing that nationalism.

But as the debate begins, most Americans oppose ceding control of the canal, and as the debate grows warmer, opposition will too. The arguments that are easy and fun to make, the ones that stir the soul and satisfy animal spirits, are for keeping the canal. Yielding the canal may be prudent, but prudence, although a virtue, is not a heroic virtue. That is why Thurmond, shaking hands and shaking his fist, is a force to reckon with. As was said of Jefferson Davis when he was sworn in as Confederate President, the man and the hour have met.

September 5, 1977

Harold Macmillan: The Fox in Winter

At this moment of rearrangement, with Washington even more self-absorbed and sunk-in-the-momentary than usual, a visitor from another place and time has passed through, and his presence has gently insinuated into this city's mind a salutary sense of the long sweep of large political lives.

Harold Macmillan, the fox in winter, is 86. He was lucky to live to be 26. As an officer in the First World War, he was among the point men for a doomed generation. He was wounded three times, and his name became a byword for bravery in his brigade. He was the only honors entrant in his year at Balliol College, Oxford, to survive the war. Perhaps one reason he shows none of the melancholy that often afflicts old men is that he had so much occasion for melancholy when he was young, in the war that killed so many friends.

To come home from the carnage of Flanders to the frivolity of London in the twenties could instill an unthawable chill in a man. It may have done so in Macmillan, who entered Parliament in 1924.

There was perfect continuity between Churchill's public and private lives: brooding or acting, he had no facade. But Macmillan seems to have played out his political career behind a facade of studied diffidence, almost languor. It was as deceptive as was (or so 'tis said) the monocle he wore (it was corrective, not merely decorative, as he insisted) when enlisting in the army.

Every combatant but the United States emerged from the First World War diminished. Britain, especially, was diminished by the Second. The 1950s, which promised revival, were instead a decade of letdown for Britain. Shortly after Suez, Macmillan came to power, remaining Prime Minister until 1963.

When urged to give Britons "a sense of purpose," he said, "If people want a sense of purpose they can get it from their archbishops." And in 1963, invited to sum up his political life, he said:

I usually drive down to Sussex on Saturday mornings and I find my car in a line of family cars. . . . Ten years ago most of them would not have had cars, would have spent their weekends in their back streets, and would have seen the seaside, if at all, once a year. Now— now, I look forward to the time, not far away, when those cars will be a little larger, a little more comfortable, and all of them will be carrying on their roofs boats. . . .

Again, the facade, the studied offhandedness. But those statements were more than a pose. He defined the stakes of politics as far as possible from the terrors of Flanders. Better conservative materialism than the idealism with which Europe went to war in 1914. He still faces resolutely forward and believes Britain can find in technology what America found in the frontier: an invigorating challenge.

During Macmillan's tenure as Prime Minister, Britain's needs (especially the need for bracing contact with more vigorous societies) seemed to coincide with the principal idealism left to the survivors of Europe's wars: European unity. Macmillan's greatest contemporary, and his great adversary regarding British membership in the European community, was Charles de Gaulle, whose greatest challenge, Algeria, compelled him to be a ruthless liquidator.

Macmillan too was a brave liquidator, of empire and of an attitude. In politics as in war, orderly retreat calls for special skills, and Macmillan understood that "the will at the center" was gone—Britain's will to maintain Great Power status.

British television has recently specialized in Edwardian nostalgia: *The Forsyte Saga, The Duchess of Duke Street, Lillie, Edward the King, Upstairs/Downstairs.* The Edwardian epoch was the Indian summer of Britain's ascendancy, the moment before the world went smash. Macmillan, the last Edwardian, is half Hoosier, half Highlander: His mother was from Indiana, his father from Scotland. Macmillan insists that everyone is "half Cromwellian, half Cavalier" or "half John Knox, half Mary Queen of Scots"—half severe, half romantic. He is, to me, part of the romance of our time.

Two years ago, he spoke at a dinner given by *The Economist,* which published his remarks as a graceful editorial. *The Economist* noted: "Mr. Macmillan spoke without notes; his words are reproduced here without change." The boy is father to the man: when not much more than a boy, this man read Aeschylus while lying wounded in no-man's-land.

Today his manner is, as always, elegant ease, and understatement raised to the level of art.

"We had this thing called a 'permissive society,' but now there is a general feeling, 'Look here, this has gone a bit far.'" It is as though seventy years ago some Joshua commanded the Edwardian sun to stay at its zenith, and it did. Would that it had.

November 30, 1980

Ted Kennedy: Heavy Hitter in the Dugout

Ambling to the Senate chamber the other day, Edward Kennedy met a Western senator and fell to recalling, as politicians will for small talk, wonderful experiences in the other fellow's wonderful state. Kennedy remembered campaigning at a rodeo and riding, for about five seconds, a bronco named Skyrocket. That was eighteen years ago. The hero of D-Day was President, and Kennedy was bucked into the dust for the sake of his brother's Presidential campaign.

Time is a great healer of life's bruises, and today he walks jauntily, with the slightly rolling gait of certain large-framed men, half sailor, half cop. He is the personification of vigor and animal spirits. When he meets constituents, his buoyancy becomes like that of the Graham Greene character who resembled "a warship going into action, a warship on the right side in a war to end all wars."

He has a large laugh, likes large cigars and has a heart happy in Senate toil.

But he has seen the skull beneath the skin of life. Two weeks ago, he reached the exact age at which John Kennedy was assassinated. So he has lived longer than any of the three other sons born to Rose and Joseph Kennedy. Small wonder the last son is not conspicuously eager to campaign for the office that has cost his family so dearly. And it would be uncharitable to assume him incapable of what George Eliot called "the unapplauded heroism which turns off the broad road of achievement at the call of the nearer duty whose effect lies within the beating of the hearts that are close to us."

Edward Kennedy was born on the bicentennial of George Washington's birthday (February 22, 1932), and if elected in 1980 he would be the fourth-youngest man elected, after John Kennedy, Theodore Roosevelt, and U. S. Grant. Kennedy knows that the cheers he hears today are, in part, cheers for the dead. But Jimmy Carter knows he would not have been the star of the 1976 season if Kennedy, the heavy hitter, had not stayed in the dugout, and Carter knows that Kennedy can be, if he chooses to be, the Democrats' designated hitter in 1980. A reasonable surmise is that a decision about 1980 will be made in 1980, and a decision to run will be made only in response to certain events, such as Carter's losing primaries to Jerry Brown.

It might seem that with all the blood in the water around Carter, only an unreasonably apathetic shark would turn away. But Kennedy does not seem hungry. Neither does he seem like a man nagged by unrealized ambitions. And the nation is not really calling with parched tongue for him to run. Millions who say they want him to run do not know what his ideas are, and a substantial number of those people would not want him if they knew.

It is said that the nation is feeling conservative, but it is wrong to dignify today's mood with the noble word "conservative." Conservatives generally may be grumpy, but there is more to conservatism than collective grumpiness about government. And the "tax revolt," which is rather less than a revolution, is also less than a rounded expression of conservative values. Still, the nation would be relatively satisfied if the government would just quit ruining the currency. And Kennedy, as President, would not practice what Disraeli called "masterful inactivity." He would be like a boy stirring a beehive with a stick. He favors more judicial activism, more progressive taxation and, generally, more of the redistributionist activities of a welfare state. He favors those things, but he is not adamant and aflame as Robert was.

Kennedy talks animatedly and intelligently about public health, and the business of the Judiciary Committee, over which he will preside beginning next year. He has more seniority than all but sixteen other senators, but it is unclear what, if anything, stirs him, deep down: the Kennedys almost invented the modern politics of shiny surfaces. He, even more than the nation, was emotionally exhausted at the end of the 1960s. But as the end of another decade draws near, it seems possible that whatever fires once burned hotly within him have been banked for the foreseeable future.

When asked to name a national problem, he expresses "disappointment" about the "failure of Americans to be challenged" and about the "cooling off" of the people. John told the country to get "moving"; Robert exhorted it to "do better." Edward wants heat and challenge, but today the now-familiar words and cadences do not ring as they once did. John vowed to infuse new ideas into a Washington gone stodgy. But Edward's industrial-state liberalism does not seem at all new, and the nation, having seen and winced at much since 1961, no longer finds that liberalism satisfying.

The issues of the 1960s were so satisfying to some liberals because the issues could be expressed in simple injunctions ("End Segregation," "End the Bombing") or crisp legislative proposals (protecting voting rights, cutting off appropriations for the war). And the issues were personalized by focusing on "villains": "Hey, hey, L.B.J., how many kids did you kill today?" But today, neither inflation nor the problem of black youth nor any other substantial issue lends itself to slogans or simple legislative acts or identification of "villains."

Today, there is this paradox: Carter barely beat the most conservative President since Calvin Coolidge, and he won only because voters concluded that although he is a Democrat, he would be an exceptionally mild priest of that faith. Yet Kennedy, one of the most liberal senators, has a more powerful appeal.

Some people, says Michael Oakeshott, the British political philosopher, consider government "an instrument of passion; the art of politics is to inflame and direct desire." On the other hand, he continues, a person of conservative disposition "understands it to be the business of government not to inflame passion and give it new objects to feed upon, but to inject into the activities of already too passionate men an ingredient of moderation; to restrain, to deflate . . ." The nation today is conservatively disposed, but the unquenchable—indeed, intensifying—fascination with Kennedy suggests a public restlessness that is seeking satisfaction.

Kennedy's appeal derives less from what he is than from what he intimates. He is an intimation of political electricity, and the strength of his appeal in the summer of Proposition 13 suggests a flaw in today's conservatism. Such conservatism neglects the craving for ennobling passion and enlarging public enterprises, a craving that great conservative statesmen such as Disraeli and Bismarck and Churchill understood because they shared it. Kennedy, the legatee of the liberal party's tradition, is ascendant even in a conservative season because he is a thread of scarlet in an otherwise faded fabric of public life.

September 4, 1978

Juan Carlos: King on a Tightrope

Those who savor irony, and the dissolution of political categories, should rejoice in King Juan Carlos of Spain. This monarch was the indispensable director, and to a considerable extent the author, of the drama that restored to Spain the essence of republican government—a legislature of elected representatives. If democratizing an authoritarian regime of the Right constitutes an "opening to the left," a Bourbon may have been the most effective achiever "on the left" in postwar Europe.

His wait in the wings could have ruined him, as waiting ruined Queen Victoria's son Edward VII. And there were rumors of dissipation. Juan Carlos is tall and somewhat sleepy-eyed, which may have helped foster the false impression that he is mentally slow and awkward. But he is neither languid nor laconic. When Franco died, the moment found its man in Queen Victoria's great-great-grandson.

And now, at 41, brimming with the vigor of a physically powerful and politically seasoned man in his prime, Juan Carlos is in the peculiar position—gratifying but also melancholy—of having done, or at least earnestly hoping he has done, the great work of his life. That work was the peaceful dismantling, from within, of Franco's system, persuading the old parliament to vote itself out of existence and to summon political parties into existence.

In his final years Franco boasted that he had Spain *"atada y bien atada"*—tied and well tied. But Juan Carlos already was planning how to untie the knots. Not since Eisenhower has there been a military man whose political skills were so judiciously disguised and helpfully underrated.

The remarkable consensus that sustains Spain's new democratic order is reinforced by the belief that the choice is "this order or the army." There were more than fifty military plots, mutinies, coups or other political eruptions by the military in Spain between 1815 and General Franco's rebellion in 1936. But Juan Carlos is a soldier, an officer, a graduate of Saragossa academy (Spain's West Point), a jet pilot, and his most crucial and delicate task is to tranquilize the military.

He has had to walk a fine line, reassuring the military about the course of change, but not seeming too solicitous toward the military. He surely has in his mind's eye the example of his wife's family, the former royal family of Greece. In the Greek referendum that rejected the monarchy, much was made of allegations that the royal family had been too close to the armed forces.

Some terrorist attacks on officers almost certainly are designed to provoke the officer corps to attack democracy. Some terrorists have the *"Nach Hitler kommen wir"* mentality. That slogan —"After Hitler, we come"—was coined by German Communists fifty years ago. It expressed the theory that Hitler must come to power to provoke a proper revolution.

As a symbol of national unity in a nation riven by sectionalism—even by rival nationalisms—Juan Carlos understands how little he can involve himself in politics and policy. He has asked the government for more funds for Madrid's Prado Museum, but that was just one national monument helping another. His problem is less maintaining self-restraint than restraining others who do not yet understand, or will not respect, the rules and delicacies of constitutional monarchy. Because the King is accessible, and remarkably candid in private conversation, he has been embarrassed by people who, upon leaving the Zarzuela Palace, invoke his name and opinions in political arenas.

When Franco was dying, Santiago Carrillo, head of Spain's Communist Party, was asked how long Juan Carlos would last as King, and he said "as long as a caramel by a schoolhouse door." But Carrillo has been photographed bowing over the royal hand. This is, of course, only another in a lifelong series of Carrillo's cynicisms. But it demonstrates the King's power to evoke at least the forms of deference. And among the public benefits from that power is that people like Carrillo are required to advertise their cynicism.

As historian Hugh Thomas says, the transformation of Franco's tyranny into Juan Carlos' democracy is "one of the success stories of modern times"—not least because where Euro-communism was supposed to prosper, Euro-monarchism has prevailed.

June 3, 1979

Ray Kroc: Artist of the Hamburger

Ray Kroc is a small, energetic 75-year-old, as unpretentious as hamburger, as salty as French-fries, as American as frozen apple pie. He is worth upwards of half a billion dollars, which is not bad for a man who started his business when he was 52, who paid his secretary stock in lieu of salary (stock now worth many millions) and whose most expensive product costs less than a dollar. Born in Chicago, he joined the Army when he was 16 and trained with a Chicagoan named Disney. So Company A contained two prodigies of mass marketing, one who would create the Big Mac and one who would create Mickey Mouse.

Kroc was a cheerful Willy Loman, a salesman with a heavy sample case and boundless enthusiasm for his products, especially the Multimixer, a machine for mixing five milkshakes simultaneously. Selling had taken him into a zillion restaurant kitchens by the time, in 1954, he heard that two brothers were using *eight* Multimixers at their quick-service restaurant in San Bernardino, California. He went west to investigate and, like Keats's Cortez staring at the Pacific, looked on with a wild surmise. He got the right to franchise what he saw, including the brothers' name and the golden arches. In 1955, he opened his first McDonald's in Des Plaines, Illinois, and began grinding it out.

Today, McDonald's ranks first among retailing companies in terms of net income as a percentage of sales. When McDonald's went public in 1965, one hundred shares cost $2,250. On December 31, 1975, that investment, adjusted for splits and dividends, was worth $107,176. McDonald's U.S. stores average gross sales of $857,000 a year. Some gross more than $2 million. This year McDonald's will probably open its five thousandth store. It has sold twenty-five billion hamburgers, and is selling a billion every three months. Twenty-five billion hamburgers would make twenty piles the size of the world's tallest building, Chicago's Sears Tower, a monument to another retailing genius. The flour for twenty-five billion buns would make five feet of powder on the ski slopes of Aspen and Vail. McDonald's has sold enough shakes to fill every gas tank in America.

The earth must slope before a river can flow, and the public must be predisposed before a success on the scale of McDonald's can happen. The Second World War got many American palates accustomed to standardized fare, from C rations and from factory canteens. Europeans linger over meals; Americans regard food as fuel to be taken on the way steam locomotives took on water, scooping it at full speed from troughs between the rails. This vast and polyglot nation has never pretended to have a national cuisine. Americans generally want food that is hygienic, copious and fast.

What Isaac Singer's machine did for clothing; what Charles Walgreen did for drugs; what Aaron Montgomery Ward, Richard Sears, Alvah Roebuck and F. W. Woolworth did for "dry goods"; what Gail Borden did for condensed food; what Philip Armour and Gustavus Swift did for fresh meat; what George Gilman and George Huntington Hartford and their Great Atlantic & Pacific Tea Co. did for produce, Kroc has done for fast food. He did not just launch a company, he energized an industry. The fast-food industry—$14 billion a year—is one reason that one of every three American meals is eaten out. Kroc has been called "the service sector's equivalent of Henry Ford." Consider Peter Drucker's description of Ford:

. . . There is no machine, no tool, no new product, no process that bears his name, was invented by him, or could have been patented by him. Everything he used was known. There were plenty of automobiles on the market before he brought out his first one. And yet Henry Ford was a true innovator. What he contributed were mass production, the mass market, the profitability of the very cheap . . .

At McDonald's hamburger university, students earn degrees in hamburgerology by mastering computerized French-fries and other technology that enables unskilled teen-agers in Tokyo or Trenton to produce hamburgers as alike as Model T's were. This uniformity is especially remarkable because McDonald's is primarily a confederation of small-business men, the franchise owners who buy all materials from independent suppliers. Franchising is a solution to the problem of distributing goods in a continental nation. Automobiles, gasoline, motels, fast food: many franchised products are for mobile people who value familiarity because they want to feel at home away from home. Franchised products are part of the homogenizing of experience that a nation of travelers finds more reassuring than boring.

Kroc has a nineteenth-century feeling for the romance of enterprise. Like the English industrialist who cut down a grove of trees so that he could gaze from his parlor at smoke from his factory, Kroc cherished his first California home because it was on a hill from which he could watch, through binoculars, a McDonald's. His autobiography, *Grinding It Out*, recalls a popular nineteenth-century literary genre, the entrepreneur's lyric. "It requires a certain kind of mind," he writes, "to see beauty in a hamburger bun. Yet, is it any more unusual to find grace in the texture and softly curved silhouette of a bun than to reflect lovingly on . . . the arrangement of textures and colors in a butterfly's wing?" Warming to his theme, he praises buns and Fred Turner, his aide, for studying them:

> At first they were cluster buns, meaning that the buns were attached to each other in clusters of four to six, and they were only partially sliced. Fred pointed out that it would be easier and faster for a griddle man if we had individual buns instead of clusters and if they were sliced all the way through. The baker could afford to do it our way because of the quantities of buns we were ordering. Fred also worked . . . on the design of a sturdy, reusable box for our buns. Handling these boxes instead of the customary packages of twelve reduced the baker's packaging cost, so he was able to give us a better price . . . It also . . . streamlined our operations. With the old packages, it didn't take long for a busy griddle man to find himself buried in paper. Then there was the time spent opening packages, pulling buns from the cluster, and halving them. These fractions of seconds added up to wasted minutes.

Kroc's book, like his life, is as ingenuous as an American primitive painting. His prose, like his enterprise, expresses the prosaic idea on which American prosperity rests: *things add up*. Enough billions of fractions of anything (seconds, pennies) add up to a lot of something. Obsessive attention to detail—to boxes of buns, to time-and-motion studies—pays because America is the realm of mass effects: throughout American life you see astounding cumulative consequences of minute increments. Kroc's genius, like that of many entrepreneurs, is for acting on the obvious—or what seems obvious after he has acted on it.

February 20, 1978

Mary Marvich: American

In 1873, three years after General Robert E. Lee died in Virginia and three years before General George Custer died in Montana, Mary Zynovich was born in Belgrade, Serbia, in the Austro-Hungarian Empire. U. S. Grant was U.S. President, there were thirty-seven states and forty million Americans, and Mary was sixteen years from joining them.

Recently, in a courtroom in Fairmont, West Virginia, Mary Marvich, 107, became a citizen, ninety-one years after arriving in New York on a wooden sailing ship. She had much on her mind in 1889, and decades passed before she sought citizenship. When she did, she had problems, such as with a rule requiring her to recall the name of her ship. More decades passed—time flies when you're having fun—but as she entered her second century she decided to tidy up her citizenship. And when at last she took the oath, the Governor was on hand. He is descended from French Huguenots who, fleeing religious persecution, changed their name from Roquefeuille to something similar but less French and arrived in America, via Germany, in 1723. His name is John D. (Jay) Rockefeller IV.

(As often happened, a Polish tailor who arrived in 1903 had his name shortened and "Americanized" at Ellis Island by immigration officials who could not cope with the name Marciszewski. Today, the tailor's son, Edmund Muskie, is Secretary of State.)

The oath of citizenship says: "I hereby declare, on oath, that I absolutely and entirely renounce and abjure all allegiance and fidelity to any foreign prince, potentate, state, or sovereignty . . . that I will support and defend the Constitution and laws of the United States against all enemies, foreign and domestic . . . that I will bear arms on behalf of the United States . . . so help me God." It is stirring, especially the part about princes and potentates, but the judge exempted Mrs. Marvich from the clause about bearing arms.

In 1892, three years after the apple-cheeked Mary set a button-top shoe on American soil and went to work in a cigar factory, Thomas Bailey Aldrich, who probably liked cigars, wrote a poem for *The Atlantic Monthly*. Aldrich had been fastidious in his choice of ancestors, who got here before the riffraff began pouring through the nation's gates. His poem, which expressed widespread views, was called "The Unguarded Gates":

> *Wide open and unguarded stand our gates,*
> *And through them presses a wild motley throng—*
> *Men from the Volga and the Tartar steppes,*
> *Featureless figures from the Hoang-ho,*
> *Malayan, Scythian, Teuton, Kelt, and Slav,*
> *Flying the Old World's poverty and scorn;*
> *These bringing with them unknown gods and rites,*
> *Those, tiger passions, here to stretch their claws.*
> *In street and alley what strange tongues are these,*
> *Accents of menace alien to our air,*
> *Voices that once the tower of Babel knew!*

I'll wager dollars against doughnuts that Mary Marvich has kept her tiger passions tolerably well leashed. West Virginia, according to the song, is "almost heaven," so it has survived her claws. The wonder is that the immigrants survived as well as they did the hostility and other hazards in the New World.

Harried immigration officials had to decipher such written destinations as "Pringvilliamas" (Springfield, Massachusetts) and "Linkinbra" (Lincoln, Nebraska). Before many immigrants could head for "Szekenevno Pillsburs" (Second Avenue, Pittsburgh) and points west, they had large letters chalked on their clothes: "H" for suspected heart trouble, "L" for lameness, "X" for mental defects. Or "E" for eye trouble, such as trachoma, a disease that blinded and killed until a cure was found—by a Japanese immigrant. Many who, after the rigors of a transatlantic voyage in steerage, failed an often slapdash medical examination were deported. Families were broken. An adult was sent back with a very young child, but some 10-year-olds were simply sent back alone and turned loose in the port from which they had embarked.

Consider these numbers when someone says America is in danger of being "inundated" by today's "flood" of immigrants: In 1907 alone, 1.2 million immigrants arrived, 1 million of them at Ellis Island. On April 17, a record 11,745 were admitted there. Almost exactly ten years later, the United States declared war, and some of the new citizens were dressed in khaki and sent back to put the kibosh on the Kaiser and on the Austro-Hungarian Empire. When there were wars to be fought or railroads to be built, or when the servant problem became acute, uses were found for the "wild motley throng."

Mary Zynovich married an immigrant named Marvich from Belgrade. She has lived for eighty-six years in Marion County, West Virginia, where her daughter, Betty Nicoletti, lives with her husband, whose parents were born in Italy. "Once," wrote Oscar Handlin, a Harvard historian, "I thought to write a history of the immigrants in America. Then I discovered that the immigrants *were* American history."

They still are. Individuals with the grit and families with the cohesion to make their way here from Indochina and Cuba are going to be, many of them, overachievers, leavening and invigorating America. Before long there will be, if there are not already, a

lot of high-school valedictorians named Nguyen and Lopez.
It is said that many immigrants who have recently arrived are
having trouble adjusting to American life. I believe it. I arrived in
1941, and *I'm* having trouble adjusting to American life. But the
newest citizens have the clearest idea of what we're celebrating
when we raise a red-white-and-blue ruckus on the Fourth of July.
So this year, light a sparkler for all the Nguyens and Lopezes, and
Mary Marvich.

July 7, 1980

John Merrick: Measured by Soul

John Merrick has come a long way from London's Whitechapel
Road to Broadway, and now to the silver screen. His short life,
which ended ninety years ago, is the basis of a long-running and
award-winning play, and a new film, and a masterly little book.
There is a timeless beauty in the story of "the Elephant Man."

He was afflicted from infancy with a hideous and progressive
disease, neurofibromatosis. Photographs in Michael Howell and
Peter Ford's book show that the 5-foot-2-inch Merrick had a head
with the circumference of a large man's waist (36 inches); "a misshapen mass of bony lumps and cauliflower-like growth of skin";
the forehead disfigured by bony material bulging forward in
mounds, almost obscuring one eye. His face was distorted by a
mass of flesh protruding from his mouth, forcing the lips back into
folds. This "trunk" made speaking and even eating an ordeal.
Pendulous layers of flabby skin hung from his chest and back. His
right arm was enormous; his right hand was more like a fin than
like a hand. One radish-shaped finger measured five inches
around. His left arm was normal, even delicate.

Imagine his mother's terror when his transformation began. She
died when he was 10; his stepmother rejected him. Too crippled to
work, he—like Blanche in *A Streetcar Named Desire*—"always

depended on the kindness of strangers." For years, he found none. To escape the sorrows of the workhouse, he became an exhibit, in a traveling one-man freak show which, fortunately for him, and us, came in November, 1884, to Whitechapel Road, opposite London Hospital. Frederick Treves, a young surgeon, went to see him and found "the embodiment of loneliness":

> The showman pulled back the curtain and revealed a bent figure crouched on a stool. . . . The showman—speaking as if to a dog—called out harshly: "Stand up!" The thing arose slowly. . . .

"Thing"?

Treves assumed, because he hoped, that this creature—whose face was as incapable of expression as a mass of mud, and whose cumbersome limbs frustrated even gestures—was mentally blank.

But there was a sensitive, if undeveloped, intelligence in that grotesque shell, as Treves and members of London society discovered when, by extraordinary luck, after several years, Merrick found haven in London Hospital. He read Jane Austen, visited the theater and enjoyed visits from upper-middle-class British ladies, those paragons of composure, who followed the lead of his most distinguished visitors, the Prince and Princess of Wales. Using his one good hand, he expressed his romantic sensibility by making remarkable cardboard models of churches.

His emotional and intellectual awakening was, like that of a child, as lovely as the opening of a tulip. Treves, who became one of England's great doctors, wrote, in old age, that Merrick had been an extraordinary moral as well as a medical phenomenon. Ennobled by passage through an unimaginable furnace, Merrick exemplifies the fathomless mysteries of "the evolution of character."

Merrick could not even sleep as others do, and when he tried, he died. He slept crouching or sitting, his burdensome head resting on his knees. He died at 29, when he lay back to sleep and the backward pull of his head suffocated him, or dislocated his neck.

When Treves died, in 1923, his friend Thomas Hardy wrote, in memoriam, about the dream of humane science, the quest for

> . . . *modern modes to stem despairs*
> *That mankind bears!*

Hardy knew that most of mankind's despairs are not amenable to physical remedies; Merrick showed how unembittered a man can be who will not despair.

Merrick was fond of verses from a poem by Isaac Watts, the Nonconformist clergyman who wrote such hymns as "O God, Our Help in Ages Past":

> *Were I so tall to reach the pole,*
> *Or grasp the ocean with my span,*
> *I must be measured by my soul;*
> *The mind's the standard of the man.*

Mind, that is, meaning not intellectual power but the distinctively human capacity to love, suffer loneliness and cherish life.

The play and especially the film take liberties with the facts and use Merrick's story to spin social parables. Read the book, *The True History of the Elephant Man.*

In every age, but especially in this age, mankind's tendency is to navigate by social stars. People judge their success and others' worth by outward signs—and achievement and acceptance. Merrick, besieged by his own hostile flesh, became a reminder of the transcendent importance of the spark within.

October 19, 1980

Cicely Saunders: Just a Very Good English Nurse

As all rivers flow to the same home, the sea, all lives reach the same end, death. But in a modest residential neighborhood south of the Thames, Dr. Cicely Saunders and her colleagues at Saint Christopher's Hospice in London are demonstrating that some ways of dying affirm and enhance life. Saunders, 59, a gray-haired 6-footer, radiates the determination of one who hears birds chirp, leaves rustle and people say "It can't be done," and regards it all as just sound, mere music of nature. She is nurse, social worker, physician and founder of Saint Christopher's. As a hospice it provides care to terminally ill patients and their loved ones. Its primary purpose is to alleviate chronic pain. Families are treated as units and cared for in bereavement.

Perhaps not until this century did the average visit of a patient to a doctor do more good than harm. But now medical proficiency, while making living better, is making dying more problematic. Medicine should prolong life, not the process of dying. There comes a point in a degenerative disease when further "aggressive" treatment would intensify the patient's suffering without substantial benefit. Then concern for the patient should become concern for a dignified death, for palliative care for symptoms and needs. This point is difficult to determine, because much is unknown about the behavior of advanced malignant diseases. But the point must be determined.

Saunders believes that doctors treating terminal cancer frequently are concerned too much with the disease process and too little with the patient as a person. "It seems that we first learn how to do things and only later *when* to do them." It is not always obligatory to use every medical technology as long as possible. For example, doctors should "consider what has been done to a patient who dies in the isolation of a laminar-flow room, perhaps unable to touch another person's hand for the last weeks of his life." At some point in terminal cases, such measures as chemotherapy, radiation and surgery could be described as treating the doctor, not the patient. Before recent medical advances, doctors had little technology to give, so they gave much of themselves at bedside. Today, when mistakenly prolonged attempts at cures are at last abandoned, many doctors desert the dying, who are left unsupported at the most demanding point of their illnesses.

Dying of a prolonged disease is less an event than a difficult process, which, like birth, requires understanding help. But understanding is scarce—not only because death is a mystery from which people flinch, but because it no longer is a reality with which people are acquainted. Until recently, death was woven into the fabric of life. A rural death was a village affair, and the impersonality of cities was tempered by large Victorian homes where grandparents died with grandchildren at bedside. One reason people had large families was that many children died of diseases no longer feared. Today life is healthier, families are smaller and dispersed. And death is too remote to be readily conceivable.

Saint Christopher's is not just for the dying (there is a wing for the frail elderly), but 90 percent of those admitted do not go home. The mean length of stay is twelve days. All but about twenty of the more than six hundred persons who died there in 1977 died of cancer. Saint Christopher's also is a teaching and research facility in the field of terminal care. Its premise is that no patient must remain in chronic pain. Its purpose is *efficient* loving care, hard medicine with a humane dimension in the treatment of all aspects of pain—physical, social, emotional and spiritual. Seventy percent of Saint Christopher's patients are on powerful analgesics—usually morphine taken orally, every four hours, in doses suited to each patient's requirement for keeping pain from breaking through. No patient is anxious about adequate medication, or unbearable pain.

Hospices here and in the United States are an answer to demands for euthanasia (meaning not the patient's legal right to demand withdrawal of life-support treatment, but the right to demand a killing act). Support for euthanasia legislation derives, in part, from the mistaken fear that doctors are obligated to prolong life with all available technologies, however severe the ordeal and cost, and the mistaken fear that unremitting pain in terminal diseases, especially cancer, is unavoidable. With hospice care as an alternative, there would be little demand for euthanasia. Without the hospice alternative, legalization of euthanasia would exert vicious pressure on people who are old and frail and believe society does not think much of them. When incurably ill, such people would think of an administered death as the only alternative to terrible suffering for themselves and terrible cost to their families, so their "right to die" would come to seem like a "duty to die."

Saunders speaks of "a positive achievement in dying" when terminal illness is "a time for reconciliation and fulfillment for the patient and his family, and may well be the most important period they spend together." Remember, she is a professional, not a sentimentalist, and she has earned the right to speak of dying, as she sees it daily. Aside from sophisticated pharmacology, Saint Christopher's specialty is simple words and gestures. The dying and those who attend them struggle, Saunders says, to make what T. S. Eliot called "a raid on the inarticulate." Patients' needs, she says, are summed by the words "Watch with me," meaning: "Be there."

The hospice is a therapeutic community within the community, helping the dying to live until they die and helping families to live on. At weekly staff meetings, members brief one another about patients in the hospice and as many at home, and about the grieving. A recent meeting was led by a remarkably poised, tranquil and businesslike young woman with that glowing complexion which is a blessing of life in a misty nation whose genius is not expressed in central heating. Saunders says, offhandedly, that the young woman, who radiates health and serenity amidst distress, "is just a very good English nurse." In Saunders' pride you sense the steel that made another English nurse, Florence Nightingale, such a force for improvement. Saint Christopher's staff generally has the placidness of a gentle river which, over time, cuts canyons in granite.

In her masterpiece *Middlemarch*, Mary Ann Evans (George Eliot), another extraordinary English lady, said of "the finely touched spirit" Dorothea: " . . . The effect of her being on those around her was incalculably diffusive: for the growing good of the world is partly dependent on unhistoric acts . . . " If the good of the world is growing, the hospice movement is one reason. It is a result of the concentrated intelligence and charity of the finely touched spirits at Saint Christopher's, and their predecessors and colleagues around the world.

January 9, 1978

Part Seven ◈

PREJUDICES

"Old": The Loveliest Word

The slow distillation of civilization has created a jewel where, long ago, oxen forded the River Isis. Oxford University, a jumble of yellow-gray stone, and gardens unreasonably green the year around, is as pretty as it is crowded. The university has much to teach the universities that teach other nations.

Crowdedness is Oxford's last medieval quality. Its architectural richness is a legacy of centuries that were blessed with an abundance of craftsmen, and were not cursed with plate glass and precast concrete.

The university resembles a toy carved from ivory by a delicate giant. Few sights are as pleasing as the intricate outline of the college walls and spires seen against a winter sky at dusk. Architecturally, as well as in the life of the mind, Oxford is a case of extreme elaborateness in a small place. Like civilization, it is cumulative, complicated, old and densely packed.

Oxford was founded before culture was nationalized; it is a crystal precipitated from the medieval class of truly European scholars. Because Oxford does not seize the causes of the day, it has been called the "home of lost causes." Were that true, it would be alarming, because Oxford's only cause is civilization.

Not since the "Oxford Movement," a nineteenth-century theological row, has Oxford been thoroughly preoccupied with a doctrinal fight. This is partly because the university is a creative anarchy of little states, the colleges. Another reason Oxford has outlived most doctrines taught within its walls is that it is less a place where things are settled than a place where things are discussed.

Oxford is a conversationalist's paradise. To come here as a student is to join a great conversation that has been in progress for centuries and that you know you will not see concluded. The heart of this endless conversation is the tutorial system.

Oxford's teachers are apt to teach many more hours than their American counterparts. Perhaps fewer books get written here than would be written were there no tutorial system. And conceivably that is unfortunate. But the tutorial system keeps Oxford's mind concentrated on the fact, frequently forgotten on American campuses, that the proper purpose of a university is as much teaching as research.

Furthermore, there are aspects of education, including perhaps the essence of education, that can be acquired best in the one-on-one encounter of an unformed mind with a formidable mind. Tutorials, in whatever subject, are ideally suited to teach several invaluable lessons. One is that there is a level beneath which an argument should not fall. Another lesson is that, as Samuel Johnson said, one can be convinced, if not pleased, against one's will.

American undergraduate life is increasingly regarded as a parenthesis between childhood schooling and the intellectual seriousness of graduate school or professional education. Undergraduates spend four qualifying years, not four serious educational years, to acquire a bachelor's degree that is a ticket for getting another ticket. The result is intellectual underutilization.

A system of large lectures (a system made measurably worse by "reforms" that have decreased required courses and expanded the academic cafeteria of electives) leaves less of a trace on students than the tutorial system leaves. At Oxford, the rule is intimate exposure to the best, as soon as possible. The tutorial system says: What you are doing *now* is important.

Tutorials can be close encounters of the strangest kind. Not long ago, Oxford had a distinguished professor of divinity who delivered tutorials while lying beneath a blanket. Many young men seeking instruction in things divine received it from a blanket-covered lump with a Scottish accent.

But some tutors who have good reason for hiding under a blanket do not. In the annals of English fortitude there are few examples as stirring as that of Geoffrey Warnock. He endured, without solace of distraction, my attempts at philosophy, and responded with stoical courtesy: "If I understand what you are trying to say . . ."

What I am trying to say now is that Henry James was wrong. He said that "youth" is the loveliest word in the language. For those who favor "old"—old ideas and institutions—this ancient community is the rainbow's end.

January 1, 1978

Progress Was All Right Once, but . . .

The fear that war may blow civilization to smithereens loses some of its sting when you see Denver's Colfax Avenue. It is one of those thoroughfares—most cities have at least one—which nuclear devastation would improve.

I used to consider Colfax Avenue second only to Rome's Victor Emmanuel Monument as evidence of mankind's capacity for excess. But the memorial in Rome has been just sitting there while Colfax has been evolving, and Colfax is no longer second.

It is lined with fast-"food" places selling deep-fried cholesterol, "book" stores offering the literature of unspeakable acts and unnatural practices, cinemas devoted to similar themes and other forms of enterprise more defensible but not measurably more eye-pleasing. This unsightly river of commerce reflects the malice of Destiny, which did not have elegance in mind for an avenue named after Schuyler Colfax.

Colfax was President Grant's first Vice President. Republicans refused to renominate him, even before they knew about his involvement in the Crédit Mobilier railroad scandal. Think of it: so deep was the doubt about his ethics, he failed to measure up even to the standards, such as they were, of the Republican Party of the 1870s.

But recently, amidst the rank growth of eyesores on the avenue named for that reprobate, I found an orchid: a fine used-book store. There I bought, for $2, a tiny volume published in 1922. It is *The Victorian Age*, a Cambridge University lecture by W. R. Inge. It was clever of Destiny to bring Inge to Colfax.

Inge was an eminent theologian and ecclesiastical historian, and remarkably opinionated. In 1922 he had lived only sixty-two of his allotted ninety-three years, but his lecture was a curmudgeon's summing up, an exercise in letting chips fall where they might. It was a bristling phalanx of passionate opinions, or bigotries, depending on your point of view.

Its tone may be understood from the short shrift he gives the Irish ("In Ireland the barbarous and illiterate peasantry multiplied until the population exceeded eight millions, when the inevitable famine illustrated nature's way of dealing with recklessness") and the French ("Our nation has a great tradition in fiction, and we shall be wise to stick to it, instead of preferring a corrupt following of the French, whose novelists . . . seem to me frequently dull and usually repulsive"). His opinions were not always appreciated. He once received a letter that said, "I am praying for your death. I have been very successful in two other instances."

Colorado, where every prospect pleases and only man and Colfax Avenue are vile, is an appropriate place to stumble on Inge's reminder that "Until the reign of George III a town was regarded as improving a landscape." Inge believed that "ugliness in the works of man is a symptom of social disease," and that the disease of industrialism had brought about the extinction of "handicrafts and the temper which inspired them."

This idea recently bubbled up in a biography of Samuel Johnson by John Wain, Oxford professor of poetry. In a bracingly reactionary digression, Wain writes:

Yes, perhaps that is what we should notice first, we twentieth-century people, if we could take our deafened ears and ugliness-affronted eyes back to the England of Johnson. It was a place in which ugliness was very rare; indeed, with the important exception of the ugliness that disease and disfigurement produce in human beings and animals, ugliness was unknown. . . . To us any object, from a city to a teaspoon, that is anything but hideous is immediately recognized as something special. . . . In [Johnson's] day there was probably no such thing as an ugly house, table, stool or chair in the entire kingdom. . . . [The main reason] is that industrialism, by moving people away from the natural rhythms of hand and eye, and also from the materials which occur naturally in their region and to which they are attuned by habit and tradition, cannot help fostering ugliness at the same time as it fosters cheapness and convenience.

Perhaps that is a trifle strong, as regards both then and now. But consider, if you dare, the possibility that the natural rhythms of modern life attune people to Colfax Avenue and similar urban sights. As has been said, progress was all right once, but it went on too long.

August 10, 1978

Junk

In the bad old days, artists depended on princes and Popes. Today, Mark di Suvero, a sculptor working with thirty-five tons of scrap metal at the Hirshhorn Museum and Sculpture Garden, enjoys the patronage of the Institute of Scrap Iron and Steel, which supplied the raw materials, and Joan Mondale, who is attentive to the avant-garde. The raw materials include enormous I-beams, a submarine float, a section of a ship's prow and the cab of a diesel locomotive. A spokesman for the Scrap Metal Institute says Di Suvero has "a feel for our industry."

Mrs. Mondale dropped by the construction site the other day and embraced the artist, her pretty blue hard hat narrowly missing his welder's shield. There was no shade except the shadow of the crane that Di Suvero calls "the *sine qua non* of this kind of art," and the site resounded like a foundry. A sign admonished onlookers:

Artist at Work

Please Do Not Disturb

In 1928, a court ruled that Brancusi's *Bird in Space*—a graceful shaft symbolizing flight, but not resembling a bird—was sculpture and not subject to import duties. Although one judge thought it pertinent to ask if a hunter seeing something like that in a forest would shoot it, the ruling acknowledged the "liberation" of art from convention.

Peter De Vries satirizes (but barely) "minimalist" art, describing a sculpture exhibition consisting of empty pedestals, an "area of virgin space unoccupied by anything save what the viewer himself might imagine it to contain, rather than what the artist has arbitrarily imposed." And he describes "centrifugalists," whose aim is to use disagreeable conformations and nauseating colors to drive people out of galleries, "away from pictures threatening to imprison their vision within arrangements of inherently parochial materials."

De Vries is joking. Not so the gallery that displayed a pile of bricks. Or the "earth artist" whose art was a curtain across a Colorado valley. Or the "conceptualist" who spent sixteen days on the Trans-Siberian Railway placing a different slate beneath his feet each day, then burning his notes, smearing the ashes on the slate and exhibiting them. It was not De Vries being mirthful but a critic being solemn who praised a sculptor like Di Suvero for creating "a perceptual experience that is aggregate in character and that unfolds non-holistically in time."

Abstract art developed, in part, as a reaction against the "academicism" of art that is especially meaningful to a viewer with a tutored eye, a capacity for contemplativeness and, in some instances, some knowledge of history or literature. The program of abstract art was anti-intellectual, to create "flat," "fast" art that is entirely and immediately "understandable" to every eye that is assisted by an appropriate rationalization. Stripes will do nicely. So will drips.

Such art is inseparable from theorizing that is at once comic and oppressive. For example, a critic says of Jackson Pollock, who is famous for a drip style: "Pollock's strength lies in the emphatic surfaces of his pictures, which it is his concern to maintain and intensify in all that thick, fuliginous flatness. . . ."

As the intellectual content has been drained from art, the role of critics has swollen. They manufacture theories and invest with significance whatever artists manufacture.

Pity the artists. Try as they might to shock the bourgeoisie, the bourgeoisie remains "understanding." However fast the avant-garde moves its camp, it cannot shake its camp followers. Even Pop Art (such as Andy Warhol's paintings of Campbell's Soup cans), which began in part as a jape at ludicrous theorizing about abstract art, was quickly embalmed in solemn tones of "criticism."

Such "criticism" is sold to people who are grimly determined to "understand," come what may. There is no philistinism more prevalent than the fear of being considered a philistine.

Unintelligible works are most frequently praised as "vital" or "lyrical," although "playful" is the preferred encomium for the sort of work begun in 1913 when Marcel Duchamp exhibited a snow shovel entitled *In Advance of the Broken Arm.* But people who make themselves tiresome by making distinctions say that geometrical shapes, such as those of machines, can be pleasing; machines can produce pleasing designs; and any material can be displayed playfully. But does fine art encompass every pleasing design or playful assemblage?

Di Suvero's work will be called *Isis*—the name of an Egyptian fertility goddess, and the acronym of Di Suvero's scrap-metal patrons. It is too early to judge this work in progress. As I write, it is unclear how the submarine float will connect to the ship's prow, or the prow to the locomotive cab. Such choices, are, presumably, crucial.

July 16, 1978

"It Doesn't Mean a Damn Thing"

Political conventions—the crowds, the noise, the strange fauna— put me in mind of Noah's ark, and of Mark Twain's thought that it sometimes seems a pity Noah didn't miss the boat. When Noah's boat finally came to rest, it was against a mountain, which just goes to show that God, who created deluges and conventions as punishments, created mountains as mercies. And just as Noah leaped from the ark to the mountain—from tribulation to deliverance—I leap from Detroit to Aspen.

Perhaps the only thing to be said for living far from the mountains is that we flatlanders experience a restoring rush of pleasure when we come into the mountains. Folks who live in Aspen don't know what they're not missing. As Emerson said, if the stars appeared only one night in a million, how mankind would adore them.

The world looks best in long light—early in the morning or, better still, at sundown, especially just as the sun dips behind mountains. This mountain town, which in winter is infested with skiers, is in summer redeemed by a music festival—some of mankind's cultural gems in one of God's grandest settings.

Musically, I am like Ulysses S. Grant, who said, "I know only two tunes. One of them is 'Yankee Doodle' and the other isn't." As a musician, I peaked a little early. I played the triangle tolerably well in kindergarten. Then my parents tried to make a violinist out of me, which was like trying to make a silk purse out of an ear which no self-respecting sow would have minded losing.

Still, I know that if Aspen's famous festival has a flaw, it is the flaw of this age: it is too receptive to the new.

There is one, if only one, thing to be said in defense of modern painting, and Solomon Guggenheim said it: "All day long I add columns of figures and make everything balance. I come home. I sit down. I look at a Kandinsky and it's wonderful! It doesn't mean a damn thing!" The most I can find to say for most modern music is what Rossini said about Wagner's opera *Lohengrin*. He said one could not judge it after just one hearing and that he had no intention of hearing it a second time.

But I favor performing modern music, for reasons Jascha Heifetz gives: "I occasionally play works by contemporary composers, and for two reasons. First to discourage the composer from writing any more and secondly to remind myself how much I appreciate Beethoven."

Happily, there is loose in the world an elemental force of talent and personality, a musician who believes that people who appreciate the Bee Gees can be brought around to appreciate Beethoven too. This year's guest artists at Aspen's festival, which runs until August, include James Galway, "the Man with the Golden Flute," whose flute, like a dozen of his recordings, really is gold. He combines his Irish charm with the confidence of Reggie Jackson, and he sees no reason he should not be able to make classical music as popular as "popular music" is:

Haydn was the Mick Jagger of his day. He used to make more than three hundred pounds for a performance. And the aristocrats paid through the nose to get in—three guineas each, I think. I don't know why classical musicians shouldn't make money the same way today.

Today, most people who know Haydn was do not know who Jagger is, and—emphatically—vice versa. But if anyone can insinuate Haydn into whatever remains of the inner ears of those who "appreciate" the Rolling Stones, it is Galway. For six years he was principal flutist for the Berlin Symphony, under the baton of the exacting Herbert von Karajan. Today, without relaxing the rigor of his standards, Galway has recorded jazz and popular compositions. Five hundred thousand people have bought his recording of "Annie's Song," written by John Denver. Denver's mountainside home looks down on the meadow where, as the light grows long in the Rockies, people flock to Aspen's music tent.

I have gone to earth here to steel myself for the shocking sight of

Madison Square Garden wall-to-wall with Democrats. I can't honestly say columnists deserve vacations, but readers deserve vacations from their columnists. You, gentle reader, may find the silence as soothing as I shall find the sound of music in the meadow.

July 24, 1980

A Knack for Misery

It is our bounden duty to broaden our minds to a fare-thee-well. So I recently put myself in an anthropological frame of mind and repaired to several saloons that feature "country" music. With my elbow on knee and my chin on hand, looking distinctly like Rodin's *Thinker*, I listened carefully—because "country" music is said to be a slice of terribly real life.

If such music does indeed answer the question about how "country" folks are getting on, the answer is: Poorly. This music speaks feelingly of lives in which one thing has led to another, which in turn has led to much more, all of it dismal. I have pieced together from many lyrics this picture of the misfortunes that attend typical "country" lives:

You wore my high-school ring and letter sweater before bright neon lights made you up and walk away from standing by your man/ leaving the crops in the field and me jamming gears with nothing to do but keep on trucking in my eighteen-wheeler/ listening to the windshield wipers when I'm not drinking Falstaff and Wild Turkey and putting the last dime from my faded jeans into a jukebox to help me make it through the night/ wishing I could make the alimony payments and visit little Billie and Betsy Sue.

So in the Elko, Nevada, Greyhound depot I shot the man, my best friend, who took you and even my pickup truck/ and I wound up here on Death Row listening to the lonesome whistle of the

*night train rolling south through the cotton fields from Nashville to
that little bit of Heaven, Biloxi/ where we were dirt-poor, eating
beans and gravy, and didn't even have a gun rack for the pickup/
but we were happy until you became a good-timing woman and left
me with nothing to look at but four walls of the cheap hotel room/
where I drink black coffee and read the Good Book, just like my
daddy, a preacher man, and Mom, a widower sharecropper's
daughter, back in the dusty one-room shack where/ we didn't have
much and wouldn't take welfare and loved this great country in
spite of gun control.*

Well, now. If such lyrics are an accurate survey of bucolic life,
that life hurts like the dickens, and we might as well admit that
civilization has come a cropper and the fabric of society is unravel-
ing, even in the country. But there is this to be said for the forthright sorrowfulness of country music: it is a timely assertion of an
endangered right—the right to be unhappy.

In his new book, *Passions and Prejudices*, Leo Rosten praises
the ability "to be unhappy soundly, without apology or rationalization," and adds:

> Once upon a time (very long ago) a man could stare glumly out a
> window, or grunt at his wife, or slam the door, or stalk off on a solitary
> walk, without having his loved ones rush to his rescue with bright
> psychiatric phrases and psychotherapy handy-dandy.
>
> Once upon a time (believe it or not) we were not silly enough to
> expect everyone to walk around in a state of bliss . . . or give hourly
> demonstrations of being "well-adjusted."
>
> Once upon a time (oh blessed time!) sensible men simply knew that
> life, even at its best, is beset with difficulties, that frustration or disap-
> pointment or defeat is natural and as inevitable as changes in the
> weather.

In an age when people assume that "everybody was intended by
God, or fate, or biochemistry to be contented all of the time," it is
hard to remember that "as recently as 30 years ago, no one questioned your right to be unhappy . . . Men were permitted the
dignity of periodic discontent."

Mr. Sears and Mr. Roebuck, TVA, rural electrification, the soil bank, price supports, Ezra Taft Benson and Earl Butz should have made country life a little smoother than country music suggests that it is. But when Pollyannas proclaim that life is smooth sledding, at least country-music fiends understand that, as Rosten says, "Pollyanna was a pretty silly, to say nothing of tiresome, little girl."

August 13, 1978

Marc Chagall and Mayor Daley

Orange boxcars of the Illinois Central railroad rumble between wings of the Chicago Art Institute. The museum exuberantly leaps across "the Main Line of America."

To get from the museum's main section to the one on the other side of the tracks, you pass down a walkway toward the luminous blue of the stained-glass windows created by Marc Chagall in honor of—really—the fine arts in America and the memory of His Honor, Richard J. Daley. Its setting and its history make the Art Institute, one hundred years old on May 24, a symbol of this city, and an illustration of an admirable relationship between commerce and culture.

Seen from offshore, Chicago presents one of the world's loveliest cityscapes. The "Gold Coast" apartments are perhaps the nation's most striking concentration of the rich. But Chicago still is a working-class city of those small, proud houses you pass on the way in from O'Hare Airport. It is still, to some extent, Carl Sandburg's city of the broad shoulders, hog butcher of the world, stacker of wheat, and all that. Yet in addition to being a great blue-collar metropolis, and because it is that, it also has a magnificent museum.

Its collection is less comprehensive than that of New York's

Metropolitan or Washington's National Gallery, but it is second only to those American museums, and its collection of Impressionists is unsurpassed in America. It is a monument to the entrepreneurs, and civilizing women, who built Chicago after the 1871 fire.

The Art Institute was begun as a brave assertion of civility in a rough-and-tumble city. Those who have done the asserting through the years have included some of the most famous names in American business—Armour, Palmer, Ryerson, Field, Ward, McCormick.

But as a Chicagoan has written of the Art Institute, "in a larger sense, it is also a product of numberless stockyard laborers and department store clerks, plant employees and sawmill workers, all of the anonymous hordes whose toil built the fortunes that purchased it. In that sense, they built it with their own rough hands."

The rough, or at least unpolished, manners of some of the men who bought the Institute's first paintings provoked ridicule. When a Chicagoan said of his purchase of fine Dutch paintings, "They are corkers, every one of them," a New York newspaper said, merrily:

> . . . we have no doubt whatever these corkers are the largest specimens . . . that Mr. Hutchinson could find in Europe. He probably paid $1,000 a foot for them, and we assume the citizens of Chicago will give him a triumphal procession along the lakefront when they arrive, carrying them and him in huge floats, drawn by a team of milk-white Berkshire hogs.

But when the laughter died, Chicago had a collection of corkers, built with the self-confidence characteristic of the city. Without waiting for learned opinion to give its imprimatur to the Impressionists, Chicagoans made pilgrimages to Monet at his lily pond, and with the help of a friend, Mary Cassatt, the American painter, they made superb use of their money.

Today the Institute has more dues-paying members (65,000)

than any other American museum. In the mid-1960s, about 750,000 people visited it each year. Now 1.5 million do, and 2 million when there is a popular special exhibit.

There is a general boom in museum attendance, and no single explanation seems satisfactory. There is, of course, more leisure time; and a larger portion of the population has attended colleges. But it also is true that museums are one measure of society's attitude about the present. The more complex and bewildering the world seems, the more people think they should know about the past.

One of the Institute's most exhilarating exhibits is not in a room, it is a room. It is a piece of Chicago's past: the restored Trading Room from the old Chicago Stock Exchange. It is a splendidly ornate space which suggests how relatively impoverished our senses are in today's public places.

And it is altogether right that works by two alumni of the School of the Art Institute, Edward Hopper's *Nighthawks* and Grant Wood's *American Gothic*, elemental American urban and American rural, hang side by side, beside the railroad tracks, in the elemental American city.

May 20, 1979

The National Cathedral: Symphony in Stone

Among the twentieth century's many defects is this: it affords few opportunities to join a noble profession, that of cathedral builder. But Easter is a time to note how people can join, and why they should.

Like a runoff of melting snow, the flow of tourists through Washington becomes a torrent in spring. Unfortunately, only a small fraction visit the Cathedral Church of Saint Peter and Saint Paul, commonly called the National Cathedral. The architecture is fourteenth-century Gothic, but one need not be inclined, as I am, to think civilization peaked a bit early (about the fourteenth century) to delight in it.

Washington is rich in visual pleasures, but none matches the cathedral's newest rose window in late afternoon, when slanting sunlight dapples the nave with color. The cathedral is faithful to the Gothic principle: every stone adds strength as well as weight. The flying buttresses are functional. Four 100-foot columns, 27 feet in diameter at the base, support the main tower and its 100 tons of bells.

Virtually every nook and cranny has decorative detail, and there are lots of nooks and crannies in a building one-tenth of a mile long. A cathedral is a place for a bishop's cathedra, or chair, and near the main altar is a chair made of stones from Glastonbury Abbey, founded by Saint Joseph of Arimathea about A.D. 43. The stone for the altar comes from the quarry near Jerusalem that supplied the stone for King Solomon's temple.

Ten small stones from the Chapel of Moses on Mount Sinai are set in the floor in front of the altar. One pulpit was carved from limestone quarried nine hundred years ago for Canterbury Cathedral. The only President buried in Washington, Woodrow Wilson, is buried in the National Cathedral.

In the great cities of the civilization from which this Republic is descended, the noblest works were built to serve religion—the Parthenon in Athens, Saint Peter's in Rome, Notre Dame in Paris, Westminster Abbey in London. They are stone memories of a premodern age when cities were supposed to be something other than mere arenas for acquisition, when civil society was supposed to serve ends other than the pursuit of self-interest, when civil law was supposed to be patterned after a higher law.

Washington has no premodern past, and the monuments people flock to see are, like the Capitol Building, places where power is exercised or, like the Lincoln Memorial, temples for democracy's civil religion, the worship of those who epitomize popular government. The inscription above Lincoln's statue begins: "IN THIS TEM-PLE . . ."

The National Cathedral is different. Beneath it lies the world of strain and uproar. More than any other city, Washington represents a civilization founded on self-interestedness. But because the cathedral is mounted on such a splendid pedestal—Mount Saint Alban, the city's highest hill—it seems, from a distance, to be the institution beneath which the city has reverently arrayed itself. Obviously, Washington presents a misleading profile.

Last year, construction on the last phase of the cathedral virtually stopped. The cathedral had gone deeply into debt to complete the nave in time for the Bicentennial. The energy crisis is an appalling burden when you are heating a "room" with a 100-foot ceiling.

It would take $15 million today to complete the facade and twin towers on the west front. So in a town where billions evaporate, a shortage of a few million is halting a collective work of genius that has been rising for seventy-one years. If more people would visit the cathedral, and if they and others would give a bit more generously, they would be important participants in what may be the last pure Gothic work the world will see built.

One of the first and finest expressions of Gothic architecture is Chartres Cathedral. Its completion in 1164 was a sign of spiritual springtime as European culture bloomed after the long winter of the Dark Ages. It is perhaps unlikely that a thousand years hence, the National Cathedral will be seen as a sign of twentieth-century America's real values. But a thousand years hence, whatever else remains along the Potomac, this cathedral will remain, like a sailing ship on the swell of a rolling sea.

March 23, 1978

Saint Bartholomew's: An Island of Human Scale

The day dawned sunny, in marked contrast to me. Then I saw an uplifting headline:

St. Bartholomew's Officials Refuse
To Sell Their Church at Any Price

I am fond of obduracy in noble causes, and am fanatically fond of resistance to "irresistible forces" represented by large numbers. If you too derive mental refreshment from contemplating such pluckiness, come with me to Saint Bartholomew's Episcopal Church.

Saint Bartholomew himself is said to have been flayed alive—a particularly painful, because protracted, martyrdom. Many urban churches are suffering an analogous fate. Saint Bartholomew's Church, organized in 1835, came to New York's Park Avenue and Fifty-first Street in 1918 because its congregation—which included Vanderbilts and Whitneys—had moved to posh Park Avenue apartments.

But the apartments have long since been replaced by towers of commerce, and the parishioners today are, by and large, neither rich nor WASP. The church is living hand to mouth, and off its past—off the endowment built by the Vanderbilts and others. Its deficit will approach $400,000 this year. Repairs, heating—everything is crushingly expensive. The rector, the Reverend Thomas Bowers, says it is expensive almost to the point that when the organ needs fixing, someone must be fired. City pollution injures the organ.

But the church sits on the most valuable bit of land in America, the most eligible remaining place for a skyscraper in midtown Manhattan. Many corporations ache to plant one there. The representative of one discussed a price of $100 million. That is $2,000 a square foot, and he suggested that $3,000 might be possible. But the church will not be led into temptation.

The church's adjacent garden and community building could be sold or, better, built around and over. The Reverend Dr. Bowers, a man of faith, has faith that some modern Michelangelo could design a tall building that could enrich the church without desecrating its beauty.

With its rich, dark interior, mosaics and domed ceiling, Saint Bartholomew's is, fortunately, of Italian Romanesque style. Fortunately, because a Gothic church, such as Saint Patrick's Cathedral on Fifth Avenue, with its delicate spires competing feebly with the brutal skyscrapers, is more diminished by buildings towering over it.

If Saint Bartholomew's is rescued from penury by an ingenious architect who designs a skyscraper compatible with the church and satisfactory for some titan of commerce, it will be because God is at it again, moving in mysterious ways His wonders to perform. Or so I fancy.

The second-worst invention of the modern age (second to the hydrogen bomb, but worse than the third-worst thing, designer jeans) is the elevator. Without it, the skyscrapers would be impossible, and so would this city, with its oppressive density and inhuman scale. I think of skyscrapers and New York the way Oscar Wilde thought of poetry and Pope: "There are two ways of disliking poetry: One way is to dislike it, the other is to read Pope." If you cannot see that skyscrapers are wrong in theory, visit New York.

But it is the skyscraper's ability to pile up so much onto so little land that accounts for the astronomic values of midtown real estate. And that may be Saint Bartholomew's salvation. That, and the unwillingness of the church's leaders to put a price on the sacred enterprise they conduct here amidst enterprises built by reverence for the price mechanism.

Manhattan, the capital of world economics, is a slightly scary place to true conservatives because commerce, although indispensable and endlessly creative, is, because of its revolutionary energy, inimical to existing institutions, always. Saint Bartholomew's, nestled next to the Waldorf and amidst banks and multinational corporations, is a little Israel, a small salient of gentler values in a region not altogether congenial.

In the last chapter of his book *Civilisation*, the chapter titled "Heroic Materialism," Sir Kenneth Clark writes:

> Imagine an immensely speeded up movie of Manhattan Island during the last hundred years. It would look less like a work of man than like some tremendous natural upheaval. It's godless, it's brutal, it's violent—but one can't laugh it off, because in the energy, strength of will and mental grasp that have gone to make New York, materialism has transcended itself.

I do not know what Clark means by "heroic" and I suspect he doesn't know what he means by materialism's transcending itself, but this I know: it is jolly that Saint Bartholomew's may harness the forces represented by skyscrapers to preserve itself as an island of human scale in the canyons of commerce.

December 4, 1980

"Liturgical Fidget" and the Prayer Book

Unaccustomed though I am to approving change (and I am not really going to do that here), I now offer a very partial and tepid defense of those who have tried, and of course failed, to improve the Episcopal Church's Book of Common Prayer.

Intelligent people disagree about whether miracles occurred in first-century Palestine. But something miraculous obviously occurred in sixteenth-century England: Thomas Cranmer's prose.

Miracles are hard to define but easy to recognize, and Cranmer's Prayer Book is one. It is not just stately; it helped create our idea of stateliness.

The revisers of the Prayer Book have diminished it. But they are not guilty, as some critics charge, of thoroughly vandalizing Cranmer's work. And some critics reason too much from aesthetic, and too little from theological, premises.

Several of the new rites preserve most of Cranmer. But, for example, this moving passage is gone from the burial service: "Man, that is born of a woman, hath but a short time to live, and is full of misery. He cometh up, and is cut down, like a flower; he fleeth as it were a shadow, and never continueth in one stay." Charity, a duty of Christians and others, prevents me from commenting on some of the new rites, except to wonder what becomes of the very idea of "common prayer" when the Prayer Book resembles a multiple-choice quiz.

The revisionists' ranks included some essentially conservative liturgical experts whose aim was to restore practices of the early Church. It is arguable, for example, that by deleting from the General Confession the phrase "miserable offenders" and the passage "there is no health in us," what they have sought to excise is the medieval gloominess that eclipsed the early Church's joyfulness. Still, a glance at contemporary society suggests that this is not a propitious moment for encouraging mankind to think better of itself.

Some revisions reflect what C. S. Lewis called "liturgical fidget."

Why else did the revisers flatten "till death do us part" into "until we are parted by death"? Yes, of course, language like Cranmer's sounds "artificial." All art is artifice, and the art of liturgy, being of unsurpassable seriousness, should be especially artful. Yes, of course, people today do not talk the way Cranmer wrote. But people then did not talk that way either. Except when talking to God.

As Lewis said, liturgical writing "needs to be not only very good but very good in a very special way, if it is to stand up to reiterated reading aloud." Much of what is being done to religious language in the name of "relevance" is something a sensitive person cannot face, even once, without shuddering. God is not dead, but he is powerfully embarrassed by books like *Are You Running with Me, Jesus?*

Frank Mankiewicz, one of Washington's finer wits, has subjected himself to the "Good News Bible," and he says that "Thou shalt not kill" is there rendered "Don't murder." The perpetrators of that improvement did not heed that commandment when they assaulted the cadences of what they doubtless call the King Jim version.

In order to bring the Prayer Book closer to the "language of the people," the revisers had to ignore the laity's emphatically expressed preference for Cranmer's language. It is hard to suppress the suspicion that ecclesiastical egalitarians are scoring ideological, not theological, points. They probably are vaguely put off by language that is not as immediately and universally comprehensible as a Pepsi jingle.

Among the dismally remarkable achievements of the modern world is this: life is, simultaneously, indescribably noisy and impoverishing to the senses. So the revisionists are, in a sense, right: Cranmer's Prayer Book is out of place here. Perhaps Christianity's many revisers are, as a matter of fact, bringing Christianity into conformity with the spirit of the age. But I thought it was supposed to work the other way.

Now, a postscript.

My tutors about the Prayer Book include Ed and Jane Yoder, North Carolina's gift to Washington. Ed is just a journalist (editor of *The Washington Star*'s editorial page), but Jane does something useful and dignified. She is a student of homiletics, the art of preaching. As a sermon auditor at Virginia Theological Seminary, she is a critic of student sermons. Theirs is a marriage which must have been made in heaven when heaven was feeling kittenish: imagine, an editorial writer married to a stern judge of bad preaching! Yet it is a happy marriage. Another miracle.

September 23, 1979

The Conversation of Bells

As a foreign policy, the ringing of church bells may leave something to be desired. But President Carter's suggestion that bells be
rung all around the nation until the hostages are home is desirable.
And it gives me an opportunity to address a subject near to my
heart: bells, the unfortunate neglect thereof.

The world is divided, by no means evenly, between the enlight-
ened few of us who think bells are an important aspect of commo-
dious living, and those who never have given this serious matter any
serious thought.

I have never disguised the fact that I am no friend of up-to-date
thought, and high on my list of reasons for regretting the twentieth
century is this: the sound of bells is no longer a part of society's life,
and people are poorer for this change. In his book *The Waning of
the Middle Ages*—the very title is enough to break a sensible
heart—John Huizinga wrote:

> One sound rose ceaselessly above the noises of busy life [in the Middle
> Ages] and lifted all things into a sphere of order and serenity: the
> sound of bells. The bells were in daily life like good spirits, which by
> their familiar voices now called upon the citizens to mourn and now to
> rejoice, now warned them of danger, now exhorted them to piety.
> They were known by their names: big Jacqueline, or the bell Roland.
> Everyone knew the difference in meaning of the various ways of ring-
> ing. However continuous the ringing of the bells, people would seem
> not to have become blunted to the effect of their sound.
>
> What intoxication the pealing of the bells of all the churches, and of
> all the monasteries of Paris, must have produced, sounding from
> morning till evening, and even during the night, when a peace was
> concluded or a pope elected.

Bells were part of society's communication system, part of the
conversation of the community, in some places until recently.
Amoret and Christopher Scott write:

> Another charming custom which survived into the present century was

the ringing of bells not only to warn St. Peter that a soul was on its way but to frighten off the devils which might impede its passage.

Ronald Blythe, in *Akenfield*, recorded the memories of a bell ringer in Suffolk, England:

> The bells tolled for death when I was a boy. It was three times for a man and three times two for a woman. . . . Then the years of the dead person's age would be tolled and if the bell went on speaking, "seventy-one, seventy-two . . ." people would say, "Well, they had good innings!" But when the bell stopped at eighteen or twenty a hush would come over the fields.

Proper bells produce one of the man-made sounds worth preserving, but they have been largely dispensed with everywhere. Of course, we hear bells all day long, thanks to cash registers and telephones. Many homes have feeble, lisping doorbells that are doing the work that once was done by hefty, shiny brass door knockers that made a healthy THUMP. The bells we have indoors are pesky nuisances; the bells we used to have out of doors provided decorous counterpoint to the symphony of nature's sounds.

It is hard to rise to Newtonian heights of scientific detachment about the boneheadedness that has caused people to bring this about. After the revolution of true conservatism, doorbells (and a few other things) will be illegal, and proper bells will be heard everywhere.

If you are one of those pitiable people who do not understand that bells are part of the magic of life, consider this true story, recounted by the Scotts:

> When the Duke of Wellington died in 1852 the Dean of his old parliamentary constituency at Trim ordered the bells be tolled in full peal. No sooner had the ringers begun than the tenor bell, the pride of the church, shattered. When it was examined, it was found to have been cast in 1769, the year the Duke was born.

If that doesn't give you pause, well, the more's the pity. Chekhov wrote of someone, "He was a rationalist, but he had to confess that he liked the ringing of church bells." Me too.

December 2, 1979

Signs of Decay

It was mealtime aboard the San Francisco flight, so the stewardesses were in the galley electrocuting what you might, if very drunk, call food. To steel myself for the ordeal of an airline meal, I went to the lavatory to run cold water across my wrists and splash it over my drawn and ashen features. On the lavatory mirror I read a familiar little sign:

"AS A COURTESY TO THE NEXT PASSENGER, MAY WE SUGGEST THAT YOU USE YOUR TOWEL TO WIPE OFF THE WASH BASIN. THANK YOU."

You're welcome. No, come to think about it, you're not. I don't like that guilt-inducing sign.

Signs. They are everywhere. I will read anything—cereal boxes, candy-bar wrappers, airline safety-instruction cards, the *New York Post*—rather than not read anything. So I am always reading remarkable but generally unnoticed words.

Consider the words on the camera that takes your picture when you cash a check in some stores: "WE ARE TAKING YOUR PICTURE FOR YOUR PROTECTION." Uh huh. And consider these words that are on many hot-air hand dryers in public rest rooms:

> *To serve you better, we have installed pollution-free electric hand dryers to protect you from the hazards of disease which can be transmitted by cloth towels or paper towel litter. This clean, quick, sanitary method dries hands more thoroughly, prevents chapping, and keeps washrooms free of towel WASTE.*

This hymn of concern for our health, this paean to hot air, would be more touching had it not been written by, and affixed to the machines by, the manufacturer of the machines.

There is a mad profusion of signs in Washington, where right-turn-on-red recently became legal. Legal, that is, except where forbidden. It is forbidden at 80 percent of Washington's intersections. So at all but 20 percent of the intersections, there are up to four "NO TURN ON RED" signs.

In New York subways, I am told (I am not crazy enough to venture down to check), signs say: "NO LOITERING. NO SPITTING." Surely the sort of people who spit are not the sort who care about signs ordering them not to. Furthermore, New Yorkers are so aggressive, it would be an improvement if many would just stand around loitering and spitting.

New York is not the only place with eyebrow-raising signs. An elegant lady of my acquaintance once found herself in the ladies' room of a New Mexico airport, where she read this sign: "GIRLS: IF YOU HAVE BEEN MOLESTED OR RAPED, AND ARE IN NEED OF ASSIST-ANCE, CALL . . . " Jeepers, I know life on the frontier is rough-and-tumble, but colorful New Mexico is too colorful if the "girls" are in such constant, routine jeopardy that permanent signs are placed to advise victims.

The signs (in several senses) are better elsewhere. Out in central Illinois, where virtue is valued and I am from, folks subscribe to the Doctrine of Preventive Signs.

In the village of Savoy, at Skateland, a roller-skating rink (which also has some of the finest pinball machines in Christendom), signs stipulate strict limits on the ruckus-raising that can break out in such an arena of pleasure. There are injunctions against intoxication, drugs, reckless skating, destruction of property—injunctions backed by threats of arrest, and worse, "eviction" from the rink.

But that is just the beginning. Skateland is a major-league Moses when it comes to communicating the Moral Law. Skateland's signs say, *inter alia:*

No hats, sunglasses, scarfs, headbands, curlers, halters, midriffs, see-thrus or short blouses, tight or short shorts allowed on floor. All females over 10 yrs. to be fully bloused.

No muscle shirts on males 10 yrs. or over. All clothing and persons must be clean.

Neatness of dress is expected of every skater.

No necking or indecency allowed.

No smoking or gum chewing allowed anywhere except in smoking room for 16 yrs. and older.

No foul language allowed.

Boys and girls forcing their attention on each other, not allowed.

We reserve the right to refuse admission to anyone not meeting the good standards listed here.

They are, indeed, "good standards," and Skateland expresses them in stately cadences. But Skateland could be more concise. What it means is simply this: libertines and others inimical to established institutions should not plan to roller-skate in Savoy.

March 13, 1980

Salt, Pepper and Semicolons

In an age of flaccid consensus and too much tolerance, robust prejudices are welcome. But Paul Robinson, a contributing editor of *The New Republic*, has gone too far in an essay in that journal. He has said rude things about semicolons and parentheses.

He says the period and the comma "are the only lovely marks of punctuation" because they are "simple," and the period is especially lovely because "innocent of ambiguity," whereas

> More than half the semicolons one sees, I would estimate, should be periods, and probably another quarter should be commas. Far too often, semicolons, like colons, are used to gloss over an imprecise thought. They place two clauses in some kind of relation to one another, but relieve the writer of saying exactly what the relationship is.

Halt right there, Robinson. What is so marvelous about simplicity? Why this dislike of ambiguity?

Semicolons do indeed signal, rather than shout, a relationship. Therefore they require a reader to read—really read. The reader must bring an active mind to bear on what the writer is doing. A semicolon is a compliment from the writer to the reader. It says: I don't have to draw you a picture; a hint will do.

If you don't believe me about the noble semicolon, believe a doctor, Dr. Lewis Thomas, president of the Memorial Sloan-Kettering Cancer Center, who writes a column for *The New England Journal of Medicine*. He says:

> The semicolon tells you that there is still some question about the preceding full sentence; something that needs to be added; it reminds you sometimes of the Greek usage. It is almost always a greater pleasure to come across a semicolon than a period. The period tells you that that is that; if you didn't get all the meaning you wanted or expected, anyway you got all the writer intended to parcel out and now you have to move along. But with a semicolon there you get a pleasant little feeling of expectancy; there is more to come; read on; it will get clearer.

Surely there is one supreme rule: that punctuation is best which best serves to make writing subtle, supple, delicate, nuanced and efficient. Of course you can write using only periods and commas for punctuation. You can cook using only salt and pepper for seasoning. But why do it when there are so many seasonings pleasing to a mature palate?

Robinson also frowns on parentheses (and dashes—they often serve similar needs). He says they "are of course indispensable," but that all of them are "syntactical defeats." Indispensable defeats?

He says parentheses and dashes "generally betoken stylistic laziness," an unwillingness to present things "in the most logical order." Thus "every random thought, every tenuous analogy gets dragged in." Come now.

Of course parentheses can be used promiscuously. So can salt, pepper, dill, sage and cloves. Parentheses are for thoughts that are related to other thoughts not randomly or tenuously, but parenthetically. Parentheses are for writers (such as, I am sure, Robinson) whose minds do not lumber along like a truck on a straightaway, but rather soar and swoop and change direction gracefully, like a swallow at home in the whole sky.

On this subject, among others, I allow Dr. Thomas the last word, playfully:

> There are no precise rules about punctuation (Fowler lays out some general advice (as best he can under the complex circumstances of English prose (he points out, for example, that we possess only four stops (the comma, the semicolon, the colon and the period (the question mark and exclamation point are not, strictly speaking, stops; they are indicators of tone (oddly enough, the Greeks employed the semicolon for their question mark (it produces a strange sensation to read a Greek sentence which is a straightforward question: Why weepest thou; (instead of Why weepest thou? (and, of course, there are parentheses (which are surely a kind of punctuation making this whole matter much more complicated by having to count up the left-handed parentheses in order to be sure of closing with the right number (but if the parentheses were left out, with nothing to work with but the stops,

we would have considerably more flexibility in the deploying of layers of meaning than if we tried to separate all the clauses by physical barriers (and in the latter case, while we might have more precision and exactitude for our meaning, we would lose the essential flavor of language, which is its wonderful ambiguity))))))))))).

May 8, 1980

Oh, Cleveland!

Long ago, when mankind was young and wit was fresh, if someone in an audience called out, "Say something funny," Mort Sahl, the comic, would say: "John Foster Dulles." Today's last-gasp laugh-getter for desperate comics is some reference to Cleveland, a city disdained by those who pluck their values from the prevailing wind.

Cleveland has the problems of an old industrial city. It also has the most acrimonious government in Christendom; and, yes, the Cuyahoga River did catch fire once. But such problems do not obscure the city's fascinating dimension. That dimension, which may be what Cleveland's despisers despise, is that Cleveland embodies the American middle: Midwest middle-class civilization.

Ohioans were, in a sense, the first Americans. Ohio's northern part was once "New Connecticut"; the southern part was the Virginia Military District. "Ohio," said a nineteenth-century writer, "is at once North and South; it is also—by grace of its longitude and its social temper—both East and West. It has boxed the American compass."

Ohio was the first defined wilderness area made into a state, and the names of its communities include London, Dublin, Berlin, Geneva, Moscow, Holland, Poland, Smyrna, Cadiz, Lisbon, Antwerp, New Paris and New Vienna. Walter Havighurst suggests why Ohio has produced eight Presidents: "To any other part of the nation, an Ohio candidate could not seem alien."

In 1784, George Washington examined a map of the wilderness and predicted that "where the Cuyahoga River flows into Lake Erie shall arise a community of vast commercial importance." A century later, a Clevelander explained his city to a squinting Easterner: "Smoke means business, business means money and money is the principal thing." Ohio's largest city is bound up with America's basic commodities.

Edison was born 60 miles west of Cleveland, which became the first city in the world with electric lighting in a public place, and the first to unite electricity and steel in transportation (in streetcars). One of Cleveland's thoroughfares, Superior Street, is a reminder of the link between Cleveland and the Great Lake, Superior, that is surrounded by iron-ore deposits. Those deposits were shipped to Cleveland's mills and turned into rails and locomotives.

Oil was needed before transportation could move from steel wheels to rubber tires (tires are giant industry in the state bisected by the National Pike, U.S. 40). The world's first producing oil well was 100 miles east of Cleveland, and its potential was best understood by a product of Cleveland's Central High School (John Davison Rockefeller).

Cleveland is the only major American city where the original city center is still the city's hub. Public Square is the site of the Soldiers' and Sailors' Memorial, which a guidebook gently describes as an example of "the literalness of Victorian art." It is a stupendous pile, a granite-and-bronze clutter of guns and fierce warriors. It is not quite as exuberantly martial as some monuments in Indianapolis, but it adequately expresses late-nineteenth-century patriotism.

One purpose of public architecture is to create a mood: the Supreme Court Building in Washington is designed to instill awe for the majesty of the law. But the Court is a mere cabin compared with Cleveland's Federal Reserve Building. This temple to currency has stirring symbolic statues, and a lobby worthy of a place of worship. Whatever an aura of strength can do for currency, this building does.

Today many banks resemble hotels, and many branch bank offices are built in a style that might be called Neo–Dairy Queen. No wonder the dollar is a ghost of its former self. Cleveland's downtown is planted thick with thick banks, and is a reminder of the way things were.

Euclid Avenue no longer is America's noblest collection of stately homes (my nominee is Audubon Place in New Orleans). But Cleveland, as much as any city, has been the home of spacious homes of the sort suited to the life of large families. Such homes were monuments, of sorts, to the energy and confidence of America, and especially of the Midwest, when the nation was gathering strength.

My guilty secret, cheerfully confessed, is that I admire Cleveland. But then, I also admired John Foster Dulles.

June 15, 1979

Mormons: A Community Within the Community

An administrator of a private elementary school in Washington recently explained the school. "We have desks," she said, "and doors." Her listeners, parents aware of today's educational doctrines, understood perfectly. The school favors "structure" rather than "open classrooms."

I am agnostic about the desks-and-doors doctrine, but I admire schools that know their own minds. One such is Brigham Young University. Like its namesake, and like the state it adorns, BYU is pleased to be a bit different.

BYU is, broadly speaking, a desks-and-doors school. The honor code mandates "graciousness," and the dress-and-grooming "standards" say that beards and "bushy" sideburns are "not acceptable," mustaches are "not encouraged," women's hemlines are to be of "modest length" and jeans are not acceptable women's wear for classes.

Who, you indignantly ask, do BYU's administrators think they are? The point is that they know exactly who they are, and what they are about. Mormons are short on identity crises, and long on certitude. Where but among Utah's Mormons can you hear President James Buchanan denounced? That may seem like denouncing rye bread—an inherently disproportionate investment of passion—but Buchanan sent the Army to break the Mormons to the saddle of federal authority. The government was slow to believe that Mormons could be a community within the national community without being a community against the national community.

Utah, writes Daniel Boorstin, "remains even now a living monument to the scope that the West offered to the genius of the organizer." Utah's organizer was Brigham Young, who led the Mormons west.

> Rejected in one place after another [Boorstin writes], their westward movement was a staccato series of enforced group transplantations, each more remarkable than the last as a feat of organization . . . For the long march across Iowa, the Mormons built roads and bridges, and even planted crops to be harvested by those who came after them the next season.

Mormons constitute the most singular great church to come into existence in the United States, and it is quintessentially American. It is about doing things, triumphing in this world, turning faith into works. There are no Mormon monasteries; it is hard to imagine Mormons given over to the purely contemplative life. Today, these "American Zionists" are conservative in distrusting dependence on a welfare state, but they practice the ethics of common provision through a remarkable church welfare program.

They were and, to an extent astonishing in this homogenizing nation, still are as distinctive as the first Americans, the Puritans. They, like the Mormons, considered themselves "visible saints" with a divinely ordained "errand into the wilderness." Mormons do utterly lack the Puritans' gloominess, and could, perhaps, be improved by just a touch of it.

It is against the laws of nature to be as upbeat as Mormons can be over a 7 A.M. eye-opening cup of hot chocolate. But then, one of Utah's charms for people like me (people so straight that they would not recognize marijuana if a bale of it fell on them) is that in Utah they often can feel conspicuously, thrillingly improper by just drinking coffee.

Recently, Barbara Walters interviewed Donny and Marie Osmond, the Henry Fords of show business. (They mass-produce entertainment, each product indistinguishable from all the others.) Donny and Marie are Mormons who, supported by their extended family, live in Utah, and avoid the contaminations of entertainment capitals.

The interview turned, as Walters' interviews occasionally do, to the subject of sex. Would they, Walters asked, consider premarital sex? No, said he. No, said she. Not "No, except . . ." Or "No, unless . . ." Just: No. Walters waited for the qualifying clauses; sought them; then surrendered to astonishment.

Walters has a veteran journalist's worldliness and could cover the General Resurrection with an air of having seen it before. But she seemed never to have seen the likes of the Osmonds.

The Mormon sensibility sometimes makes Utah seem to others like an enclave surrounded on four sides by reality. Certainly a different reality is just an hour's flight away, in Denver, where a nightclub advertises: "THE NEWEST ENTERTAINMENT RAGE—MUD WRESTLING: BEAUTIFUL GIRLS FIGHTING TOPLESS IN A PIT OF REAL MUD."

Some people evidently think it matters that the mud is "real." And those people probably think Mormons are peculiar.

January 21, 1979

Out-Porning the World

It seems to me a distressing oversight that the National Trust for Historic Preservation—of which I am a card-carrying member— has not undertaken to preserve San Francisco's North Beach area.

As a student of American commerce, I believe the nation should preserve the birthplaces of giant industries, such as the Titusville, Pennsylvania, oil field, the Wright brothers' bicycle shop in Dayton and F. W. Woolworth's dry-goods store in Watertown, New York. America's economy is the most marvelous example of productivity since the episode of the loaves and fishes, and it deserves monuments for worship and shrines for pilgrimages.

San Francisco's North Beach is a small strip of tenderloin, a jumble of seedy nightspots, cinemas and "bookstores." It is as similar to areas of other cities as one K-Mart is to another. But there is a difference: North Beach has a good claim to being the symbolic birthplace of one of the nation's significant growth industries, "the sex business."

Of course, that business did not really begin there. But in the 1960s, when legal restraints on the exploitation of sex were falling, the Bay Area was the spiritual center of student and other ferment. And North Beach symbolized the American genius for marrying a new opportunity ("liberation") and an old motive (profit).

Now *Forbes* magazine, in an entertaining report by James Cook, shows that at least in the pornography business the American gift for economic growth survives.

The California Department of Justice estimates that U.S. pornographers do $4 billion of business annually. That is as much as the "conventional" movie and record industries, combined. And the sum may be more than twice that high. The 10 leading "skin" magazines alone have a combined monthly circulation of 16 million and will have revenues of about $475 million this year, almost $400 million of it from circulation.

About 2 million people a week pay an average of $3.50 at the

780 "adult" cinemas that will gross more than $365 million this year. The movie *Deep Throat* cost $25,000 and has grossed $50 million so far. The average pornographic film returns about 200 percent on investment in eighteen months.

"It's a very hard business to lose money in," says a happy man, David Friedman, chairman of the Adult Film Association of America. Yes, pornographers too have a trade association and eventually, no doubt, will have a Washington lobbyist.

But the days of the small operator may be numbered. With significant money at stake, it is only a matter of time before major studios get into the act. Cook reports that already many producers "are making their films in two or even three versions—hard-core, soft-core and R—so that their films can play in a variety of markets."

The lion's share of the sex business is done by the thousands of "adult" bookstores and peep shows. A Times Square store can easily gross $10,000 a day. Los Angeles stores gross $125 million a year, three times the retail sales of I. Magnin in the Los Angeles area. The glorious free market is working its wonders: competition has brought down the cost of dirty movies for home enjoyment from $50 to about $13. Yankee ingenuity is adapting new technologies to the pornography trade, including X-rated video cassettes for showing on home television sets.

The pornography industry's only substantial sorrow is that its audience still consists primarily of people over 35. But as Cook says (drolly, I think), that is "merely a marketing problem" and it will be tackled by "someone from Hollywood, *Hustler* or the Harvard Business School."

In these trying times of declining trade balances which damage the dollar, let the record show that America's pornographers are doing their bit to reduce the nation's dependence on costly imports. "At one point," proclaims a Customs official, "most of our pornography came from foreign sources. Now the United States can out-porn any country in the world."

A wonderful verb, "out-porn." And here is a stirring thought: If the United States has beaten a foreign cartel—an OPEC of pornography exporters—some credit is due to the pioneering and heroic rascality of North Beach.

October 1, 1978

Rodeo Drive, Street of Dreams

Some facets of American civilization are—let us face facts—less than excellent. The saxophone, for one. Football halftime shows, for another. Frozen French toast, for a third. But there is, I insist, a form of excellence for almost everything, even excess. So let us now praise (sort of) two and a half blocks of Rodeo Drive here.

Beverly Hills (5.7 square miles, 33,500 population) is blessed with 678 law firms—one whole firm for every 49 residents—according to Marcia Seligman, a student of Beverly Hills' strangeness. "There are," she says, "no hospitals or cemeteries. . . . A place in which there is no birth or burial is not a serious place."

Perhaps. But according to a serious source (a country-music song): "All the gold in California/Is in a bank in the middle of Beverly Hills/In somebody else's name." But that money is just resting there, en route to Rodeo Drive, where it belongs.

You can walk the stretch that matters in three minutes. The tone of this stretch is so, well, tony that the Gucci store is just a kind of K-Mart, and Hermès is, at best, a Woolworth's. Even Juschi, a boutique that cost $3 million to decorate, is a pale fire in comparison with Bijan, a men's store.

If excess is, in its way, a fine art, then Bijan Pakzad is its Bernard Berenson, a stern, standards-setting critic. He was born in Iran, but is at pains to mention that he is an American citizen. He is, I assure you, the kind of Iranian that gives ayatollahs the willies.

He says his store averages three to five customers a day and this year will gross more than $8 million. Each customer must spend thousands of dollars. Many customers are foreigners, some from OPEC countries, so think of his store as, among other things, a national asset and patriotic enterprise—a device for recycling petrodollars.

You can, of course, window-shop on Rodeo Drive. A recent window display at Bijan included a $42,000 item for the man who has everything except a bedspread made of gray fox fur from China or Mongolia. But don't plan on dropping by to browse in the store.

Customers must make appointments—a precaution Pakzad has taken against what he calls, with magnificent impudence, "the Rodeo Drive riffraff." He says you should not make an appointment unless you earn $100,000. A month. Those of you in that bracket can get some nice, oh, $300 cotton shirts.

Why so much? Well, Pakzad explains that he takes the finest cotton, from Egypt, and sends it to Switzerland to be woven into cloth. The cloth goes to Italy to be made into shirts. They are displayed for customers here on a table made of marble from Versailles, by salespeople whose manicures he personally checks.

"I like America," he says, with unquestionable sincerity. "In America you have opportunity." But he thinks the American male is an inexcusably drab creature, and that a little more peacockery would serve the cause of world peace. He says that European men, who have a civilized sense of style, see Secretary of State Cyrus Vance on television and say, "I don't believe him—look at his tie."

I knew there was something wrong with our foreign policy but I couldn't quite put my finger on it. Now I blame Vance's haberdasher.

Speaking more in sorrow than in anger, Pakzad says: "The American man wears something because he must cover his skin." Clod that I am, I had hitherto thought that covering skin was, indeed, the heart of haberdashery. But Pakzad insists that America will not measure up to its potential until its men start wearing, among other things, perfume. To hasten the day, he is bringing out a man's perfume, $400 for 4 ounces in a Baccarat crystal bottle.

Rodeo Drive, and especially those stores which sell things (belts, ties, shoes, handbags, and so on) with the store's name or symbol all over them, is a monument to the fact that some people are nothing if not earnest in their pursuit of whatever status can be purchased and worn. In a new novel (*The Pope of Greenwich Village*, by Vincent Patrick) that is alternately funny and gruesome, one character impresses his girlfriends, and makes himself feel good, by tipping toll-booth attendants. There is the unconquerable American spirit. It turns the New Jersey Turnpike into the average guy's Rodeo Drive, a street of dreams.

December 9, 1979

Nebraska: The Fairest Girls, the Squarest Boys

The man who greeted me at the plane was the soul of Middle Western agreeableness, than which nothing is more agreeable. He was, on the surface, as normal as Nebraska, than which nothing is more normal, on the surface. Then, fool that I am, I asked: "How are the 'Huskers?"

His brow narrowed; his face clouded; his mouth took on the hard, narrow set of a mail slot. "They're only number two," he muttered.

The 'Huskers are the University of Nebraska Cornhuskers, the football team. They were, that day, "only" number two in all of Christendom. What ails Nebraskans that they fret so about not being number one?

Out here you can find anything, including a bathtub, emblazoned with a big red "N." One of the 'Huskers' coaches has a little red "N" inlaid in a false tooth. For just $69.95 you can get for your car a horn that plays the opening notes of the Nebraska fight song.

When Gary Hamilton's mother died, he had carved on her tombstone:

MARY L. HAMILTON
1916–1977
GO BIG RED

His father and brother were slow to warm to the epitaph, but, Gary says, "when they got to realizing that was Mom's life, they understood too." She was an extraordinary fan, even though she never saw a game in the university's stadium (which on home-game Saturdays is the third-largest "city" in Nebraska). She died hours after Nebraska lost to Iowa State. According to Gary: "I wouldn't say it [the game] did her any good, but I wouldn't say that killed her."

Dorothy Weyer Creigh, a Nebraska historian, says Nebraskans are so used to deprecation, including self-deprecation, that when they get a chance to brag, they tend to go overboard. When Nebraska was the nation's leading producer of beef, the legislature had the unfortunate idea of cluttering license plates with the words "BEEF STATE" (a slogan that, come to think about it, fits a football-crazed state).

As recently as 1975, *The Omaha World-Herald* headlined: NYC DANCER FINDS OMAHA AS GOOD A PLACE AS ANY. Obviously, the state has a pent-up need to toot its horn. Hence car horns that toot ol' NU's fight song.

Maybe the problem is that Nebraska was for so long The Great Highway, the way west for people—350,000 of them between 1841 and 1866—just passing through on the Oregon Trail, whose ruts remain. "Nebraska," writes Creigh, "was not the goal; she was the means to an end."

She was also the end for many. The Great Highway was not a place for the fainthearted, and many who tried to pass through passed instead into Nebraska's soil. Creigh says that one traveler in 1850 "estimated an average of four deaths from cholera per mile of travel across Nebraska." Many who were not killed by disease were drowned fording rivers, kicked to death by horses or crushed beneath wagon wheels. Those who survived and stayed were the tough stuff of which Big Eight football players are made.

Nebraska's borders are just too geometrical. The state is a space too obviously drawn arbitrarily, rather than by natural, organic influences. Furthermore, the land within these borders is so very flat that the state seems to lack definition. I am not saying that the land is less than beautiful. To me, the sweeping prairies are as sweet to behold as is the histrionic scenery of, say, Colorado. Still, people from flat places sometimes feel, well, flat.

Loyalty to the state's football team is one way a sparsely populated state defines itself, one way prairie people assert a sense of community. And it reflects deep attachment to the state-building, equality-engendering, pride-producing state university. The university's song is:

> There is no place like Nebraska,
> Dear old Nebraska U,
> Where the girls are the fairest,
> The boys are the squarest,
> Of any old school that you knew.
>
> There is no place like Nebraska
> Where we're all true blue.
> We'll all stick together
> In all kinds of weather,
> For dear old Nebraska U.

Fairest girls? Squarest boys? Golly, haven't Nebraskans been told they are supposed to be morose, as befits people suffering "malaise"? Yes, they've been told, but people who live where the land is flat learn to lean against strong winds.

There certainly are too few places like Nebraska. I don't know what ails it, but whatever ailment makes it unable to abide being "only" number two is a disease I wish the country would catch.

November 18, 1979

The Chicago Cubs and the Decline of the West

I have come, suddenly, to a jolting conclusion: Chicago Cubs fans, of whom I am one, are at the least symptoms of what ails the West, and may be what ails the West.

This thought broke like thunder in the quest of my sluggish mind when, on opening day, a Cubs fan cheerfully said that all the team needed to be a winner was "three starting pitchers and an outfielder."

The fan was not being witty, as Oscar Wilde was when he described a particular woman as "a peacock in everything but beauty." Rather, that Cubs fan, like most of them, fits the description of Lord Halifax, Britain's Foreign Minister at Munich: "He had an infinite capacity for being trodden on without complaint." But Cubs fans can complain, as I learned when, on the eve of the season, I said (on the *Today* show) approximately this:

> When the Mets were dreadful, they were cute. When the Red Sox blew the pennant, they had tragic dignity. But the Cubs are just mediocre, and if they play this season they will just embarrass themselves and their fans. If, however, they flatly refuse to come out of the dugout, they can give the world a shining example of a heroism suited to an age of anti-heroes, lowered expectations, tempered hopes, contracted horizons and expensive beef: heroic resignation. A white towel hoisted over the dugout would be a banner to which realists could repair, a symbol of unconditional surrender to undeniable facts.

This thought touched the flaming, tigerish spirit for which Cubs fans, unlike their team, are noted. Many fans have communicated with me in simple, austere terms—the philosophic gist being that I am the sort of person who would be much improved by being drawn and quartered.

But Cubs fans exemplify the muddiness of mind that made

Munich (and Suez, the Department of Energy and other calamities) possible. They fancy themselves idealists, but theirs is a dotty idealism that confuses athletic and ecological criteria. They idealize the team for playing at home on real grass, illuminated by solar energy. An idealist, as H. L. Mencken said, notes that a rose smells better than a cabbage and concludes that a rose also will make better soup.

But I have received a letter from a Virginia lawyer whose professional address—on Jefferson Davis Highway—suggests that he should be heard on the subject of losers. John Nies says that my strategy for the Cubs—unconditional surrender—is "by Washington standards rather barren." And:

> As Mr. Califano will tell you, the situation in which the Cubs find themselves is not of their own making. The basic truth of the matter, at least in Washington, is that failure in *any* enterprise is always someone else's fault. This is the corollary, of course, of the proposition that success is a product of avarice and related vices.

Nies has some suggestions:

> First, consider the possibilities of affirmative action. The Cubs' ineptitude is obviously the product of years of neglect. This can be corrected by requiring the Yankees and the Red Sox to accept as starters those Cubs who, because of broken homes or other socioeconomic reasons, have a batting average of less than .100 or who can't throw a ball straight more than five feet. This program, called Ineptitude Transfer (IT), if carefully monitored, should be productive.
>
> Next, let us think about whether it is really fair to retire a Cub hitter after three called strikes, which is the same standard used to judge the skills of a Ted Williams or a Reggie Jackson. . . .

It is too much to hope that government will accept the truth taught by competitive sports, and even by uncompetitive sports, such as the Cubs play. The truth is that, as a carpenter once said to William James, "There is very little difference between one man and another; but what little there is, is very important."

A concluding unscientific postscript:

Since my season-opening fit of foul temper, the Cubs have been, if not awesome, at least marginally adequate. This year the June Swoon did not come, as it usually does, in early May, which may, or then again may not, prove something.

May 17, 1979

Baseball, Metaphysics and the Universe

When last I addressed the subject of baseball, the lark was on the wing, the snail was on the thorn and my Chicago Cubs were in first place. That was last June. The lark and snail had good seasons, but the Cubs floundered. Now several sadists have called my attention to the fact that another season is at hand, and they have dared me to say something cheerful.

That is a daunting challenge, but if the challengers had done their homework in the Will Family archives, they would have known that we are a family rarely daunted. So here goes a cheerful thought:

Not even practitioners as inartistic as the Cubs can spoil something as sublime as baseball.

To understand why this is so, you should begin at the beginning of baseball, and that does *not* mean Abner Doubleday. Doubleday, who was a captain of artillery in the Union Army at Fort Sumter, was present at the creation of the Civil War, but not of baseball. His *New York Times* obituary did not even mention baseball. Yet such is the power of myth that baseball's Hall of Fame is at Cooperstown, New York, because Doubleday was a schoolboy there.

Nevertheless, the hall does contain a plaque honoring the one American whose achievements of mind rank with those of Aristotle, Newton, Hegel and Einstein. I refer, of course, to Alexander Cartwright, whose middle name was, appropriately, Joy. On the plaque, the list of his accomplishments begins: "SET BASES 90 FEET APART."

In 1845, Cartwright, then 25, joined some friends in a meadow beside a Manhattan pond. He had a chart in hand. Red Smith the columnist says the dimensions of the baseball field Cartwright laid out that day may have been determined by the size of the meadow, or perhaps Cartwright just stepped off 30 paces and said, "This seems about right." But Red Smith the metaphysician says:

> Ninety feet between bases represents man's closest approach to absolute truth. The world's fastest man cannot run to first base ahead of a sharply hit ball that is cleanly handled by an infielder; he will get there only half a step too late. Let the fielder juggle the ball for one moment or delay his throw an instant and the runner will be safe. Ninety feet demands perfection. It accurately measures the cunning, speed, and finesse of the base stealer against the velocity of a thrown ball. It dictates the placement of infielders. That single dimension makes baseball a fine art—and nobody knows for sure how it came to be.

Perhaps baseball players are occasionally inclined to slight the life of the mind. (After being introduced to Ernest Hemingway, Yogi Berra said, "Quite a fella. What does he do?" "He's a writer," said a friend. "Yeah?" said Yogi. "What paper?") But baseball is the sport most satisfying to the mind, perhaps because of its use of space and time.

Other sports are played in a strictly defined space, like a basketball court or football field, but baseball has what one writer (George Grella) calls "potential for infinity." Even foul balls are in play until they land in the stands, and if you removed the stands, the field of play would extend forever through 360 degrees. The Republic, the planet, the *universe* would be an extended baseball field. What a jolly idea!

Even when confined by fences and stands, a baseball field is remarkably large. Yogi, who once said "you can observe a lot just by watching," made this observation about playing outfield in the late afternoon: "Out there it gets late early."

In baseball there is no clock, and no tie game. As Grella says, "Baseball's unique freedom from any external time [means that] the game succeeds in creating a temporary timelessness perfectly appropriate to its richly cyclical nature." In theory, a game could (and I am sure that in Heaven all games do) go on forever.

Of course, in this life, all things must end, even the best things—baseball games. But baseball games call to mind the title of a poem by Robert Frost: "Happiness Makes Up in Height for What It Lacks in Length."

April 2, 1978

Part Eight 🙌

ON THE HOME FRONT

Quick! Relax!

I know Thoreau was right, that it is an art to saunter, and I intend to study the art tomorrow, or maybe the day after; but today, after a reasonably restful five-hour sleep, interrupted only by a child searching for his cap pistol at 3:45 A.M., I am at my desk at 8:30 A.M. with my third cup of coffee and my seventh phone call (the eighth is on hold) and I am only half listening because, even though the cab is waiting and I may miss my plane, I am fascinated by a newspaper article in front of me.

The article, from *The New York Times*, is headlined "CHANGING BEHAVIOR MAY PREVENT HEART ATTACK." It explains that we "Type A" people are even more doomed that everyone else.

Research confirms that the "achievement-oriented, competitive behavior" of "Type A people is a significant risk factor in heart disease. Furthermore, behavior modification can dramatically reduce the rate of heart attack among such people.

Here are some Type A characteristics:

"Thinking of or doing two things at once." (Only two?)

"Scheduling more and more activities into less and less time." (A Yiddish proverb: "Sleep faster, we need the pillows.")

"Failing to notice or be interested in your environment or things of beauty."

"Having difficulty sitting and doing nothing."

"Becoming unduly irritated when forced to wait in line or when driving behind a car you think is moving too slowly."

"Measuring your own or others' successes in terms of numbers (numbers of patients seen, articles written, etc.)."

"Playing nearly every game to win, even when playing with children."

Whoa!

What's this "even" against children? Especially against children. Few pleasures rival watching a smarty-pants 6-year-old roll the dice and come careening around the corner of the Monopoly board, only to land smack on Boardwalk, where you have just placed your second hotel. Such catharsis can't be bad for a parent's heart. But of course, cardiologists are right about Type A-ness.

For decades, and simultaneously with the elaboration of high-technology medicine, science has been coming to a thumping conclusion: Grandma was right. Research shows that longevity is indeed enhanced by not smoking, drinking only moderately, eating three proper meals, not eating between meals, keeping your weight down, exercising and sleeping eight hours a night.

Once upon a time we believed Grandma because she was Grandma. Today we believe Grandma because UCLA or MIT says what she has said all along.

Now cardiologists are saying what she has always said about what she calls, with nice concision, "nerves."

It is unclear why stress of the sort Type A people put themselves under is apt to increase blood cholesterol levels and clot formation. Therefore it is unclear why it helps to practice "exercises"—cardiology's answer to Saint Ignatius of Loyola's exercises for the spirit—to develop "Type B characteristics. But the exercises do help.

One, for example, involves learning how to stand in line without succumbing to exasperation. When I'm in a line, all I can think about is this iron law: The other line always moves faster. A Type B person would reflect about something soothing, or talk to a stranger about nothing much. A psychologist says Type A's try to become Type B's when convinced that Type A behavior is "inefficient" and reduces productivity. That is, Type A values drive the ever-driven Type A's to become Type B's.

The basic problem is that, as Emerson said, solitude is impracticable and society is fatal. We are taught that it is better to wear out our shoes than our sheets, the early bird gets the worm, a man's reach should exceed his grasp, and all that. As Arthur Hugh Clough said:

Thou shalt not covet, but tradition
Approves all forms of competition.

Type A Americans are produced by what one psychologist calls "the Little League syndrome . . . the belief that everyone has to be No. 1." My Little League team labored under no such illusion. Indeed, it taught me that someone has to finish fourth in a four-team league—but that did not prevent me from becoming a Type A.

Still, as the song says, you've got to stop and smell the roses. Therefore, I am going to make a list of all the kinds of roses, and I'm going to set an exacting schedule, smelling more roses today than yesterday, more tomorrow than today, more roses per minute than anyone ever thought possible, until I am an Olympic-class rose-smeller and the most disciplined all-around practitioner of finely honed Type B skills in international competition.

September 28, 1980

Toys

Depending upon your temperament, the skies of early December are a pretty pewter, or a dull gray. Depending upon your temperament, early December is a time of profound and elemental pleasure, or of grumpiness because the Christmas season begins so early. But Christmas is for children, and society should give a full month to their eager anticipation of Christmas toys. During the other eleven months, adult society is preoccupied with the consumption of adults' toys.

If a toy is something bought primarily for the fun of it, for amusement, then "developed" nations have developed toy-based economies. Look—really *look*—at advertisements. *The New Yorker* magazine, for example, is a toy catalog for adults who buy porcelain birds and Greek fisherman's hats. Few ads anywhere are as forthright as the one in a boating magazine (itself a toy): "Big Boys need playthings, too . . . like no toy you've had . . . most exciting plaything on the water . . ." But tobacco and spirits and cosmetics, cameras and campers and jewelry, most clothes and many appliances are for amusement. Millions are being spent on videotape machines—toys to attach to toys (TV sets). A car is a necessity, but most cars are toys, too. They are built for *Homo ludens*, playful man. Why else call them "Stingrays," "Firebirds" and "Broughams"? Why else design dashboards that enable drivers to feel like Luke Skywalker? SALESMAN: "Do you want the Le Mans racing-style glove-compartment-light package? The Louis XIV upholstery? Genuine simulated-wire wheels?" ME: "Yes, yes, *yes!*"

Play and toys are increasingly important to adults. Most work, in law or medicine or teaching, as on an assembly line, is repetitive. But variety is inexhaustible in play. Almost all work has almost always been drudgery. What is new is that many people are surprised by the drudgery. They have believed that all of life, and *especially* work, can be fun, or, in the current argot, "self-fulfilling." Such a strange idea could come only from institutions of higher learning, and when it is refuted by reality, people assuage their disappointment by turning with awesome intensity to the search for fun in consumption. In affluent societies, most people have acquired the "necessities" (*very* broadly construed), so the consumption that refreshes, briefly, is the consumption of adult toys.

Children's toys are more serious. For example, electric trains taught me the terrible weight of philosophic choice. In the late 1940s, the world, or at least the heart of the habitable world, central Illinois, was divided into warring camps. On one side were loutish children who preferred Lionel trains. (Lionel tracks had— and still may have, for all I know—*three* rails, for Pete's sake.) On the other side were precocious and discerning children who rejoiced in American Flyers, like my model of a Pennsylvania Railroad steam locomotive. I believed then, and still do, that children who embraced Lionelism had dark pasts and dangerous futures.

Alas, my side now has the disappearing-railroad blues: American Flyers have gone the way of the Pennsylvania Railroad. From toys, I acquired my taste for lost causes.

The obsessions of today's children lack the severe grandeur of those I had. "What is man but his passion?" asks Robert Penn Warren. What, then, is a 4-year-old boy in Chevy Chase, Maryland? He is a little satchel crammed with a large passion for figurines of *Star Wars* characters. Civilization has been rocked irreparably by that movie, which lacks the dignified scholarship of the Davy Crockett movie and song that launched the coonskin-hat craze twenty-four years ago.

> *Born on a mountain top in Tennessee,*
> *Greenest state in the Land of the Free,*
> *Raised in the woods so's he knew ev'ry tree*
> *Kilt him a b'ar when he was only three.*

The music from *Star Wars* is music in the way prunes are fruit: only technically.

Ah, well. As the rising generation goes to wrack and ruin, there is one constant: proprietors of toy stores are an austere and iron race. They are hardened by constant exposure to the torrid directness of children. A mere parent pitted against a child in a test of wills in a toy store is a terrible spectacle. Sad to say, the strain of being a parent unhinges many minds, and opens those minds to the unsound ideas of advanced thinkers.

One idea is that realistic toys will stunt a child's imagination, so parents should buy "creative" toys, like "cars" that are lumps of unpainted wood with wheels. Such toys are supposed to stimulate Billy's gift for abstract thought, and thus launch him toward Yale. Some parents (often the same ones) say it is toy guns that make boys warlike. Granted, many shelves in toy stores resemble altars consecrated to Mars. But give a boy a rubber duck and he will seize its neck like the butt of a pistol and shout "Bang!"

Children are an enlarging, if sobering, experience, and often amusing. But childhood is frequently a solemn business for those inside it. A child's high ratio of desires to memories accounts for what George Eliot called the "strangely perspectiveless conception of life," the "bitter sense of the irrevocable" and the storms of grief that seize children because they are "soothed by no memories of outlived sorrow." As Eliot wrote in *The Mill on the Floss*, children, especially, are "gifted with that superior power of misery which distinguishes the human being and places him at a proud distance from the most melancholy chimpanzee."

But as Eliot also wrote:

> There is no sense of ease like the ease we felt in those scenes where we were born . . . Where the outer world seemed only an extension of our own personality: we accepted and loved it as we accepted our own sense of existence and our own limbs. Very commonplace, even ugly, that furniture of our early home might look if it were put up to auction; an improved taste in upholstery scorns it; and is not the striving after something better and better in our surroundings, the grand characteristic that distinguishes man from the brute . . . ? But heaven knows where that striving might lead us, if our affections had not a trick of twining round those old inferior things—if the loves and sanctities of our life had no deep immoveable roots in memory.

That is why "we could never have loved the earth so well if we had had no childhood in it." Toys are the most important furniture of childhood, so it is not fanciful to number *Star Wars* figurines among life's "loves and sanctities." A Christmas toy, even when it has become only a Christmas memory, is what Eliot called "the long companion of my existence, that wove itself into my joys when joys were vivid."

December 11, 1978

My Car: A Shock Absorber

Rising over orchards, the helicopter skimmed mountains, dipped beneath the cap of smog, and suddenly, I beheld one of this planet's awesome sights: the crossing of the San Diego and Santa Monica freeways at 8:20 A.M. It was the perfect moment for meditation about America's indissoluble marriage—as vexing and passionate as any marriage—to the automobile.

Just as European intellectuals at first disparaged automobiles as aristocrats' toys (like Lord Peter Wimsey's roadsters), American intellectuals considered automobiles symbols of the "materialism" of merchants: Babbitt's Buick. Only the learned could be so wrong. The automobile is one of technology's greatest gifts to the common man. The French say there is no such thing as a pretty good omelet. But almost anyone can own a pretty good car.

The automobile and television have been the two great democratizers of experience. Automobiles take experiencers to distant places; television brings distant experiences near. Automobiles instill and serve the modern ideal, absence of restraints. In automobiles, American boys and girls first sample the delights of mobility, and of independence from parents. (Not to mention the delights of girls and boys.) The automobile is a paradigm of the modern, democratic product. It was first a luxury, soon a universal aspiration, then a necessity.

The first Model T (1909) cost $900. Thanks to Ford's assembly line (a precursor was Swift's "disassembly line" for hogs), the 1916 Model T cost "only" $345. Still, as Daniel Boorstin says, "For the first time there was a mass-produced consumer's item that cost between 10 and 20 percent of a family's annual income." It required a revision of the thrift ethic, and new credit practices. Henry Ford considered installment buying immoral: if you couldn't pay full price, you couldn't "afford" a Ford. Instead, he approved a plan whereby customers paid weekly deposits until they had the full price. Then they got a car.

But that required Americans to do what they hate to do: wait. In

America, we *pursue* happiness, we don't wait for it. And in America, moralities are like cars: "new, improved" models are always being manufactured. So the old notion of thrift was junked. You could "afford" to own a car if you could commit future income on an "installment plan." The extension of consumer credit to the common man, answering a need for the automobile industry, was one of the great democratizations of life.

Automobiles made possible the golden age of American crime. As Boorstin says, the "getaway car" enabled crooks to flee cops, and enabled crime to disperse to "roadhouses" in suburbs like Chicago's Cicero. Automobiles produced supermarkets, drawing customers from beyond the neighborhood and selling them more than they could carry in their arms. Automobiles stimulated a "fast food" industry and other "franchise" phenomena, such as motels, offering what people away from home often want, familiarity.

When Detroit sneezes, the economy catches cold, and today Detroit has various flus, including the Asian flu: Tora! Tora! Toyota! But look on the bright side. As in 1941, Japan has overdone it a bit, and has awakened a giant. GM and other survivors (if any) will soon have a competitive "world car." And if Chrysler goes bust (and if New York City does; both are becoming more likely), the nation will learn a timely lesson about the folly of trying to outlaw failure.

In *Death of a Salesman*, Willy Loman whines, "I would like to own something outright before it's broken! . . . I just finish paying for the car and it's on its last legs . . . They time those things. They time them so when you've finally paid for them, they're used up." But the average American doesn't change cars for that reason. Fashion may be, as Shaw said, an induced epidemic, but Americans didn't have to be induced to like annual model changes. Indeed, Ford paid a stiff price for resisting such changes. Cars have never been just transportation: they have been personal statements. Why, General Motors is an almost theological institution, serving the full range of American aspiration, the great chain of human goals, from Chevrolet to Cadillac.

Besides, it is antisocial to be satisfied with your car. Keep it too long, the economy may crash. The average new-car buyer keeps his car about 3.5 years. Were that to become 5, the economy would sag. Six, and grass would grow in the streets.

Mea culpa! My car is as old as, and is becoming a menace to, my marriage. Mrs. Will ('78 station wagon) says the neighbors are more neighborly than they should have to be about the unsightliness of my '67 coupé. She says that although an antiquated, broken-down wreck is an appropriate car for me, I really shouldn't drive a car whose door flies open and whose mirror falls off in traffic. I call such criticism picky. Besides, holding on to cars is a Will tradition. My father drove a Model A until 1953, when I betrayed embarrassment by asking him to let me out a block from the Little League field. But I've seen enough cowboy movies to know life's essential ceremonies. Soon I'll have to shoot my lame ol' hoss in the carburetor and get a new mount. So I recently visited a dealer.

"Here," said the salesman, proudly, "listen to this one." Listen? He seated me at the wheel, switched on the radio and, wham! I was assaulted by music from all directions. "QUAD SPEAKERS," he bellowed, barely audible above the disco beat.

Detroit's emphasis on interior details is a result of "down-sizing"—a horrid word for a horrid fact: cars will never again be what they were when America was respected and Buicks looked pregnant. Back when a car was as big as Kansas, designers trying to make cars distinctive had lots of chrome and sheet metal with which to do wonderfully rococo things. So the exteriors of cars resembled the interiors of Bavarian churches.

Today, designers express themselves in details like a combination door lock: little spots on the door, sensitive to light touch. When touched in the right order, the door unlocks. Excelsior!—a new way to get locked out of your car: forget your combination.

The quadraphonic, touch-sensitive car I didn't buy is not a luxury make, but it costs about what my parents paid in 1950 for the four-bedroom house in which I grew up.

April 28, 1980

Raising Boys, Not Grass

The Will Family has, I'll warrant, the only Pontiac station wagon with automatic pilot. Switch on the ignition and, if you don't meddle with the steering wheel, the wagon will drive straight to the emergency ward at Sibley Hospital.

Okay, I don't actually know it will do that. But it ought to; it has had enough experience. And okay, perhaps other station wagons will do that—wagons belonging to families with children of the male persuasion. I know that what I am saying may some day be Exhibit A at an international tribunal convened in Iran to expose sexism in Chevy Chase, but I believe that boys bang themselves around more than other types of children do.

I could, but will not, exhaust you with the details of the episodes that have made this December somewhat testing. Suffice it to say the following.

Geoffrey, 5, is given to trying to run through things (walls, closed doors, large children, and so on) that he would be well advised—and in fact has been advised—to run around. When he recently showed up at Sibley for the second time in ten days, he was still wearing the identification bracelet from his earlier visit. (The first visit was to stitch up his nose. The second was to see if another collision had broken the nose. It hadn't.)

My friend Hal Bruno of ABC News raised football-playing boys who, Hal says, could conduct learned discussions about which of the local rescue squads most skillfully deliver you to the emergency wards, and which wards are preferred by discriminating casualties. I am less experienced than Hal is, but I think there is much to be said for Sibley's emergency ward, if only because down near the X-ray machines there often are some old *New Yorker* magazines. When your nerves are frayed, it is soothing to read *The New Yorker*'s Novocain prose, the on-the-one-hand, on-the-other-hand prose that trickles along between advertisements for Greek fisherman's hats and porcelain birds.

I have found that two of the small, unanticipated benefits of raising boys is that you never know what is going to happen (read: break) next, and you meet some nice young men and women of medicine who are nimble with needle and thread. The Will boys aren't really impressed by fewer than three stitches. But when Jonathan (now 7, then 5) totaled his Big Wheel into the creek at the bottom of the hill, even he was impressed by the amount of bleeding he was able to do before the folks at Sibley went to work on him.

(You say you don't know what a Big Wheel is? It is a few pounds of red and blue and yellow plastic that, when pedaled by a wound-up child, rips along at about 147 miles per hour and stops on a dime, or on a father's instep, whichever is handy. If you get your child a Big Wheel for Christmas, get it assembled. 'Tis the season to remember that the three most terrifying words in the English language are found in small print on toy boxes: "SOME ASSEMBLY REQUIRED.")

It is, I'll admit, tiresome to have to pull oneself away from the more-or-less-adult violence of a Sunday football game to cart a child away to the emergency ward. But it is nice for your child to be greeted there with the sort of friendly casualness that bartenders reserve for regular patrons. "Hi, Geoffrey," the doctors and nurses say, barely looking up, and he nods, curtly, making a beeline for the *Sports Illustrated*s in the waiting room.

Children who move fast bump into things. But who wants children who let grass grow beneath their sneakers? In his fine new book *The Death of an American Game: The Crisis in Football*, John Underwood of *Sports Illustrated* tells a story about the late Amos Alonzo Stagg when that wonderful football coach was nearly 100:

> Until he went to the rest home . . . to live out his days, Stagg mowed his lawn with a hand mower. "He mowed that lawn to death," said Stella Stagg. One day a neighbor advised him that kids had been playing on it daily, ripping up the turf. "You'll never raise grass that way," the neighbor said. "Sir," answered Stagg, "I'm not raising grass, I'm raising boys."

That's what I'm doing, and loving every (well, almost every) minute of it. Raising boys, and being raised by them.

December 13, 1979

Cheer Up, You Could Be Camping

Remember, in grade school, when each September you were reinducted into academic rigors by an assignment to write an essay on "My Summer Vacation"? Just to get a jump on the rest of you kids, here's mine:

As usual, the flight to Colorado confirmed Robert Benchley's rule that in America there are two forms of travel—first class and with children. The flight, a foretaste of close confinement, also called to mind the terror of two years ago, when it rained for eight straight days in Aspen, and there was not a Monopoly game to be bought anywhere. An hour after we arrived this year, our housesitter called from Maryland to tell us about the burglary.

Acting on the principle that the surest way to forget small troubles is to acquire big ones, I joined several other parents in taking our children (at least, we think they were ours, give or take one or two) camping. It has been said that the only time a woman wishes she were a year older is when she is pregnant. But pregnancy is its own reward when there is a camping trip to be avoided. Mrs. Will, two months away from delivering, was for that reason delivered from camping.

Up we hiked, two miles into a secluded mountain valley. The parents were trying to feel like Hillary and Tenzing leaving the last base camp for the final assault on Everest, but were finding the mood hard to maintain as they looked up the trail at the long bobbing line of children's backpacks, from many of which hung

Teddy bears and stuffed Snoopys. We pitched eight tents in what became, for sixteen hours, the noisiest city in the Mountain West. It is a wonder (and a blessing) we did not have to file an environmental-impact statement.

Aside from a not-very-clever deer, which seemed stunned by the sight of us, all wildlife fled to other valleys. But in the cathedral of the wilderness I heard life's sweetest music—the sound of other people's children charging that children other than mine had thrown them into the creek, or their sneakers into the fire.

Coloradans are a hardy and neighborly breed, and besides, company loves misery, so some friends without children hiked up to see us. They came for the exquisite pleasure of then returning to their Jacuzzis before sundown.

When those visitors were gone and we were alone with our fate, we fell to rationalizing it: Camping is good for the children because . . . well, it teaches them what toughness it took to conquer the continent. More precisely, it teaches them what that conquest would have been like if the pioneers had done it one night a year, carrying nylon tents, aluminum stoves and granola bars. The children were impervious to the point, but their parents got it. Most ambitious attempts to teach children teach parents instead.

By 10 P.M., the children were unconscious and the parents were using tequila and something called Yukon Jack to prepare for an attempt at sleep. Shakespeare said that sleep knits up the ravell'd sleave of care. Shakespeare was no camper. At about two minutes past midnight, a father's voice drifted across the campsite: "Okay. That's it. I said we'd stay until tomorrow. This is tomorrow. Let's go." Go we did, but not until morning, and then in the kind of high spirits that comes to people who know they are a full year away from the next camping trip.

I brought back two imperishable memories. One was of my friend (provisionally) Dale Shaffer trying to stanch the flow of blood from the wound on his head. The wound was inflicted by a Will boy with a rock, but without malice. The other golden memory is of wit in an extreme situation. As we sat in the dark, watching a breathtaking moonrise, a father stuck his head from his tent and called to his wife: "Do you know where my knife is?" Without a second's hesitation, she asked in reply: "Why? Won't the children be quiet?"

Every year at about this time I am in the same frame of mind. I understand intellectually, but cannot accept emotionally, that annual vacations represent a hard-won and precious victory for toiling mankind. I don't know quite how civilization came to be saddled with summer vacations, but I'll say this for them: they do rob winter of its sting. A man shoveling snow can console himself with the thought that things could be worse: he could be camping. Vacations also help parents and children know each other better, but time usually heals that wound.

August 21, 1980

On Turning 40

To the average 7-year-old boy (the average 7-year-old boy is a bit below average), there is no other pleasure as pleasant as the sight of his father falling flat on his face. Unlike pleasures of the flesh, this pleasure of the spirit is not diminished by repetition. We adults are tomorrow's past, and hardhearted 7-year-olds are tomorrow.

That melancholy thought came to me recently while I was providing much pleasure to son Geoffrey, in a situation conducive to thoughts of mortality. I was on skis, teetering on the top of Vail mountain and on the edge of my fifth decade, heading downhill. Soon I shall be a wizened 40-year-old, purged and purified of the grosser passions of youth, loaded down to the Plimsoll line with the wisdom of age and riddled from head to toe with the whimsy suitable for a gentleman in gentle decline.

The 40th is, truth be told, a boring birthday. My 30th was exhilarating, because I was delighted to join the age group despised by the youths I deplored. The 35th is notable as the halfway mark in the Biblical threescore and ten. But the 40th just means middle age, which is so, well, middling. I have been eagerly anticipating my "mid-life crisis," that moment when the middle-aged male does something peculiar—buys a Porsche or grows a mustache or takes up yoga or yogurt—to prove he is not a spent force. "To his dog," Aldous Huxley said, "every man is Napoleon; hence the constant popularity of dogs." I think I'll get a dog.

Actually, my mid-life crisis is that I am not having a crisis. Like Napoleon pacing the deck of the *Bellerophon*, I pace my study, my forehead corrugated by concentration, wondering why I have been denied this crisis, this badge of seriousness, this excuse for going off the rails. The problem, I have decided, is that I made a shrewd choice of parents and have been happy ever since, damn it.

Perhaps, too, the problem has to do with the special openness of the horizon in the Midwest, an openness that reveals no obstacle to travel in any direction. The remarkable flatness of the prairie suggests that God had good times in mind—perfectly smooth infields for countless baseball diamonds—when He created central Illinois. We who wisely chose to be born there have a talent for cheerfulness. But a happy childhood is considered cultural deprivation by those who consider rebellion a necessary growth stage. It has been said (by Anthony Powell, whose twelve-volume *A Dance to the Music of Time* provided the greatest reading pleasure of my first forty years) that we date ourselves by the standards against which we rebel. But the opportunity for doing that is limited for those who live in an age that refuses, as a matter of principle, to have standards.

I wish I could serve up, on a silver salver, some glistening original thought gleaned from forty years' experience. But the essential wisdom of life is deflating. It is that the great task of life is transmission: the task of transmitting the essential tools and graces of life from our parents to our children. The two most important things to be transmitted are a mastery of logic and a capacity for sympathy. The Will children shall, in the fullness of time, study logic as taught by Lewis Carroll, a mathematician, logician and (hence) author of *Alice in Wonderland*. Carroll showed how to derive the conclusion that "babies cannot manage crocodiles" from three premises:

1. Babies are illogical.
2. Nobody is despised who can manage a crocodile.
3. Illogical persons are despised.

Sympathy is harder to teach than logic, but it is as essential, because a world of rigorous logic, unwarmed by sympathy, would be cold indeed. The well-lived life involves reversing the instinctive tendency to be subjective toward ourselves and objective toward others. Sympathy, a humane subjectivity, enlarges the sympathizer, and as Disraeli said, "Life is too short to be small." But providing children with better lives complicates the task of making them better people. The more a child has security, serenity and opportunity, the harder it may be for him to imagine the lives of those who do not. "Poverty," said Walter Bagehot, "is an anomaly to rich people. It is very difficult to make out why people who want dinner do not ring the bell."

Journalism can illustrate life's thorns and thistles, but literature must convey what George Eliot conveyed in *Middlemarch*: "If we had a keen vision and feeling of all ordinary human life, it would be like hearing the grass grow and the squirrel's heart beat, and we should die of that roar which lies on the other side of silence." The themes of great literature—love, disappointment, the texture of time—are the themes of ordinary life. Indeed, the older I get, the more I see the inexhaustible interestingness of the ordinary.

What could be duller than some "extraordinary" people, such as Lenin? He is supposed to be interesting because he was important. But he was important because he was potent, and he was potent because he was single-minded. Thus, in the most important particular he was simple. We speak of "childlike simplicity," but no child is simple. That is an adult, an acquired, failing. One reason why there is so much politics but so few good political novels is that "public figures" often are too much that: public, with little interesting inwardness. Mussolini's surface was interesting, but he was surface clear through.

Longevity, like literature, is a splendid teacher. By age 40, almost everyone has experienced enlarging sadnesses, such as the deaths of loved ones; enriching delights, such as introducing a child to *Huckleberry Finn*; deepening astonishments, such as contemplation of this fact of life: physically, you ain't what you used to be. Every instant, every cell in your body is changing. This 40-year-old jumble of space and electricity is not the jumble it was at 30. Our continuity is more in our memories than in our physiologies.

It is said that God gave us memory so we could have roses in winter. But it is also true that without memory we could not have a self in any season. The more memories you have, the more "you" you have. That is why, as Swift said, no wise man ever wished to be younger.

April 27, 1981

Hail, Victoria!

The struggle to reelect the 39th President, or to elect the 40th, though not insignificant, has been eclipsed by a far larger event, the birth of the 48th President: Victoria Louise Will. Her two brothers, aged 8 and 6, have said "We are not amused" that she chose to be born female, and they gloomily wonder what other eccentric things she will do. I, in turn, have advised them of Stephen Leacock's axiom: "The parent who could see his boy as he really is would shake his head and say, 'Willie is no good; I'll sell him.' "

Another philosopher once offered this proof that we learn from experience: A man never awakens his second baby to see it smile. Others say that if we really learned from experience, no one would have a second baby. I say, with novelist Peter De Vries, that "the value of marriage is not that adults produce children but that children produce adults." I am a slow learner and need the help of three children to get the hang of adulthood.

Leaving aside how children shape parents, it is problematic how much heredity and how much environment shape a child—and how much parents can control the child's environment. Most people believe in heredity only until their children begin to act like children, or even worse. On the other hand, as Abraham Myerson says, those who believe that environment is everything "seem to believe that if cats gave birth to kittens in a stove, the offspring would be biscuits."

Clearly, social environment is something, and today's is frequently unfit for human consumption, so care must be taken.

For a dozen or so years Victoria will, I assume, be quiet and delicate and inclined to sit reading Louisa May Alcott and making doilies. She will be dressed in blue velvet dresses decorated with small yellow flowers.

I am told by parents of little girls—parents who, unaccountably, look as distracted as do parents of little boys—that I am daft. They say I can buy blue velvet dresses until I am blue in the face, but even if the child consents to wear one, even once, it will look odd with the soccer shoes she certainly will not consent to remove.

Perhaps. But as soon as she takes an interest in popular music or popular boys she will be sent to school at a thick-walled convent on a high mountain overlooking an inaccessible valley in a remote region of Portugal.

Because our Washington child was born on the first day of the Federal Government's new fiscal year, perhaps we should have named her Deficit (just as, in healthier times three centuries ago, Mr. and Mrs. Mather named one of their sons Increase). But as responsible parents we have given her a name resonant enough for someone from whose Venus-like and brain-crammed head will come the great American novel and dozens of epoch-making Supreme Court opinions.

James Agee could have—must have—had a premonition of Victoria when he wrote, "In every child who is born, under no matter what circumstances, and of no matter what parents, the potentiality of the human race is born again." Actually, history will record, in awe-struck tones, that the potentiality of the human race was redefined on October 1, 1980.

Therefore, all the names we considered we tested in hypothetical but predictable news stories, such as:

Stockholm, Sweden—In a move as obviously right as it is unprecedented, the Nobel committee today awarded prizes in physics, chemistry and literature to a single recipient, Victoria Will.

Or:

Washington—The Supreme Court today overturned 70 years of what it called "willful perversity" regarding the due process and equal protection clauses of the 14th Amendment, demolishing a line of precedents extending back to the Warren Court in the middle of the last century. In the most important opinion since Marbury v. Madison, Chief Justice Victoria Will said . . .

Mrs. Will favored the name Victoria for the sensible reason that it is lovely. To that sufficient reason, I added some rococo reasons.

My philosophy of life can be put in five words: "The world needs another Victoria." I am a card-carrying member of only one group, The Victorian Society in America, which celebrates an era when literature and manners and other things that matter were grand. And what student of history would not enjoy ordering a Victoria to go clean up her room?

If—Heaven forfend—the name Victoria is ever desecrated by being contracted into a nickname, at least there is a tolerable possibility. "Vicky" is icky, but for obvious reasons, I think "Tory" Will is musical. Mrs. Will says it is child abuse.

October 5, 1980

Index

farmers' strike (1978), 48–50
Federal Farm Loan Act (1916), 50
Federalist Papers, 191
Federal Reserve Building (Cleveland), 344–45
Federal Trade Commission, 219–22, 226–27
Fermi, Enrico, 249
Ferreria, Joseph, M.D., 255
Field, Marshall, 327
First Amendment, 69–70, 72, 81–84
  and abortion, 103–04
  and Christmas displays, 92–93
  and freedom of religion, 118
  and the Nazi party, 84–86
  and pornography, 93
First Amendment and the Future of American Democracy, The (Berns), 85–86
Flamingo Road, 73
Fonda, Jane, 153
football, 352–54, 372, 373–74
Forbes magazine, 348
Ford, Gerald, 184, 242
Ford, Henry, 286, 301, 369–70
Ford, Peter, 306
foreign policy, U.S.
  under Jimmy Carter, 149–50, 154–57, 163–65, 289, 290–91
  toward China, 149–50, 155–56
  and the India-Pakistan war, 148
  and the Iran crisis, 167–69
  toward Japan, 150
  under Lyndon Johnson, 201–02
  under John Kennedy, 22
  Henry Kissinger and, 146–49
  and the Panama Canal, 289, 290–291
  and peace agreements, 139–41
  Republican *vs.* Democrat, 36–38
  See also Cold War; détente, U.S.-Soviet
Forster, E. M., 249
Forsyte Saga, The, 77, 293
Fortas, Abe, 291
Fourteenth Amendment, 126, 129–30

Fowler, H. W., 342
Frampton, Peter, 99–100
France, 152
  and Algeria, 150–51, 293
  and the French Revolution, 250–251
  W. R. Inge on, 318
  and the Kellogg-Briand pact, 139–140
  in World War I, 143
  in World War II, 144–45
franchise businesses, 302, 370
Franco, Francisco, 298, 299
Franke, Linda Bird, 107
Franklin National Bank, 239
Friedman, David, 349
Frost, Robert, 359

Gagarin, Yuri, 22
Galway, James, 323
gambling, state-run, 59–61
General Motors, 238, 370
George VI, 144
Germany, in World War II, 143–45, 170, 269, 278–79
Gierek, Edward, 171
Gilman, George, 301
Gilson, Étienne, 271
Gladstone, William, 189, 218
Goldwater, Barry, 201, 202, 262
Good Morning America, 120
"Good News Bible," the, 335
Gothic architecture, 329, 330
Gouzenko, Igor, 282
Graham, Katharine, 174
Grant, Ulysses S., 295, 317, 322
Gray, Thomas, 196
Great Purge (U.S.S.R.), 164
"Great Society" program, 201
Great Terror, The (Conquest), 160–161
Greece, 298–99
Greene, Graham, 294
Grella, George, 358, 359
Grinding It Out (Kroc), 302
Gromyko, Andrei, 282
Gucci (shop), 350